MARKET STRUCTURE
AND
CORPORATE BEHAVIOUR:

Theory and Empirical Analysis of the Firm

Edited by

KEITH COWLING

Professor of Industrial Economics
University of Warwick

GRAY-MILLS PUBLISHING LTD
10 JUER STREET
LONDON S.W.11

First edition, 1972
© Keith Cowling
ISBN 0 85641 004 7 (cloth)

Figures drawn by Bailey & Bailey.
97a Albert Bridge Road, London, SW11 4PF
and printed in Great Britain by
Page Bros (Norwich) Ltd., Norwich

CONTENTS

PREFACE

This collection of papers is taken from a symposium held at the University of Warwick in April 1972. Those present comprised chiefly university researchers in the field of industrial economics together with representatives from industry and government departments.

The papers fall rather loosely into three groups. The first group, consisting of papers by Hindley, Kuehn and Samuels and Chesher, explore theoretical explanations for the mode of growth of firms, and provide new empirical evidence on the characteristics of takeover raiders and the growth of firms in recent history. These papers help in an understanding of the evolving size-structure of firms and the resulting evolution of market and political power.

Hindley's paper poses the question, why should firms seek to merge? and is concerned specifically with the pure theory of merger, unrelated to market power, technological links or pecuniary economies. Various alternative hypotheses, traditional entrepreneurial, non-entrepreneurial (for example, concerned with conditions leading to divergences in valuation) and managerial, are explored and the empirical evidence is reviewed. Kuehn's paper compares the predictions of alternative models of firm behaviour (for example, growth-maximizing and profit-maximizing models) in the context of the observed characteristics of raiders. The predictions relate to the growth rates, profit rates, valuation ratios and retention ratios of raiders relative to other firms in the same industry. Samuels and Chesher, using as their sample companies quoted on the London Stock Exchange, examine the growth rates of firms in relation to their initial size over recent history and also document births and deaths of companies and establish the probability of survival of companies of different size.

The second group of papers, by Jacquemin and Thisse, Cowling and Cable, contribute to an understanding of another aspect of market structure namely barriers to entry created via the product-differentiation activities of the firms in question. These papers explore theoretical models of firms' product differentiation and pricing strategies and provide empirical evidence on firms' behaviour and on inter-market differences in the importance of these activities.

Jacquemin and Thisse examine the application of optimal control theory to advertising and R & D activities and also analyse some of the dynamic aspects of pricing policies. The important thrust of the paper is to emphasize the impact on market structure of the conduct and behaviour of firms and to suggest new ways of looking at this link. Cowling is concerned with comparing the actual advertising behaviour of firms in a variety of markets with the predictions of various optimizing models. The empirical work is essentially concerned with generating estimates of price and advertising elasticities of demand at the firm level. The analysis of advertising behaviour is taken a stage further in Cable's paper where a theoretical and empirical explanation of inter-market differences is attempted. The main contribution of the paper lies in establishing links, theoretically and empirically, between the size-distribution of sellers and advertising intensity, a particular aspect of barriers to entry.

The third group of papers are provided by Williamson and Bhargava,

Yarrow and Phillips. Again the group has both a theoretical and empirical component but this time the focus is on the links between structure, both internal and external to the firm, and performance. The first two papers are concerned with managerial discretion and the control of it via internal and external mechanisms. The third paper analyses attempts by firms to control their external environment via collusive arrangements.

Williamson and Bhargava pose the problem of testing hypotheses about the M-form (multi-divisional) firm when various types of divisionalized structure exist. They suggest a classification scheme for firms according to the type of internal control and apply this to a sample of eight corporations. Yarrow's paper is concerned with the competing hypotheses concerning executive compensation offered by neoclassical, managerial and organizational theories of the firm. His paper includes a careful respecification of the neoclassical model, together with empirical analysis, using U.S. data. The neoclassical predictions turn out rather well, although further testing is required. The last paper, by Phillips, looks on the conduct and performance of firms as being inter-dependent variables. He estimates a model, where price-cost margins and price-fixing agreements are both treated as endogenous variables, using a unique set of data on price-fixing in the UK in the early fifties.

The symposium from which these papers are derived was made possible by the generosity and encouragement of Shell International. We are most grateful.

Coventry
July 1972.

RECENT THEORY AND EVIDENCE ON CORPORATE MERGER

by

BRIAN HINDLEY

Though corporate merger* has never been a major focus of research for economists, there has recently been an increase in professional activity in the area. To some extent, this is due to the larger number of mergers of late, and the correspondingly increased attention to issues of public policy. But there are at least two reasons for supposing that interest will continue at a higher level than in the past. The first of these is the conglomerate component of recent merger activity. The second is the appearance of the new theories of the firm.

Conglomerate merger is not a new phenomenon. The novelty lies in a situation in which a majority of mergers can be classified as conglomerate.† When the bulk of mergers are from the same or technically connected industries, and are to that extent compatible with the traditional merger categories of monopoly or economies of scale or integration, conglomerate merger is all too easily dismissed as an aberration. But when the bulk of mergers are conglomerate, the traditional hypotheses lose whatever force they once had. The pursuit of hypotheses appropriate to conglomerate merger takes on a heightened interest because such hypotheses may generalize to provide alternative explanations of intra-industry mergers.

The pursuit of new hypotheses also provides part of the reason that merger is a potentially fruitful topic in the context of the new theories of the firm. Barred from technological or monopolistic links, it seems very likely that explanations of conglomerate merger must focus on the entrepreneurial factors that are at the heart of the new theories; and they thus hold the possibility of refining and expanding the new theories.

But there is another aspect of merger which is probably more important from this point of view. Merger is an important part of the takeover mechanism which, as I have argued elsewhere (Hindley 1969), is the sole *external* constraint on management which can in principle compel them to operate the firm in the interests of the owners. Some empirical assertion about merger is therefore logically prior to any new theory of the firm based upon the separation of ownership and control.

However, in at least one sense, these latter issues are peripheral to the content of this paper. Its primary concern is with 'pure' theories of merger—that is, theories which do not rely upon market or technical links between merging firms; or on such inevitable connections as discounts on the combined firms' purchases of advertising, computer, or car rental services.‡ To this end, it will be assumed that managerial services are completely non-specialized with respect to industry.

The problem then is to explain why the owners of a firm should find it more profitable to sell it rather than to remain independent; and why the

* Merger is used here as a generic term covering consolidation, acquisition and takeover. I should also note that, unless otherwise stated, the evidence cited in the paper refers to the United States.

† Eis calculates that market and product extension mergers in the US accounted for 31 per cent of disappearances in 1926–30 as against 71 per cent in 1960–64 (1969, p. 294).

‡ Of course, such motivations to merger may in fact be dominant—though to me it seems unlikely. However, they are eschewed here not on empirical grounds but rather because they are ubiquitous. To rely on them is to either make merger economics entirely vapid or to turn it into a search for the particular links between any two consolidating firms. It seems more useful to at least attempt a more general theory.

purchasing firm should be prepared to pay more than other acquirers for its control. Possible reasons are presented in section I. The available evidence is discussed in section II. Finally, in section III, some implications and conclusions are drawn.

I. REASONS FOR MERGER

A. Traditional-Entrepreneurial Reasons for Selling Control

Though it is obvious that entrepreneurial considerations are more prominent in new theories of the firm than in the traditional ones, they are not absent from the latter. The questions traditional theory is principally designed to handle—the response of firms to *changes* in demand or taxes or factor prices—and the analytical assumptions adopted—that the owner-entrepreneur seeks to maximize his own utility and that this derives solely from his personal wealth—minimize or eliminate any need for thought about entrepreneurial capability or personality. Nevertheless, such considerations emerge as an explanation for diseconomies of scale: decreasing returns to other factors as they expand relative to the entrepreneurial input.

This basic idea is frequently disputed on the ground that managers can be hired through the market—which is of course true. But what the entrepreneur cannot hire is managers who seek to maximize his utility function rather than their own; and it is therefore likely to be costly to make their *actions* coincide with those required for maximization of the entrepreneur-owner's utility function. Formally, diseconomies of scale have the same root as the problem of the managerial corporation: hired managers will not automatically act in the interest of the owner.

Before turning to the managerial theory of the firm, however, this hint in the traditional theory that entrepreneurs are not mechanical men—that they are prone to limitation and error and subject to return to the dust from whence they came—may be developed into a number of theories of merger. These are designated as 'traditional entrepreneurial' because—whether or not they were cited by traditional economists—they are clearly consistent with traditional reasoning and postulates.

In the first place, since managers have finite lives, it is likely that at some point they will wish to reduce their commitment of time to the firm or even retire completely. For some, with capable heirs, this presents no problem. But for those less fortunate, withdrawal of time and attention may imply a considerable loss of income—in effect, the firm is converted into a managerial corporation with the possible losses to the owner or owners that this implies. For the same reason, the current owner (or his incapable inheritors) may find that disposing of his holdings piecemeal through the market entails a considerable discount on the value they would have if his attention to the affairs of the firm were to continue undiminished. His most profitable solution may well be to sell to an already established firm which has the ability to provide supervisory services, possibly remaining himself as manager for some period.

Second, at some point in its expansion,* a successful firm is likely to require outside managerial personnel for specialist functions: marketing, production, finance, labour relations and so on. The owner of a relatively small firm may have considerable trouble in solving the inherent information problem: how to discover the best man available for the job. But he may also have a problem in that, however rapidly his firm is growing, it may not be growing rapidly enough to satisfy the career aspirations of the people best suited for the job; and even if it succeeds in attracting them, the owner may have difficulty in controlling a team which feels no particular loyalty to the firm and is likely to be highly mobile. An alliance through merger with a large firm will provide at least partial solutions to all of these problems and may in addition reduce the costs of supervision of specialist functionaries—the prospect of more lucrative jobs further up the scale in the parent organization may be a sufficient spur to performance.

Finally within the scope of pure entrepreneurial problems, an owner may attempt an independent solution of these problems and fail to an extent that he cannot himself recoup. Merger, regarded as a means of association with a larger pool of managerial skill,' may prove the most profitable means of obtaining assistance.†

B. Non-Entrepreneurial Reasons for Selling and Buying Control

Theories in this group are characterized by an inattention to entrepreneurial personality or problem. In the words of Michael Gort, who proposes one of the two theories discussed here: 'In short, before proceeding to search for special explanations of mergers, we would do well to see whether there is anything to explain beyond the phenomenon of normal turnover in income producing assets' (1969, p. 624). In other words, we pay no attention to the fact that income from the asset 'corporate control', unlike that from stocks and bonds, does depend upon who owns it.

Gort's hypothesis is that mergers occur because of differences in valuation of assets between buyers and sellers. As he recognizes, this is in itself a vacuous proposition—all transactions occur because of differences in valuation between buyer and seller. The essential part of the hypothesis is therefore the specification of the circumstances which give rise to changes in valuation. According to Gort, these are likely to be when there is rapid change in stock prices or when technical change is great. In addition to this hypothesis, Gort presents results from a cross-section study of industry merger rates. Both tests and hypothesis will be more fully discussed in the next section.

The second hypothesis in this group is old (and probably infirm). It is that a firm with a potentially profitable future may need outside capital to exploit its opportunities and yet only be able to obtain it *and* maintain its independence at a rate of interest which is prohibitive. Obviously, this implies a capital market which is imperfect, at least in the sense that the cost of transmitting

* 'Diseconomies of scale' merely implies a unique relation between minimum costs and scale for a *particular* firm at a *point* in time. *Over* time this relation obviously may change.

† In addition, there are taxation reasons for selling control. See in particular Butters *et al.* (1957) who also provide sample survey evidence of the importance of group A reasons for selling control.

and discovering information is high; but given this, it may prove more profitable to persuade a larger firm with available capital that the market is wrong rather than to persuade the market at large that it is wrong.

It has recently been argued that this situation would lead to a loan from the larger firm to the needy one rather than to a merger between them (Mueller 1969, pp. 651–2), but the logic of the objection is at least dubious. The essential point is that the situation visualized is one in which only two firms have more accurate information than the market at large: the one with capital to supply and the other able to make profitable use of capital at the market rate of interest. It is quite true that the transaction between them could be accomplished by bond issue; but it is also clear that this is not the most profitable transaction for the potential lender. Since information is imperfect the shares of the borrowing firm will be undervalued relative to the beliefs of the lending firm. It will therefore regard them as a profitable purchase and is likely to make their sale a condition of supplying capital. The potential borrower, on the other hand, must decide how much it will cost to persuade another source of funds to make capital available without the same string attached. Since that cost might be high, and since the lender can still make a profitable purchase if he pays more than the going market value of the shares, it is clear that agreement to merger may be the most profitable course for the smaller firm.

As well as the difference in emphasis on entrepreneurial factors, group B theories differ from group A in so far as they contain a hypothesis explaining buyers as well as sellers. There are, of course, very many such hypotheses, all of which identify some attribute of which one firm has insufficient and the other has an excess supply. It would be tedious to list all such possible factors; but one is clearly the managerial factor itself.

Thus for example a corporation faced with a decline in demand (or rate of growth of demand) for its existing products is likely to have an excess of managerial skills. There is no reason to break up a successfully functioning managerial team merely because the demand for the products its current assets are designed to produce falls below expectation; and the need to do so can readily be avoided by purchase of group A firms which have an insufficient (or a prospectively insufficient) supply of managerial skills.

While neither group A nor group B explanations of merger rely upon any separation of ownership and control, they are, with two possible exceptions, consistent with such separation. The exceptions are the planned retirement of the owner-entrepreneur, though very similar circumstances could derive from the expected retirement of a dominant non-owner manager; and Gort's valuation-discrepancies hypothesis. If ownership and control were separated, differences in the valuation of assets would imply changes in ownership but not in control. Since acquisition or merger frequently does entail a change in effective control, Gort's hypothesis could only with difficulty be extended to cover this case.

C. The Managerial Corporation: Theories of Buyers

Introduction of the fact that ownership and control are separated in most large corporations leads to at least two further suggestions. The first of these is straightforward. In so far as managers make use of their freedom from the direct control of the owners, it is a clear prediction of traditional economics that they will divert to themselves some part of the residual income stream 'due' to the owners. But if this is reflected in the price of shares of the firm, it implies the possibility of an above-market rate of return to a purchaser of control. Since corporations are essentially a device for cheaply gathering large amounts of capital and since large amounts of capital are involved in transactions concerning the control of corporations, it is likely to be corporations which react to this incentive. The purchase of control will then appear as a merger.*

The second hypothesis also appears to be straightforward but is in reality less so. It is based upon a particular hypothesis regarding the use to which managers will put resources diverted from the owners: that they will wish to maximize the rate of growth of the firm they control.† The principal advocate of the growth-maximizing hypothesis in relation to merger is Dennis C. Mueller. In his own words:

> The stock-market value of a firm (even at its maximum) will always be less than the discounted present value of the firm to a growth-maximizing management, since the latter's discount rate is below that of the marginal stockholder. Thus, even if the managements of all other firms maximized stockholder welfare, these firms would still be attractive candidates for a takeover raid by a growth-maximizing management. We conclude that a growth-maximizing management will be faced by a seemingly boundless set of merger opportunities, all priced below their present value to the management group (1969, p. 656).

However valid this proposition, another appears equally correct. This is that, *ceteris paribus*, a growth-maximizing firm will always prefer to purchase another growth-maximizing firm rather than a stockholder-welfare-maximizing firm. Stockholder welfare acts as a constraint on the operations of a management divorced from ownership; and it follows that a growth-maximizing management will always prefer to pay as little as possible for a particular collection of assets—that is, *ceteris paribus*, will prefer to deviate as little as possible from maximum stockholder welfare. Since the assets of a growth-maximizing firm will be valued less than the equivalent assets owned by a

---

* This also leads to a subsidiary hypothesis. Managements who are candidates for a hostile bid are likely to take defensive action. One form of defence is to contract a merger with another (and more friendly) management.

† As with all speculations on managerial utility functions, the connection of this hypothesis with the separation of ownership and control is less direct than may appear. Nothing in the logic of the separation of ownership and control leads to the conclusion that non-owner managers must have different utility functions than owner-managers. If one is content with the hypothesis that owners or owner-managers will maximize their utility by maximizing their tangible wealth, there is no reason to reject the proposition that non-owner managers will maximize *their* utility by maximizing *their* tangible wealth. Or, if one asserts that non-owner managers obtain utility from the size of 'their' firm or its rate of growth, there is no obvious reason why one should not assert that owner-managers obtain utility from the same source. The difference between the two lies rather in the constraints upon their actions. To increase revenue by a dollar or rate of growth by a percentage point, the owner-manager must give up income whereas the non-owner manager must (for example) increase the risk that he will lose control of the firm via takeover.

stockholder-welfare-maximizing firm, they will be preferred for acquisition by a growth-maximizing management.

It does not follow from this that all managements will be *in terrorem* and compelled to act as if they wished to maximize stockholder welfare. So long as there are transaction costs entailed in the purchase of control, this permits managements some leeway to diverge from maximum stockholder welfare. But the amount of the divergence must be less than transaction costs for otherwise the firm represents a costless purchase for another growth-maximizing management. The model therefore degenerates to a position in which managerial firms deviate from maximum stockholder welfare to some degree less than the transaction costs involved in purchasing control and in which mergers occur only in the case of firms which, presumably by accident, have allowed their market value to fall relative to their potential value to such an extent that their purchase does not put the acquiring firm at risk. In other words, to a system which may be difficult to distinguish from a pure stockholder-utility-maximizing model which includes some variance in the quality of managements. The crucial factor determining the difference is the transaction cost of merger.

Mueller recognizes this difficulty. He meets it by an appeal to size:

> In a pond in which all fish seek to devour one another, it is the biggest fish which will be immune to attack and the smallest which will be the most digestible. If all firms' managements desire growth, it will be the largest firms which can pursue this goal with the most abandon, confident that few other firms will have the financial resources to attempt to acquire them. Small and medium-sized firms will have to pursue stockholder-welfare-maximizing behaviour to a greater extent, in order to try to keep the stock price up and thereby avert takeovers (p. 658).

However, this is not a particularly happy resolution. Small, medium and large are not precise categories; but firms appropriately described as medium —or even small—do make conglomerate acquisitions. Mueller's starting point is that conglomerate merger is difficult and perhaps impossible to explain by other means than the growth-maximizing hypothesis. Yet the passage above goes a long way towards conceding that conglomerate acquisition by acquirable firms is not explicable in terms of growth maximization unless it is also explicable in terms of present-value (entrepreneurial utility) maximization.

Furthermore, in view of the apparent lack of a systematic observed relationship between size and rate of growth (see Singh and Whittington, 1968) resort to the defence that large firms are freer to pursue growth-maximizing policies than small firms appears to imply the following hypotheses:

1 If all firms maximized present value, large firms would grow more slowly than small firms.
2 The discrepancy between actual and potential (maximized) value is greater for large firms than for small.

The relationship between size and profitability is, and is likely to continue to be, a subject for debate; but it does not seem unfair to assert that there is no evidence demonstrating a systematic relationship between size and profitability. If this is the case, however, Mueller's thesis appears to imply that in a present-value-maximizing world, large firms would have both a slower rate of growth and a higher rate of profit than small ones. This may be possible but it is not particularly plausible. Certainly it requires some further explanation.

II

In general, empirical work on merger has not reached the stage of formally testing one causal hypothesis against another. Rather, it has been concentrated on examining certain characteristics of the merger process. These are considered here under four headings:

1   The profitability of merger for acquiring firms
2   The timing of merger activity
3   The characteristics of acquired companies
4   The characteristics of acquired versus non-acquired companies.

(1)   *Is Merger Profitable?*

Of the hypotheses listed above, only one predicts that merger should be an exceptionally profitable activity from the point of view of buying firms. This is the hypothesis that merger is a means of overcoming the imperfections of the capital market, which, to be plausible, must suppose that the buying firm has sufficient information to persuade it that shares of the seller are undervalued.

Only one hypothesis unambiguously predicts that merger is an unprofitable activity. If merger is part of a stategy of maximizing growth at the expense of profits, then growth maximizers bidding against one another should be prepared to pay something more than the acquired firm is worth in terms of expected income. However, the possibility that merger is sometimes a last defensive move against takeover by hostiles is compatible with merger unprofitability. It is perfectly plausible and even probable that the performance of the joined firms will not improve as a result of such a move.

For the rest, the position from the buyer's point of view may be likened to a competitive auction of any other asset. There is no obvious reason to suppose that the price established will give rise to an expected return in excess of the market rate.

There is, of course, an old literature dealing with the profitability of merger. A. S. Dewing, writing in 1921 and examining the outcome of a sample of turn-of-the-century American mergers and consolidations, concluded that members of his sample had typically fallen spectacularly short of their promoters' estimated earnings at the time of the merger; that the earnings of the constituent companies prior to consolidation were greater than the earnings of the consolidated companies in the first year of consolidation; that the average earnings of the consolidated companies over the ten years following the merger were less than the earnings of the first year following consolidation; and that the earnings of the first year were somewhat greater than those of the tenth year following consolidation.

These results were later challenged by Shaw Livermore (1935) on the basis of a much larger sample. Of 156 firms classified by Livermore as achieving a high degree of market control, 40.4 per cent were judged as outright failures and 10.9 per cent as doubtful. The remainder were in his judgment successes. The figures for his secondary group, consisting of 172 firms not achieving a high degree of market control, were similar. Failures accounted for 45.3 per cent and successes for 48.3 per cent.

The even split is compatible with Nelson's (1959) conclusion, based on a sample of 13 large consolidations of the period, that the average return to their common stock over the nine-year period following the mergers was about on a par with alternative portfolio investments. Nelson's measure, however, suffers from a disadvantage common to all studies of the behaviour of common stocks—it is not clear how much the anticipated gains (or losses) had affected share prices at the start of the period and therefore to what extent outcomes reflect discrepancies between expectations and performance rather than performance as such.

Nevertheless, these results suggest that the turn-of-the-century movement was not unduly profitable. Since it is eminently plausible that many of these mergers were undertaken with the object of creating monopoly power, a profitable outcome would not have been surprising. That there appears to have been no such general result, and that Livermore's two groups showed no great difference in success rates, suggests the possibility that managerial difficulties outweighed any gain due to increased market dominance.*

The Dewing and Livermore studies adopted some absolute standard of success and this introduces a considerable ambiguity in interpreting results. The basic methodology of postwar studies, in contrast, has been to compare some aspect of the performance of acquiring with non-acquiring firms. Though this is possibly the only way in which the problem can sensibly be tackled, it is not itself free of ambiguity as a means of discovering the profitability of merger. In so far as some firms elect to be active acquirers and others to pursue growth through internal expansion, there is some difference between them in the first instance. Until that difference is isolated, there is no warrant to assume that the performance of the acquires, had they not adopted that policy, would have been the same as non-acquirers.

It is, for example, plausible that acquirers (or sufficient of them to affect the results) are concentrated in relatively declining segments of industry while non-acquirers were in the relatively growing segments. In that case, the performance of the acquiring firms had they not acquired might have been distinctly worse than that of the non-acquirers; and a finding that their performance was roughly the same might reflect a high profitability of acquisition combined with a declining profitability of their original assets.

The two initial studies in the postwar group, by Reid (1968) and Kelly (1967) illustrate different responses to this problem. Kelly compared firms which had increased their sales by at least 20 per cent through merger and a control group, very carefully selected for comparability, which had increased theirs by merger less than 5 per cent. The need for careful selection of comparable

* Markham (1955) provides a useful discussion of these studies.

firms imposes a constraint on sample size. Kelly, with a sample of 21, found no statistically significant difference between the two groups for increase in the price of shares, rate of return, earnings per share or profit margins, though the non-merging firms were ahead in all of these. Merging firms were ahead in price-earnings ratio and net sales per share of common stock, the last difference being the only one with statistical significance. Kelly concludes that 'the form of investment, external versus internal, does not have a significant impact on profitability, whether judged in terms of market valuation or rate of return' (p. 70).

Reid, on the other hand, uses a sample of 478 large American industrial firms for the period 1951–61 (which between them had acquired some 3300 firms, just over half the total reported by the FTC). He concludes that high-merging firms have performed worse with respect to stockholders' interest* than lower merging firms or firms which have made no acquisitions. The variables representing stockholder interest are the percentage change in the price of common stock, the increase in the share of profits attributable to stockholders as of the start of the period relative to assets at the start of the period, and the share of profits attributable to original shareholders relative to sales at the beginning of the period of observation. Over all firms, the differences are statistically significant; when divided into 14 industry groups, acquiring firms perform significantly less well in 5, 8 and 7 (for the three variables, respectively) of the 14 groups. But despite the statistical significance of the results, the large-sample method eliminates any possibility of guaranteeing comparability: to construe the results as a negative answer to the question 'Is merger profitable?' therefore requires a rather substantial assumption of fact.†

Since confirmation that acquirers and non-acquirers were initially faced by roughly the same opportunities is crucial to interpretation, and since industry classification is probably the best proxy obtainable for that purpose, it is appropriate to trade off sample size for finer industry classification. In this sense, probably the most promisingly designed study to date is that of Hogarty (1970) who uses a sample of 43 corporations which engaged heavily in merger activity—so that at least a 20 per cent increase in their size was attributable to merger—during 1953–64. The sample spans 29 three-digit and 15 two-digit industries; and ranges over firms with opening assets of $2 million to over $700 million.

Hogarty's first test is based on the ratio of the stock-market price of the

---

* Reid also tests variables representing 'managerial interest' and finds that active acquirers are ahead on these. However, the interpretation of this result is not as straightforward as Reid suggests. The managerial interest is represented by growth of sales, assets and employees. In the short run it is not surprising to find acquisitive firms significantly ahead on all of these, but there is no reason to conclude, as Reid does, that mergers serve *only* the interests of managers.

† Another large-sample study, entirely undifferentiated as to industry, reports conclusions similar to those of Reid: 'On the basis of the twenty-year history of the sample as a whole, one would conclude that acquisitions do not pay and, in fact, are an inferior method of growth.' However, high-growth acquirers were 'distinctly superior' to non-acquirers on both price-earnings and price equity ratios when total history is considered. Further, '... acquirers in all [growth] classes were clearly more skilful in stemming a downward trend on the return on total capital employed in the firm. This is due in part to the use of higher debt leverage' (Ansoff, Brandenburg, Partner and Radosevich 1971, p. 75).

acquiring company to its stock-market price two years before the first acquisition made by the firm.* The 1964 price is adjusted for dividends by the addition to it of an arithmetic sum of dividends paid over the period; and the ratio is compared with the performance of the unweighted index of stock-market performance for the relevant SIC grouping as computed by Fisher and Lorie.†

Only 10 of the 43 heavily merging firms outperform their industrial groupings; a sufficiently small proportion, on a binomial test, to reject the null hypothesis at the 0.01 level. The mean of the sample distribution is negative (indicating an inferior stock-market performance by heavily merging firms) but not significantly different from zero.

However, when the Fisher–Laurie index is replaced with a Standard and Poor's index, weighted by value of outstanding shares and excluding dividend payments so that the comparison is between capital gains generated by heavily merging firms and their primary industry counterparts, 20 out of 43 heavy mergers outperform their industry group. Clearly, this has no statistical significance.

On a further comparison of earnings-per-share growth of the two groups, 16 of 37 high-merging firms outperformed their industry. In each of the last two comparisons, the mean was negative (indicating overall relative failure of merging firms) though not significantly different from zero.

Hogarty concludes:

> ... the investment performance of heavily merging firms is generally worse than the average investment performance of firms in their respective industries. A complementary measure of success suggests that mergers have a neutral impact on profitability; however, this measure was based on an index which, in our judgment, was less suitable for the purpose at hand (p. 325).

Hogarty gives two reasons for his preference. The first is that the Standard and Poor's index is weighted towards the largest firms in their grouping whereas Fisher and Laurie's is not weighted. The second is that the Fisher and Laurie index contains more firms than the Standard and Poor index (the median number for industries entering the sample was 7 for Standard and Poor against 25 for Fisher and Laurie). Hogarty argues that there is reason to believe that '... since the Korean war, large firms have experienced gains in market value below the average for all publicly held firms...' and from that to the proposition that unweighted indexes will outperform indexes weighted towards large firms. While this may be so, it is not demonstrated; and furthermore some of Hogarty's sample firms are themselves large. His point implies that simple comparisons between means are unsatisfactory: but to substantiate it and to correct for its effects would require much more detailed statistical analysis than Hogarty provides.‡

* Thus raising the problem of interpreting stock-price movements.

† These indexes are described by L. Fisher (1966).

‡ Hogarty's work has been extended by Gort and Hogarty jointly (1970). Using the Fisher and Laurie indexes, they there argue, *inter alia*, that merger has a roughly neutral effect on the joint profitability of the joined firms but that there is a transfer from the owners of acquiring to the owners of acquired firms.

In the meantime, there appears to be no compelling reason to abandon the hypothesis that merger is about as profitable as other forms of investment. The evidence suggests strongly that acquiring firms have performed less well for their owners than non-acquiring firms; but until one can be reasonably confident that *ceteris paribus* is satisfied, this tells nothing about the profitability of merger as an activity. On the other hand when industry classifications are held tolerably constant, merger activity appears to have a roughly neutral effect on profitability.*

(2) *The Timing of Merger Activity*

In the United States, a good deal of attention has been devoted to the correlation of merger activity and the business cycle and stock-market prices. The general conclusion appears to be that some connection does exist.

Probably the most careful analysis to date is that of Ralph Nelson (1959). His finding is that '... while the findings of this study may have demonstrated clearly the importance of the capital market as a proximate factor in merger movements, they have not so clearly demonstrated its importance as an ultimate cause' (p. 126). This is of course the nub of the issue. Merger is a type of investment behaviour. *A priori*, there is every reason to suppose that the factors which influence the stock-market, and the general level of economic activity, will also influence merger activity. It is possible to make a causal argument in almost every conceivable direction; but the perceived correlations do not substantiate these.

Nevertheless, much of the interest in these connections derives from some belief about the plausibility of a causal relation running from the stock market to merger activity. Gort's theory of merger, already mentioned, takes the relation as a major support of his argument. In this view, rapid movement of stock-market prices gives rise to a random reordering of expectations of individuals. As a result, some owners of assets will come to value them less highly than non-owners, and when this occurs, mergers will take place. There appears to be nothing wrong with this view in logic—however, the correlation is hardly strong evidence for the hypothesis. Gort's own evidence, a cross-section study of industry merger rates, is more interesting and fits properly into the next section.

(3) *The Characteristics of Acquired Firms*

The variable Gort is attempting to explain in his analysis is the merger rate:

* There are also two studies of specialized firms: in advertising (Johnson and Simon 1969) and banking (D. Smith 1971). The authors of the advertising study conclude that merged agencies performed poorly after their merger. However, despite their contrary assertion, their evidence suggests that the merging agencies were also performing badly *before* their mergers. The banking study finds that merging banks increased the yield on assets but also incurred higher operating expenses than non-merging banks which more that offset the increased yield. This is a short-period study—1960 to 1965— and raises the issue of whether merger should be expected to produce immediate gain or, in the banking context, whether operating expenses will *remain* higher for the merging banks. The same point arises with Ajit Singh's (1971) analysis of UK data, which shows a majority of amalgamating firms declining in profitability relative to their industries in the two years following merger.

the ratio of aggregate number of mergers in a three-digit industry over the period 1951–9 to the number of firms in the industry in 1954 with assets of $500000 or over. The analysis is confined to manufacturing industries and covers a total of 5534 acquisitions.

The essence of Gort's results lie in high and positive partial correlation coefficients between the merger rate and variables describing growth or change (technical personnel ratio 0.737, productivity change 0.519, growth 0.454; all over a sample of 46). In addition the merger rate is positively correlated with the concentration ratio (0.589 on a sample of 46, 0.446 on a sample of 101) but displays a small and negative correlation with the change in concentration over the period. The merger rate is less strongly correlated with rate of change of average assets (0.226 on a 101 sample) and with rate of change in firms and proprietors (0.157 over a 101 sample). These variables are reported in various combinations in multiple regression analysis with the growth variables and concentration showing the highest level of significance. There is, of course, substantial intercorrelation between the different variables.

Gort is one of the few writers on merger who establishes his analysis so that one causal hypothesis is tested against another. Unfortunately, he selects only his own valuation-discrepancies hypothesis and the traditional monopoly and economies of scale hypotheses for test. His disposal of the latter two is moderately convincing, and this outcome is then interpreted by him as a confirmation of his own hypothesis.

In terms of discussion in section I, however, the appropriate group of hypotheses to pose against Gort's is A: traditional-entrepreneurial. This is particularly so for a very large sample consisting mainly of small firms in which separation of ownership and control is likely to be very far from complete. In this view, industries which display rapid technological or other change are likely to place managerial skills at a premium. Thus there are likely to be relatively large numbers of small firms who require managerial assistance; and relatively large numbers of established firm managers who feel able and willing to supply it.

Gort recognizes this possibility but—while conceding that such differences are independent of firm size—treats the hypothesis as a sub-division of the economies-of-scale argument. It is formulated as a testable proposition in terms of the number of firms entering the industry: 'In periods or in industries in which there is a rapid increase in the number of firms, there will tend to be a more than proportional rise in the number of managers of untested ability. As a result the dispersion among firms in quality of managerial skills should increase and, in turn, should lead to a rise in merger activity' (p. 631). It is rejected on the basis that, 'Rate of change in number of firms did not contribute significantly, in any of the equations, towards explaining the variance in the merger rate and the regression coefficient had the wrong sign from the standpoint of the economies-of-scale hypothesis' (p. 637).

It is not clear, of course, that entry is an appropriate variable to test the hypothesis: the demands on managerial skills implied by a rapidly changing industry may simply shorten the life of existing firms. But a more serious objection to Gort's position is his measurement of entry, which is simply the ratio of firms and proprietors at the end of the period to that at the beginning. Thus if N is the opening number of firms, E the number of new firms established in the industry, M the number of amalgamations within the industry and C the number of purchases of firms within the industry by firms from outside it, Gort is correlating $(M + C)/N$ (the merger rate) with $(N + E - M)/N$ (the change in firms and proprietors). A low or negative correlation or regression coefficient is therefore not surprising. Certainly it cannot be interpreted as evidence against a traditional-entrepreneurial view of merger.

(4) *The Characteristics of Acquired v. Non-acquired Firms*

Research appropriately coming under this heading has largely concentrated on the efficiency—interpreted as fulfilment of owner-interests—of the managements of acquired versus those of comparable non-acquired firms. Of the hypotheses discussed in section I, those in group C predict that the managements of acquired firms will appear to be inefficient; and the same is true of the merger-as-a-means-of-obtaining-capital view, though in this case it is an error by the stock market rather than any actual inefficiency that is the cause. On the other hand Gort's hypothesis is quite compatible with every appearance of efficiency and profitability and there is no reason why group A causes should not be associated with a level of profitability in excess of the average performance for the industry. This would be less true for firms that had attempted to solve their problems and failed; but even here the effects of failure may be prospective rather than actual.

The evidence collected so far appears to show that acquired firms are somewhat, but not markedly, less efficient than those not experiencing acquisition. Firms whose managers appear to be perfectly efficient are acquired; even among large firms for which there is good ground to suppose that ownership and control are separate (see Hindley 1969 and Singh 1971).

However, a possibly much more important piece of evidence lies in the fact that firms whose managers appear to be highly inefficient and whose stock market value is low relative to their asset value, survive with the incumbent managements' control intact (Hindley 1969 and Singh 1971). Attempts to explain such survivals by the hypothesis that they are not managerially controlled, and therefore not candidates for purchase against the wishes of their owners, or by the hypothesis that they have in fact experienced control changes through less dramatic and publicized means than takeover, have met with some, very limited, success. However, this has not been sufficient to explain the continuing existence of all of them (Hindley 1969).

III

Merger is part of a continual process by which assets are redistributed among managements. Granted that managements decline and decay, it is a perfectly normal and desirable process of capitalism—whether of the owner-entrepreneurial or the managerial variety. Even if capital markets were perfect (in the sense that new resources were allocated on the basis of the present value of their intended use), cases would occur in which a particular management should receive a negative allocation: assets now controlled by them should be transferred to other hands. In the imperfect markets we actually observe, large negative allocations will also be required to redress errors of the past. Merger is a means of achieving these results.

That merger would occur in an economy operating at full efficiency does not imply that the process observed in actual economies is efficient. The correct matching of managerial skills and assets, and the changes which should take place in the matching over time, are not particularly tractable analytical problems. The strongest statement possible is that, to the extent that the purchase of a firm resembles a competitive auction, the actual acquirer is the management which places the highest value on the acquired assets. To the extent that merger has roughly the same profitability as other modes of purchasing assets, this is consistent with an efficient process. Both premises are questionable, and, even granting that the acquirer is the firm prepared to pay the highest price, an inference of efficiency would beg the question of whether this is due to superior managerial skill or (for example) to the enhanced monopoly power the acquisition will bring.

Enhanced monopoly power is, of course, one reason why merger is regarded with suspicion, and it seems very likely that some mergers are contracted for this purpose. However, abandonment of the assumption that managerial skills are completely non-specialized generates an alternative hypothesis for intra-industry mergers. Firms already in an industry, and therefore in possession of the skills required for the industry, would on that account then be prepared to pay more for a firm in the industry than would an extra-industry firm.* On that hypothesis, diversification patterns would tend to be within industries closely related to the firm's original industry—a fairly generally observed pattern.†

The temporal bunching of mergers provides a second reason for suspicion of merger. Extrapolation from merger activity at its height can provide startling predictions. However, heightened merger activity may conceivably be a permanent feature of economic organization in the future. In large part this is due to the spread of organizational techniques which are likely to reduce the costs of absorbing an alien form into the acquiring firm—a development well described and analysed in Oliver Williamson's contribution to Marris and Wood (1971). In so far as acquisition—which brings a price for the enterprise as a going concern—becomes a more likely fate than liquidation for a not entirely successful firm, it is possible that this will induce more incorporations and hence the supply of candidates for acquisition.

There is insufficient evidence to support much more than speculation on the precise nature of the overall merger process. However, when merger is regarded as an important part of the market for corporate control, the evidence is more decisive.

This is not so much because firms which are acquired are sometimes profitable or even highly profitable members of their industry. That observation is explicable in a variety of terms; among which is the dual nature of the

* Of course, the specialized skills can be purchased through the market. Merger is one means of doing this—and the hypothesis would provide a reason for the acquisition of firms which have an excellent profit record in their industry.

† For a convenient summary of the literature see Adrian Wood's Appendix on diversification in Marris and Wood (1971).

actual economic system—the bulk of assets controlled by managerial firms but a perhaps considerable majority of firms conforming more closely to the traditional owner-controlled type. Though the observation may prove to be due to the inefficiency of the market for corporate control, there are at present sufficient alternative explanations to reduce its force as evidence for that contention.

Firms whose records indicate unprofitable operation and whose assets give every appearance of substantial undervaluation relative to their potential value provide more compelling evidence. The survival of such firms with control intact despite widely dispersed ownership would provide decisive refutation* of the contention that the market for corporate control is a constraint of sufficient power to make present-value maximization a reasonable approximation of managerial behaviour.

Merely on the ground that their existence would establish the precondition for managerial theories of the firm, such firms deserve more detailed examination than they have yet received. Their examination would have significance beyond this, however. The phenomenon of a grossly inefficient takeover system seems as difficult to explain in terms of growth-maximizing models as in present value-maximizing terms: as Mueller's analysis suggests, growth maximizers should, if anything, be more eager than present-value maximizers to acquire corporations whose potential value is above their purchase price. Demonstration of an inefficient takeover system would therefore be a major step towards rejecting growth-maximizing models in favour of some form of non-aggresive 'easy life' managerial model of the firm.

* It would also have to be shown that their accounting value was not inflated relative to comparable firms and that it did not conceal commitments which would be costly to acquirers—such as obligations to pay large sums in compensation to dismissed executives.

TAKEOVER RAIDERS AND THE GROWTH-MAXIMIZATION HYPOTHESIS

by

D. A. KUEHN

I. INTRODUCTION

Recent development of the theory of the firm has taken several distinct directions, important contributions having been made with regard to the substitution of factors other than profits in hypothesized managerial objective functions. The choice between the various models may finally depend upon the nature of the behavioural predictions sought, whether they relate to internal decision-making processes or external interaction between firms. It need not be necessary for any one model to represent a general theory of firm behaviour; the model should rather give insight into the theoretical problems facing a researcher, and testable predictions with which to assess its usefulness.

Progress has been made through the explicit recognition of the separation of ownership and control in the modern company. To the extent that the shareholding is dispersed, owners will find difficulties (costs) involved in attempts to induce managers to maximize the profits (wealth) accruing to the shareholders. This is seen as a condition for the existence of managerial discretion and hence an explanation for the departure from the traditional assumption that firms will seek to maximize profits to the owners. Interest has centred on specifying the nature of the managerial objective function as well as the constraints imposed on the amount of managerial discretion available to pursue an objective not directly in owners' interests. Such constraints have been incorporated into a security variable in the managerial objective function. This desire for security which competes with the attainment of the managerial objective(s) stems mainly from two sources. First, it reflects the existence of the threat of owner sanction, which at the extreme will imply a loss of job, or possibly some curtailment in the managers' power to divert resources away from the owners (for example, removal of slack). This will depend upon the degree of departure from the profit-maximizing position and the dispersion of shareholding which reflects the difficulties involved in employing such a sanction.

Second, an externally imposed security constraint operating through the stock-market value of the company exists because of the fear of takeover and consequential loss of job. The achievement of an objective which results in a departure from the profit-maximizing position will adversely affect the market valuation of the company and hence lead to an increase in the likelihood of takeover. The impact of this source of the security constraint is dependent again on the extent of the departure from the profit-maximizing position (that is, the extent to which the objective results in a fall in the market valuation) as well as the transaction costs involved in another company acquiring the firm. There may be other factors which affect the impact of this constraint, such as the defensive position of the firm (that is, the managers' ability to move back towards the profit-maximizing position—thus raising the market valuation). At the extreme, the pursuit of an objective which directly competes with profitability may result, instead of takeover, in bankruptcy, which has an even more certain effect on the managerial security.

There have been several theoretical developments of the theory of the firm which posited alternative managerial objectives. These include sales maximizing (Baumol 1959), O. E. Williamson's discretionary model (1964) and the growth-maximizing model of Robin Marris (1964). It is the purpose of this paper to examine empirically some of the derivable predictions from Marris's managerial growth-maximizing model with reference to firms which have overtly demonstrated a desire to expand externally—that is, takeover raiders. In fairness to Robin Marris, what follows is not strictly an explicit application of the functional form of his model, for in his own words, '...through most of what follows we shall write as if internal expansion were the only method of growth ... and merger possibilities are subsumed in specifying the functional forms. Alternatively, the reader may regard our theory as representing an account of the limits on growth rates among firms which do not merge' (1964, p. 124). The development of this paper nevertheless remains an application which he implies would not be contrary to his thesis.

I shall take as my starting point the likelihood that those firms which are observed to be actively striving for external growth via takeovers are a subset of firms whose managers include the firm's growth rate as a major component in their objective function. In the UK industrial climate where takeovers are common* and such external expansion is a significant proportion of the total growth of firms, takeovers can be seen as a feasible way for many firms to supplement, or even provide an alternative to, internal growth. If, by this reasoning, raiders are firms whose managers view growth as a primary objective, then the predictions from a Marris-type growth-maximization hypothesis should be verified by empirical tests made with respect to this subset of possible growth maximizers. Moreover, in the context of the preceding discussion, if the growth-maximizing theory is to have any relevance it ought to be possible to observe some significant departure from the behaviour of the owner-controlled profit-maximizing firm.† The general procedure adopted in this paper is, in section II, to derive predictions concerning the proportion of raiders expected to achieve values of various stock-market and financial variables greater or less than that achieved by firms in a comparable industrial setting‡ for the two alternative behavioural assumptions of profit maximization and growth maximization. In section III these predictions are then examined with respect to the actual proportions found empirically.

* Between 1957 and 1970 approximately 47 per cent of all public quoted UK 'commercial–industrial' companies were taken over.

† In what follows I shall only consider the effect of attributing these two possible managerial motivations to raiders. However, much of what is argued with respect to the maximization of the growth rate of assets would hold for the sales-revenue-maximization model and without too much conceptual difficulty would fit into Williamson's discretionary model where the growth rate plays an important role in determining the amount of slack available within the system. Moreover, profit maximization is not contrasted with growth maximization simply to put up a straw man to be knocked down. It is rather seen as an alternative and not unreasonable motivational scheme having as its basis strong owner control over managerial behaviour. We are not directly concerned with an examination of the predictions of the classical long-run profit-maximization model since nearly all behaviour is consistent with this. Instead, in order to make the notion of profit maximization operational we will view profit maximization in a shorter-run sense, stemming from owners' uncertainty of the long run and consequently asserting their high rate of discount of the future upon their managers' actions.

‡ Relating raiders' performance to their respective industry median values is done to normalize the performance indicators and thereby remove differences which are solely attributable to market conditions.

It can readily be seen that not only are the two objectives imputed to raiders crucial in determining the predictions, but so also are the objectives attributed to the group of non-raiding comparable firms. That is, the derived performance predictions for raiders as growth maximizers compared with the performance of firms in the raider's own industry may change, depending on the sort of assumptions made concerning these comparable firms' motivational objectives. In what follows I shall consider the effect of imputing four possible motivational schemes to the non-raiding firms: viewing them as growth maximizers, profit maximizers, easy-life maximizers (resulting in a high preference for security), and finally as sleepy firms differing only in their degree of inefficiency. In fact the body of non-raiding companies may incorporate firms with all the above objectives and probably companies with others as well. The purpose of specifying the objectives is not to test their general validity but rather to introduce a greater degree of rigour into the analysis than would be possible in the absence of any discussion of the group of companies to be compared with raiders. If one finds general agreement between the predictions derived employing the four schemes of categorizing non-raiding firms when raiders are assumed to be maximizing their growth rate as contrasted with the predictions derived under the assumption that raiders are profit maximizers, then greater confidence can be placed upon the analysis than would be possible had not this specification of motives been undertaken. Possibly a drawback of such an approach is that the amount of

Table 1. Summary table of derived predictions

Assumption	Growth rate	Profit rate	Valuation ratio	Retention ratio
Raiders G.M. Others P.M.	+	−	0	−
Raiders G.M. Others G.M.	+	0	+	−
Raiders G.M. Others E.L.M.	+	−	0	−
Raiders G.M. Others S.F.	+	0	+	−
Raiders P.M. Others P.M.	0	+	−	0
Raiders P.M. Others E.L.M.	+	+	−	+
Raiders P.M. Others S.F.	+	+	0	0
Actual sign of proportion of raiders exceeding median ind. value				
All firms	+(111/117)	0(60/117)	+(87/117)	−(70/117)
All raiders and surviving firms	+(97/117)	−(67/117)	0(63/117)	−(78/117)

Note: Proportions greater than 67/117 or less than 48/117 are significant at the 5 per cent level.

a priori theorizing must necessarily increase in proportion to the detail of the analysis. It is nevertheless hoped that a picture of the raider as a growth maximizer which is distinct from the raider as a profit maximizer will emerge from section II and at least a majority of the analysis on which the predictions are based will be broadly acceptable. For clarity, the predictions are summarized in table 1. A positive sign is given where the prediction is that a significant majority of raiders are expected to exceed their respective industry median for a particular variable. A negative sign is given for the opposite prediction and a zero indicates there is not expected to be any significant difference between the two groups.

II. DERIVED PREDICTIONS FROM A GROWTH-MAXIMIZATION HYPOTHESIS

A. Growth Rate

The primary prediction to emerge from the hypothesis is that a significant majority of raiders (firms observed to be actively seeking growth) should in fact demonstrate growth rates higher than non-raiding firms in a comparable industrial setting. Were this not substantiated empirically, doubt would be cast on the applicability of a theory which postulated growth maximization as a general managerial objective but failed to fit a set of firms extraneously observable as seeking expansion. It is argued below that this is a general prediction from the growth-maximization hypothesis in the sense that it does not depend upon the four possible motives which will be attributed to the non-raiding firms.

As profit maximizers, comparable firms would be expected to achieve rates of growth consistent with the availability of profitable investment opportunities. Identifying this availability with a normal declining marginal efficiency of capital schedule appropriate to the opportunities available within the industrial setting, net investment would cease when the rate of return equalled the cost of borrowing. The raider as a growth maximizer on the other hand would be expected to undertake raids in excess of that warranted by profitability.* Assuming a limited supply of potentially profitable takeover opportunities, this would involve the raider growing faster than firms which were assumed to be maximizing profits. By defining raiders as firms which have undertaken three or more raids within the sample period we have allowed the set of comparable firms to undertake expansion by takeover as well as internal investment. Thus consideration of profitability can result in some raiding but in terms of this prediction active raiding is seen as primarily growth motivated.

If comparable firms are themselves growth maximizers, raiders would still be expected to demonstrate faster growth rates since, as Marris points out, raiding is subject to fewer constraints than is internal expansion. The raider must only consider the marketability (acceptability) of his equity or his ability to service his loan stock, as these form the majority of the payments made for acquired firms. The internal-growth maximizer is constrained not

---

* See section II.B where profitability is integrated into the model.

only by the above considerations when he seeks funds for expansion but also by the difficulties and costs involved in borrowing elsewhere and the constraints imposed on internal growth by retentions and the supply of technical and managerial expertise which the raider is in a sense purchasing along with the assets of the firm. Firms with growth-oriented managers may be seen as the raiders of the future, trying to establish themselves and their firms so as to alleviate these constraints and eventually become 'high flyers' in the stock market.

A third assumption about the comparable firms is that they are easy-life maximizers and possess managers who have a high priority for survival and generally undertake satisficing behaviour. Their aim is seen as the achievement of 'safe' levels of performance which is an attempt to insulate themselves on the one hand from the likelihood of bankruptcy or dismissal by the shareholders and on the other hand from the possibility of financial disaster or being taken over themselves resulting from undertaking excessive risk by attempting to grow too fast. Here again, the prediction is that raiders would grow faster than these comparable firms with this survival motivation, as only a satisfactory level of expansion would be necessary to keep their market valuation sufficiently high to discourage raids or a shareholder revolt and maintain their market share while avoiding high-risk investment projects.

Finally, one could envisage the comparable firms as simply sleepy firms which are a range of companies differing only in their degree of inefficiency. The majority either go bankrupt or are taken over. Some survive through favourable market conditions or fortuitous decisions made in the past, but in general seldom perform consistently well over a period of time. Here one would again predict that such firms would demonstrate possibly an erratic but on average low growth rate so that the raiders would be expected to grow faster than the sleepy firms.

The predictions derived by assuming that raiders are growth maximizers consistently view raiders as growing faster than comparable firms under the various assumptions concerning the nature of the objectives of these firms. This prediction differs from that derived by assuming all firms including raiders are profit maximizers in that in general the profit-maximizing raider would not be expected to demonstrate a faster long-run average growth rate as compared with the firms in their respective industrial settings. Investment projects undertaken solely on the basis of expected profitability would not be likely to result in significant differences between firms' growth rates simply due to the chosen mix between internal and external expansion. Of course, some raiders as profit maximizers would grow faster than firms in their industry as a result of extraneous variations between firms in, for example, the quality of management but not as a result of differing motivations which are by assumption identical. Since there is no reason to suppose that managerial expertise which would necessarily result in fast growth is concentrated in the hands of raiding firms, we would not expect to observe a pervasive tendency for raiders to grow faster than firms in their own industry, if one assumes raiders as well as comparable firms are profit maximizers.

The implications of assuming that raiders are profit maximizers and comparable firms are growth maximizers will not be examined in this section or in those that follow as such an assumption bears no likely relationship to reality or the theme of this paper and remains only a conceptual possibility.

If the comparable firms are assumed to be easy-life maximizers or sleepy firms, imputing profit-maximizing behaviour to raiders would be likely to result in predicting that raiders would grow faster than such firms. Neither of these posited situations is pursued here because of the direct and necessary implications such predictions have on the derived predictions for profitability which are considered in the next section.

B. Profit Rate

A second and theoretically associated prediction is that a significant majority of raiders as growth maximizers should earn lower than average profit rates than comparable firms. This is a necessary condition for acceptability of a growth-maximization hypothesis in preference to profit maximization for two reasons. First, in specifying managerial discretion in terms of the growth rate instead of profits, Marris correctly envisaged a trade-off between growth and profitability whereby firms sought expansion in excess of the level warranted by profitability considerations. Profits only enter the managerial objective function by way of a constraint on the primary growth objective to maintain some minimum level. Second, both predictions of a faster average growth rate and a lower average profit rate are a logical necessity in order to distinguish empirically the two theoretical structures. After all, if raiders tended to achieve above-average profit rates as well as faster growth rates, it could be argued that raiders were not attempting to maximize their growth rate but rather were successful profit maximizers achieving fast growth as a consequence. This prediction of a lower average profit rate for raiders as growth maximizers is not, however, general, in that it does depend upon the nature of the particular motive specified for the comparable firms.

If the comparable firms are assumed to be seeking maximum profits it is likely that our derived prediction would hold, because, as argued above, raiders were seen as sacrificing profits in favour of fast growth.

Comparable firms as growth maximizers, however, would also be sacrificing profits in favour of growth. Theoretically we have no grounds on which to distinguish whether the raiding growth maximizers would have sacrificed more or less of their profits to achieve fast growth than the comparable firms as growth maximizers.

As easy-life maximizers, the comparable firms would achieve their desired security partly through the maintenance of a satisfactory profit rate. The easy-life maximizer would not earn the maximum achievable level of profits since the easy life would involve putting up with some inefficiency and incurring some slack. But since security forms a major part of the easy life he would not be expected to allow his profits to fall to the extent of the growth maximizer where security enters the function not as an *objective* but as a *constraint*. Thus by comparison, raiders as growth maximizers who have sacrificed profits would be likely to demonstrate lower-than-average profit rates.

Were the comparable firms typified by the sleepy inefficient firm described in the section above, we again have little *a priori* basis on which to distinguish the average profit performance of the growth-maximizing raider, with his minimum profits constraint, and the sleepy firm which typically gets taken over because of a poor profit record. Some insight may be gained, based upon the empiricial evidence in section III but that still will ultimately depend upon one's personal assessment of the commonness of sleepy firms in the industrial population.

The derived profit predictions for raiders as growth maximizers when compared with firms in their respective industries under various assumptions about the nature of the motivations of the comparable firms do not yield as clear a picture as did the growth-rate predictions. No definite predictions could be made with regard to the relative performance of growth-maximizing raiders when comparable firms are assumed to be typified by sleepy firms, or growth maximizers. However, the definite prediction emerges that a majority of raiders will demonstrate lower average profit rates when the comparable firms are assumed to be profit maximizers or easy-life maximizers. We shall argue below that assuming raiders to be profit maximizers results in the opposite prediction. That is, profit-maximizing raiders would be expected to be observed earning higher profits than the firms in their respective industries and thereby the two theoretical predictions remain mutually exlusive.

To assume all firms including raiders are profit maximizers would, on general equilibrium principles, appear to imply identical, or at least not significantly different, rates of return earned within an industry regardless of the chosen mix between internal and external expansion. If, however, profit-maximizing raiders were simply less risk averse than their counterparts who seldom if ever undertook raids, significant differences in rates of return could result. By assumption raids are only undertaken on the basis of expected profitability. Even if profit-maximizing raiders were unable to maintain a higher rate of return in the long run—or came to grief in the medium term as the result of too much expansion, so that the profit expectations were not fulfilled in the long run—there would be a tendency for such firms to demonstrate higher short-run rates of return. This is especially likely to emerge when the period over which the performance is examined contains a much higher level of raiding activity towards the end, so that one would be observing the majority of profit-maximizing raiders during their short-run period of above-average profits. Furthermore, if one believes that the population of companies comprises a range of firms with profit-making potential, based either upon the degree of risk aversion or upon differences in managerial talent, it would not be unreasonable to accept the widely held view that raiders are dynamic firms with good-quality management. Here again, the expectation is that raiders' superior managerial talent, assuming it is directed at maximizing profits, would tend to result in a significant majority actually exceeding the median rate of return for their respective industries. If one assumes that the comparable firms are easy-life maximizers or sleepy firms instead of profit maximizers, this conclusion is all the stronger as these alternative modes of behaviour result in non-optimum profit performance.

C. *Valuation Ratio*

An integral part of the Marris growth-maximization hypothesis concerns the trade-off between the growth rate and the firm's valuation ratio (defined as the ratio of the market price of its shares to the net assets per share or equivalently the ratio of the total market value of the firm to the book value). Just as it was argued earlier that the growth maximizer would tend to sacrifice profits for growth, he would also be trading off the valuation ratio against his growth rate. He is restrained, however, in his attempts to maximize growth by a security constraint imposed through the valuation ratio. This security constraint is seen as operating because of the inverse relationship between the valuation ratio and the probability of takeover.* To the extent that a firm's profit performance affects its market valuation, the trade-off between growth and profits and growth and valuation ratio will amount to the same thing and therefore will involve managers adopting policies designed to maintain some minimum value of both variables for reasons of security. This would imply that internal-growth maximizers would tend to have lower valuation ratios than the median of firms in their respective industries. I shall argue below, however, that because growth-maximizing raiders achieve their growth objectives externally, a significant number would, for various reasons, tend to display valuation ratios above their respective industry medians.

Not only would growth-maximizing raiders wish to keep their valuation ratio safe, they would also wish to keep it high thereby effectively lowering the cost of the acquisition to the extent that it is financed by a share issue. The desire, however, is not sufficient to explain why the market would be expected to favour the growth-maximizing raiders' shares. Part of the explanation lies in the role retentions play in the determination of market valuation. This will be discussed in detail in section D. Briefly, I shall argue that raiders would be expected to retain a smaller proportion of after-tax earnings (that is, pay out higher dividends) in an attempt to raise the valuation ratio; high dividends would tend to be valued by the owners and hence the market. Additionally, to the extent that the market is, as Keynes described, a beauty contest, raiding would tend to make the firm known and superficially attractive; thus desired by investors as part of their portfolio. Further, any conglomerate element in the expansion will be recognized as risk spreading and thus desired by investors, in so far as the raider will be less affected by unexpected contractions in demand in one sector. On the other hand, raiders' shares would be in demand by risk takers in so far as some raiders do very well in terms of profits. Finally, to the extent that raiding is financed by loan stock or even convertible loan stock (which has come into prominence in the UK as a method of payment in the recent takeover boom) and the rate of return earned by the raider exceeds the cost of servicing the loan stock, the share of profits from the acquisitions will tend over time to be directed to the pre-acquisition owners; though with convertibles this time span will be limited. Thus, despite the fact that the growth-maximizing raider is sacrificing profits which would normally depress the valuation ratio, the method of expansion by takeover would generally result in the enhancement of raiders' valuation ratios. The security constraint may only be operable when raiders as growth maximizers fail to maintain their growth rate or fail to satisfy their minimum profits

---

* For evidence of the existence of such an inverse relationship, see Kuehn (1969). Further, as yet unpublished, work on a census of UK public quoted companies more strongly supports the existence of this relationship.

constraint, the latter possibly causing the former. This explanation is consistent with the observations Marris made that firms are reported to be taken over for attempting to grow too fast and losing control; the poor profit position having caused the firm to retrench and therefore lower its growth target.

In terms of the method of analysis of this paper, assuming raiders are growth maximizers and the set of comparable firms are typified by either profit maximizers or easy-life maximizers does not allow us to derive definite predictions. Comparable firms as profit maximizers would be able to maintain healthy valuation ratios because of the effect profits have on the valuation ratio. Similarly, the easy-life maximizers in their desire for security would be forced to keep up the valuation ratio by adopting policies which avoided the threat of takeover or shareholder intervention. Despite the basis for believing that these two motivational schemes would result in high valuation ratios, we have no basis on which to derive predictions in terms of relative levels of the valuation ratio.

If comparable firms are assumed to be growth maximizers, it is likely that a significant majority of raiders as growth maximizers would have greater-than-average valuation ratios. This follows from what was argued in sections II.A and II.B. Raiders could grow faster than their internal-growth-maximizing counterparts because they face fewer external and internal constraints. They need not, however, have had to sacrifice their profit rate any more than the internal-growth maximizer to achieve the faster growth. Thus raiders' valuation ratios *ceteris paribus* would tend to be higher than those of the set of growth-maximizing comparable firms.

If the comparable firms are typified by the sleepy inefficient firms, it is also likely that a significant majority of growth-maximizing raiders would have greater valuation ratios. There is nothing in the sleepy firm's performance to cause the market to favour its valuation of such a firm. Also, this sort of firm is typically taken over because of its low valuation ratio and the fact that an alternative management could earn a greater rate of return with the given assets. The sleepy firms that survive raiding most likely are insulated by voting control being in the hands of owner-managers or families sympathetic to existing management. Thus one would expect the raider with its healthy growth rate to command a better market valuation than the sleepy inefficient firm.

If it is now assumed that raiders are profit maximizers, the prediction for the majority of raiders' valuation ratios depends upon the accuracy of the argument put forward in section II.B concerning the profit-maximizing raiders' short-run and long-run profit performance *and* the time horizon of the stock market. If, because of a lower risk aversion than their profit-maximizing non-raiding counterparts, profit-maximizing raiders manage to earn short-run super-normal profits but tend in the longer run to be forced to retrench and if the market's time horizon is long enough to incorporate the effect of this likelihood into its evaluation of the firm's shares, then the market will tend to discount the present short-run profits in its evaluation of the profit-maximizing raiders' shares. Thus one could expect a significant majority of raiders as profit maximizers to have valuation ratios below that of profit-maximizing comparable firms. This is another way of suggesting that the stock market rewards long-run success and stability and tends to be rather cool towards short-run risky behaviour.*

If the comparable firms are easy-life maximizers and raiders are profit maximizers, it is likely that a significant proportion of raiders would demonstrate lower average valuation ratios than the set of comparable firms. Easy-life-maximizing managers would be expected to maintain healthy market valuations by adjusting their financial indicators so as to gain market (and shareholder) approval. A safe valuation ratio for such managers would then be at the level that minimized the threat of takeover and satisfied shareholders so that their job security was guaranteed in so far as was possible. This safe level would be expected to be greater in a significant number of cases than that demonstrated by the raider were he to be maximizing profits in that, as argued in the previous paragraph, raiders with a short-run profit objective would not be likely to be able to maintain this in the longer run. This, I argued, would be reflected in the market's valuation of its shares since the market was seen as being interested in a long-run view of performance. Even if the profit-maximizing raiders do not suffer a fall in profits as a result of raiding but simply display a greater variance, as would be expected from undertaking a risky method of achieving profit, the market again might well be expected to downgrade the value of such firms' shares. Finally the market does not necessarily reward firms only on the basis of profitability. Thus firms earning above-average profit rates will not necessarily have above-average valuation ratios.† For these reasons, a significant majority of raiders would be expected to have lower average valuation ratios than comparable firms typified by easy-life maximizers, whose main vehicle to the easy life is a 'safe' valuation ratio.

If comparable firms were sleepy firms, no definite prediction can be made with regard to their market valuation relative to that of profit-maximizing raiders. Both categories would tend to possess low average valuation ratios, and there is little basis on which to assert that one group's would be lower than the other.

To summarize, the pattern of the derived predictions concerning the valuation ratio for raiders versus comparable firms, while somewhat tentative and dependent upon the various assumptions made concerning the objectives of comparable firms, yields a reasonably clear-cut division between the two posited managerial objectives of growth maximization and profit maximization. In the former case, we expected either no significant difference between raiders' valuation ratios and the median value for their respective industries, or that raiders would be likely to possess higher valuation ratios when compared with their median industry values. In the latter case, assuming raiders to be primarily motivated by profitability resulted, in general, in

* This argument would not apply to growth-maximizing raiders because their profit rates have not been enhanced in the short run but rather sacrificed. It is their fast growth rate which is affecting their valuation ratio and thus a longer-term measure of performance than annual profits.

† Regressions run on each of 67 industries with average profit rates of the firms as the independent variable and their valuation ratio as the dependent variable showed profits to be significant and take on a positive sign in only 26 industries. Moreover the explanatory power of the equation was in most cases quite low.

predicting that a significant majority of raiders would have their shares valued lower in the market than the median value for their respective industries.

D. Retention Ratio

The ratio of retained to total after-tax earnings, in addition to being a variable determined at the discretion of managers, will also affect the level of the firm's valuation ratio. As with the valuation-ratio predictions, the prediction for the retention ratio differs from that postulated by Marris where growth was limited to that financed internally out of retentions and debt. Internal financing of investment implied that, to maximize growth, earnings would need to be ploughed back so that the dividend payout ratio was low —consequently the retention ratio high. Incorporating external growth via takeovers in the growth-maximizing hypothesis gives the opposite prediction for the retention ratio. Retentions no longer act as a constraint on growth since most takeovers are financed wholly or in the greatest part by the issue of new shares in exchange for the raided company.*

The choice of retention ratio would then depend upon the dispersion of ownership and control within the firm, or, in other words, the degree to which owners are able to impose their own aims on managers. With growth-maximizing raiders, this dispersion is likely to be great, as indicated by their ability to seek an objective which is not likely to be directly in the shareholders' interests. The choice of retention ratio for growth-maximizing raiders is more likely to be determined by its role as an influence on the valuation ratio. From the arguments in section II.C in terms of the valuation ratio's role as a security constraint, managers would be expected to feel that low retentions (high dividends) would serve to increase their valuation ratio thereby reducing the threat of loss of job through takeover. Additionally, high dividends in themselves could add to security by removing the likelihood of owners using their alternative sanction on managerial policies: that of dismissal. This prediction that a significant majority of growth-maximizing raiders will have low average retention ratios when compared to firms in their respective industrial settings is general in the sense that I shall argue that its application to the growth-maximizing raiders does not depend upon the four alternative motivational schemes applied to the set of comparable firms.

If the comparable firms are assumed to be profit maximizers, their retention ratio would depend upon the availability of profitable investment opportunities and the ease and cost of acquiring funds elsewhere. Even though owners (who are by assumption able to assert their influence over managers to maximize profits) are likely to have a positive preference for current dividends, it is more likely that they would prefer the capital gains and higher future dividends that could result from funds being ploughed back into profitable investment projects. Thus profit maximization is likely to result in high retentions. Therefore, by comparison with the growth-maximizing raider with low retentions, the prediction emerges that a significant majority

* Where takeovers are financed by the issue of loan stock no great additional demand will be made on retentions providing the raider does not allow itself to become too highly geared— that is, the ratio of new shares to new loan stock does not change significantly.

of raiders will have lower average retentions when comparable firms are assumed to be maximizing profits.

Similarly, if comparable firms are assumed to be growth maximizers, raiders would, in general, be likely to retain less, as firms maximizing their growth rate but for the most part confining their expansion to that financed internally, would require high retentions and hence pay out low dividends.* Raiders by comparison seeking to enhance their valuation ratio by high dividends would tend to retain less.

If comparable firms are easy-life maximizers they would choose their dividend ratio and hence retention ratio to ensure satisfactory security. All discretionary variables which affect the valuation ratio were seen as being chosen with this aim in mind. However, managers would not have to raise dividends to offset the effect on the valuation ratio of the deliberate sacrifice of some other financial variable. They would be likely to choose some level of retentions which gave them sufficient finance for growth but which did not adversely affect the valuation ratio. Growth-maximizing raiders, however, were seen earlier as having to offset their sacrificed profits by high dividends in order to raise their valuation ratios. Thus the prediction emerges that a significant majority of raiders as growth maximizers would be likely to have low average retentions when compared with firms in their respective industries which are assumed to be easy-life maximizers.

Finally, if the set of comparable firms is typified by sleepy inefficient firms, growth maximizing raiders would again tend to retain less. Since the sleepy firm's profit performance was poor, it would require a large proportion of its meagre earnings simply to invest in replacement capital in order to stay in operation. To the extent that it engages in any positive net investment the demands placed upon retentions from earnings are all the greater. Alternative sources of borrowing to finance replacement investment would usually be either fully exploited or unresponsive since such companies had demonstrated by past performance that they were poor risks. Further, it is unlikely that the managers of sleepy firms would have the awareness to attempt to increase their market valuation by raising dividends (even if it were possible, given their poor record of return on capital employed), since such firms typically are among those taken over because of low market valuation. Growth-maximizing raiders, it has been argued, would typically have a low retention ratio so that by comparison a significant majority would probably have lower average retention ratios when compared with a set of comparable firms assumed to be sleepy firms.

By examining the alternative motivational scheme of raiders as profit maximizers, a contrasting view of the relative size of the retention ratio as compared with firms in raiders' respective industries results. If all firms are profit maximizers and even if raiders do manage to earn short-run supernormal profits, there is little basis on which to argue that there would be a pervasive tendency for raiders to retain a greater or lesser proportion of earnings than firms in their respective industries. As argued earlier the retention ratio does to some extent reflect the degree of owner control within the firm. Since by assumption all managers are seeking to maximize profits

* This corresponds to the argument Marris put forward with regard to retentions in support of his growth-maximizing hypothesis.

for the owners and thus are assumed to be quite directly owner controlled so that retentions are generally kept high, there is no reason to believe that differences in the average retention ratios for the two groups should emerge simply as a result of differences in the mode of investment activity (that is, whether internal or external via raids).

Imputing easy-life maximization to comparable firms and profit maximization to raiders gives the opposite sign prediction than when growth maximization was attributed to raiders. Easy-life maximizers were seen earlier as paying out dividends at a level which would ensure that the valuation ratio was sufficiently high to minimize the likelihood of takeover. Profit-maximizing raiders, however, were seen as paying out a low ratio of dividends to total earnings because of owners' preferences for capital gains and future dividends over present dividends. Thus one would expect a significant majority of profit-maximizing raiders to display greater retention ratios (lower dividend payout ratios) than firms in their respective industries assumed to be easy-life maximizers.

Finally, assuming comparable firms are sleepy firms and raiders are profit maximizers does not allow us to differentiate between the two groups. We have argued that both classes would tend to have high retention ratios but there is no basis on which a comparison can be made in terms of which group would be likely to have a significant majority of greater or lesser retention ratios.

The picture that emerges in terms of the retention ratio is that by imputing growth maximization to raiders we would expect to observe a significant majority of them with average retention ratios below their industry median. This prediction was not dependent upon the various imputed motives of the managers of the set of comparable firms. Alternatively, by assuming raiders are profit maximizers, we predicted either no difference, or that a significant majority of raiders would be expected to show greater average retention ratios than firms in their comparable industrial setting. Thus, two distinct predictions for the retention ratio have emerged from the starting point of alternative behavioural assumptions imputed to the managers of raiding firms. A further basis then is offered on which the appropriateness of these alternative theoretical models may be judged.

In the arguments in this section, the attempt has been to derive logical implications or predictions from a starting point of assuming that firms which can be extraneously identified as seeking expansion externally by takeovers are firms whose managers possess some positive desire for growth in excess of or in place of that which would result from assuming profit maximization to be their primary behavioural objective. The next section contains a description of the data employed and the statistical procedure adopted to test the two sets of predictions against reality.

III. EMPIRICAL TEST OF THE DERIVED PREDICTIONS

A. Data

117 raiders were identified from a census of 3566 UK public quoted companies

representing the total population exclusive of several industry groups.* The companies involved can basically be described as commercial and industrial companies in existence for all or part of the period 1 January 1957 to 31 December 1969. These 117 raiders incorporate all firms in the population which undertook three or more successful takeover bids within the sample period. This group represents just over 19 per cent of the total number of firms which made successful takeovers within the period but accounted for over 38 per cent of the total number of takeovers and over 58 per cent of the total net asset value of all acquired firms. All 3566 firms in the census were categorized into 67 industry groups where any given firm was allowed to appear in one or more of the industrial classifications. Annual data were collected for each firm's share price (both high and low), profits before and after tax, net assets per share and retentions.† Using these data, average values for pre-tax and post-tax profit rates, growth rate, valuation ratio and retention ratio were calculated for each firm. Finally, the median value for each variable was calculated for each of the 67 industries. This process was then repeated omitting the non-raiding firms which were taken over.

B. Statistical Testing Procedure

Initially what was desired was to compare each of the four indices of performance of the 117 raiders individually with a group of comparable firms so that variations attributable to the industrial setting would be removed. This was accomplished by relating each of the values of the raiders' variables to their own respective industrial medians. Thus, for example, in the case of a raider having a major interest in three industries, the overall median for each variable for the combined industries was compared with the calculated value of each of the raider's performance indices. Finally, the sign test‡ is employed in order to examine any pervasive tendencies for raiders to demonstrate either higher or lower values of the performance variables than their respective industries and to relate these tendencies to the alternative sets of behavioural predictions derived in section II. The sign test is used in preference to parametric tests because it is untenable to assume that the differences between raiders' performance and the performance of companies belonging to the same industrial setting will have the same variances. The null hypothesis we wish to test is that each difference has a probability distribution (which need not be the same for all differences as required by the t-test) with median equal to zero. The null hypothesis will be rejected if there is a significant difference between the numbers of positive and negative sign differences.§ Of particular

* Foreign, agriculture and mining, investment trusts and banks were excluded from the census.

† The source of this data was Exchange Telegraph (Extel) daily and auxiliary statistical service and the *Stock Exchange Official Year Book*.

‡ For a description of the use of the sign test see Dixon and Massey (1957), p. 280.

§ The further assumption is required that the differences between raiders' performance and their industry medians are independent. Even though the existence of a raider in one industry might possibly affect the performance of firms in that industry it is exceedingly unlikely that such a raider would affect the performance of firms in other industries. Since the 117 raiders cover 65 of the 67 industries and because of the procedure of multiple industry classes for each firm only resulting in four industries where there are more than one raider, the independence condition is likely to be satisfied.

interest is whether the significant proportions of sign differences to total are in accordance with the theoretical predictions developed in terms of the growth-maximization hypothesis or, alternatively, whether the proportions tend to favour the predictions derived on the basis of assuming raiders to be profit maximizers.

IV. RESULTS AND CONCLUSIONS

Table 1 gives in brackets the actual proportion for the most frequently occurring sign of the difference between raiders' performance and their respective industry median value for each of the four variables.* Taking the level of significance at which we reject the null hypothesis that no difference exists between the two groups at the 5 per cent level of probability, signs are included corresponding to the most frequently occurring difference. Zeros indicate that the derived proportions of positive signs to total are not statistically significant.

The overall impression to be derived from these results is that they are more consistent with the predictions derived from the assumption that raiders are growth maximizers than with those derived from imputing profit maximization. That is, raiders tend to be faster growing than firms in their respective industries but this growth has not generated significantly higher profits and indeed, when compared with only the surviving firms in their industry, raiders actually earned a lower rate of return on assets. Raiders nevertheless were able to maintain their valuation ratios at healthy levels despite their profit performance. Thus 87 of the 117 raiders had ratios above their respective industry medians when compared to all firms. This fell to 63 when only surviving firms were used in the comparison. The results for retentions possibly indicate how they were able to outweigh the negative influence of their poor profitability on the valuation ratio. Both for comparisons with all firms and surviving firms, raiders had lower retention ratios and thus higher dividend payout ratios than the median of the firms in their respective industries. Logically, one would further expect that if low retentions are playing the role of offsetting the dampening effect that sacrificed profits have on the valuation ratio, the raiders with below-average profits would tend to be the firms which had the significantly lower retention ratios. By splitting the raiders into two groups comprised of those which exceeded their industry median in profit rates and those which fell short of the industry median, it is found that just under 80 per cent of these payed out more (that is, 43 of the 57 below-industry-median profit raiders using all firms in the comparison and 53 of the 67 using only surviving firms in the comparison). With the raiders which earned above their industry median profits, there was no significant difference in retention ratios. The most plausible explanation is that this is consistent with attempts to raise the valuation ratio by paying out high dividends for raiders whose low profits were negatively affecting their

* Profit rates used were before tax while the valuation ratio was measured using the annual mean share price in the numerator. When after-tax profit rates and annual low share price were used in the numerator of the valuation ratio there was no significant change in proportions for each variable given in the results.

market valuation, while this diversion of funds for expansion was unnecessary for raiders with healthy profits. Thus not only were they playing on shareholders' preferences for dividends (as well as capital gains) in high payouts when necessary to keep their share prices healthy but also their past growth record made them appear to be an attractive company to the market. In general they were allowed to pursue their policies towards growth without interference from shareholders or incurring any severe threat of being taken over themselves,* because of their healthy market valuation. And, as a consequence, in seeking growth they were permitted to trade off profits without obviously incurring any additional threats to security. By inspection of table 1 it can be seen that the alternative view of raiders as profit maximizers (or firms which are significantly owner controlled and thus induced to regard profits to owners as important) does not correspond as closely to the picture of the raider which has emerged from the results. On certain assumptions, the profit-maximizing raider may be faster growing, but it is difficult to see how it could emerge as less profitable. Even though, when considering all firms in the industry comparisons, there is no significant difference in profitability at the 5 per cent level, it must be remembered that within this group there are many firms taken over because of poor profit records. Furthermore, since raiding is risky and does not necessarily result in super normal profits it is difficult to see how the profit-maximizing raider would tend to keep the high valuation ratios observed, especially since he is not distributing significantly higher dividends and may on certain assumptions about the comparable firms even be distributing less (that is, retaining more).

It is left to the reader to draw conclusions concerning which assumptions about the nature of the comparable firms are most appropriate based upon his own judgment of the commonness of each type of firm in the population. Nevertheless, one further stage in the analysis can be made, based upon the assumption that the easy-life maximizer has a strong desire for survival. Taking it that this group of comparable firms will arrange their affairs in order to achieve this stated goal it is likely that a majority of such firms will actually be successful and survive. By examining the alternative predictions for growth-maximizing raiders and profit-maximizing raiders when comparable firms are easy-life maximizers and comparing each with the results for raiders and the group of surviving firms, a clear contrast of the two motivational schemes becomes apparent. In this case, it can be seen that the assumption of growth maximization for raiders clearly is more in line with the results than are the predictions based upon the assumption of profit maximization. That is, when comparable firms were assumed to be easy-life maximizers, the assumption of growth maximization imputed to raiders yielded the predictions that raiders would grow faster, have lower profit rates and retain less—the prediction for the valuation-ratio comparisons was uncertain and could have gone either way depending on the strength of counter-arguments. On the other hand, assuming raiders to be profit maximizers while the comparable firms were assumed to be easy-life maximizers resulted in predicting that raiders would grow faster, have higher profit rates, a lower valuation ratio and retain more. Examining the results

* Only 16 of the 117 raiders, or 14 per cent, were themselves taken over as compared with the average of 43 per cent of all firms taken over.

for the comparisons of raiders with surviving firms shows that the predictions based on the assumption of growth maximizing are more closely in line with reality than the predictions based on assuming raiders to be profit maximizers.

In this paper, I have attempted to formalize the growth-maximization hypothesis with respect to a subset of the population of firms. Some of the theorizing in section II represents a departure from Marris, though much of what is argued is in accordance with his hypothesis, at least in spirit. This fragmented approach to the examination of the relevance of this theoretical revision of the theory of the firm was necessary in order to avoid the circularity of assuming that the fastest growing firms are growth maximizers, the most profitable, profit maximizers and so forth. At the extreme, if the derived predictions had not been supported, then serious doubt would have been cast on the applicability of the growth-maximization hypothesis as a basis for a revision of the theory of the firm. Nevertheless, I believe the analysis relevant in answering the question of the general applicability of the growth-maximizing approach to the theory of the firm.

In the present economic climate, takeovers are extremely common, often recently occurring at a rate of around 30 public quoted companies per month. Raiding is by no means limited to the 117 firms examined in sections III and IV since not less than 20 per cent of the population of 3566 companies have undertaken at least one takeover at some time during the sample period and that percentage is increasing as raiding activity spreads to other industries previously relatively untouched. The motivations and predictions analysed in section II could be extended to incorporate these minor raiders as well. Furthermore, it may be the case that raiding itself is limited to relatively large firms, and small concerns must overcome some threshold size in order to indulge in takeover activity. They would, in this case, be forced to adopt policies of internal-growth maximization possibly in preparation for the time when they can also join the takeover scene—in addition to the numerous reasons offered by Marris why they might do so anyway. The results demonstrate that firms desire to become a 'high flying' raider; raiding leads to growth, security through safe levels of the valuation ratio and size, all of which are valued for themselves by managers who also value the emoluments, both pecuniary and non-pecuniary, associated with growth and size.

Thus, rather than the results contained in this paper being valid only for a limited number of 'special' firms, the implications of the analysis and results are likely to be far more general, and consequently add to the growing body of evidence supporting the appropriateness of the managerial and behavioural revisions to the theory of the firm.

GROWTH, SURVIVAL AND THE SIZE OF COMPANIES 1960–9

by

J. M. SAMUELS and A. D. CHESHER

I

This paper reports on a research project which ultimately will lead to the construction of a model representing the process of change in the size distribution of companies. There is a need for a model that represents the whole system—that is, a model that does more than examine the process of growth of surviving companies and then makes assumptions concerning the birth and death process. To be able to say anything meaningful about changing levels of concentration it is necessary to study each of the processes at work in the system, namely the birth and growth rates of new companies, the deaths due to liquidations and takeovers, as well as the growth rate of continuing companies.

In this paper the growth rate of surviving firms, and the birth and death rate, over the 1960–9 decade are considered. One of the more surprising findings relates to the growth rate of companies that have existed over the ten years. Theories such as that of Gibrat (1931) suggest that there should be no difference between the proportionate rates of growth of large and small companies (see Hart and Prais 1956; Marris and Wood 1971; Utton 1971; O. E. Williamson 1964). This law of proportionate growth has been tested and has accumulated over time considerable statistical support (see Hart 1962; Hart and Prais 1956; Singh and Whittington 1968). These earlier empirical studies have not, however, examined performance during the latter half of the 1960s, a period characterized by frantic takeover and merger activity, some of which was even initiated and supported by the government— a period when it might have been thought that large companies were growing at a faster proportional rate than small companies.

This study is based on an analysis of quoted companies over the period from 1960 to 1969. It was found that over this ten-year period, the large companies did not grow at the faster proportional rate. Indeed for the first part of this period it was the smaller companies that were growing at the faster rate. However, over the latter years, that is from 1967, the advantages of size were reflected in the above-average growth of the large companies.

A general impression given by the Press and other observers is that small companies have been finding life increasingly difficult over the last decade and that they have been losing their relative importance in the economy. The recent report of the Bolton Committee documents the many problems of the small company, it emphasizes the neglect shown by past governments to these companies, and offers little hope for their future.* Statistics can be produced to show that the largest 100 companies in the economy are continuing to increase their share of the total production and ownership of the total assets in the economy (see Utton 1970).

It is undoubtedly true that there are reasons why small companies may be experiencing difficulties. One of the problems less often discussed is the institutional investors' lack of interest in small companies. The institutions wish to invest in large amounts and to be able to dispose of large blocks of shares without affecting the share price by more than a few pennies, thus they

The authors would like to acknowledge the valuable assistance of Mr N. Nayer, and the helpful comments of Professor S. J. Prais. The research project was financed by the Acton Society.
* *Report of the Committee of Inquiry on Small Firms*, Cmnd 4811 (London: HMSO, 1971).

cannot afford to become too interested in small companies. Another reason lies in the credit squeeze of the 1960s, which forced banks to reduce the amount of loans available to companies; small companies being more dependent on bank loans than larger companies. Economies of scale, much talked about but their existence rarely demonstrated, could provide a variety of reasons favouring the growth of large companies.

These advantages were, however, not reflected in a higher growth for large companies. Those small companies that survived over the ten-year period grew at the same proportional rate as large companies. However, the chance of a small company surviving for the decade was very much less than the chance of a large company surviving. For those quoted companies that existed in 1960 and were classified in our smallest size group, there was an estimated probability of 0.42 of surviving until 1970, whereas for the largest-size classification there was a probability of 0.73 of surviving over the decade. These differences in survival probability are due both to different chances of being taken over and of being liquidated. The high death rate over the decade to 1970 among quoted companies has not been compensated for by a high birth rate.

The paper is divided into five further sections. Section II describes the sample on which the analysis was based. Section III is concerned with the rates of growth of companies. Section IV looks at concentration. Section V studies the birth and death process of companies over the decade and section VI looks at the characteristics of taken over companies.

II. THE SAMPLE

The population studied was limited for various reasons to a certain class of company. Attention was restricted to those companies quoted on the London Stock Exchange. In particular those companies which are classified as 'commercial and industrial'. The reason why only one sector was considered was that the companies were more likely to be homogeneous, therefore meaningful results could be obtained. If, for example, property companies or investment trusts had been included, the differing characteristics would have hidden many meaningful relationships.

Limiting the study to those companies quoted on the Stock Exchange meant that very small companies were excluded from the study. The Bolton Committee defined a small company as one employing 200 people or less. The smallest companies examined in this study were those with a capital employed of under £250000 in 1960. This is an open-ended group and so could include companies employing less than 200 people, but as would be expected the fact that the companies were quoted on the Stock Exchange means that they are not very small and the majority of our smallest group were employing over 200 people in 1960. It is not possible to be precise about employment figures as companies were not in 1960 required by law to give this information.

Subsidiaries of foreign companies were excluded from the analysis, for two reasons. First, it is not always possible to obtain the annual reports of subsidiaries that are 100 per cent owned by a foreign company. Second, even when the accounts are available, the situation of the subsidiary is not comparable to that of other companies, because it can receive benefits from the parent organization which may not be reflected in the accounts.

In order to be able to compare figures for each company for a ten-year period, it was necessary to include in the sample only those companies that survived the period. It is a particular category of companies that existed in 1960 that is being examined: those that survived for ten years. Companies that were liquidated during the period were excluded from the population being studied. Companies that were taken over during the period were also excluded from the population. A problem arose in that with a merger it is not always clear which company should be regarded as disappearing and which company surviving. For the purpose of the study the company that was the 'prime mover' in the merger was identified and treated as the continuing company.* The other company in the merger was excluded from the population.

Data were obtained on a number of variables. When the difficulties involved in collecting the data, particularly those for small companies, were considered in relation to the time constraint, it was decided that a sample of 200 companies would be a realistic objective and would be sufficient to enable meaningful conclusions to be obtained. The population of companies in the industrial and commercial sector with an equity quotation was, in 1960, just over 2400. However, the population from which we could sample was smaller than this figure, because we were only interested in those companies that existed in 1960 and survived throughout the period, and, as table 1 shows, the probability of death was very high for the smaller size groups. The population from which we could sample was in the region of 1500.

Table 1. Probability of surviving for a ten-year period for companies existing in 1960

Size group	Boundary (£m)	Probability of survival	Probability of being taken over	Probability of liquidation
1	65>	0.73	0.27	0.00
2	35–65	0.80	0.20	0.00*
3	15–35	0.73	0.27	0.00
4	10–15	0.67	0.33	0.00
5	5–10	0.73	0.27	0.00
6	2.5–5	0.50	0.50	0.00
7	1–2.5	0.59	0.41	0.00
8	0.5–1	0.57	0.38	0.05
9	0.25–0.5	0.42	0.48	0.10
10	<0.25	0.42	0.41	0.17

* Including Rolls–Royce.

The sample was required for two purposes. One purpose was to study certain well-defined groups of companies which differed in size as measured in some manner, and compare the attributes of these different groups. The second purpose was to make estimates of key variables for the whole of the population and compare trends in these over time.

* For a discussion of this definition, see Newbould (1970).

The first objective indicated a need to partition the population into groups, or strata, and this combined with the expected heterogeneity of the population suggested stratified random sampling as the appropriate technique for the selection of companies to be studied. The variable of classification used was capital employed; the justification for this choice will be set out later. The two purposes for which the sample would be used lead to conflicting distributions of sample units over the strata if any attempt to derive an optimum distribution is made.* Briefly, an application of Neyman allocation to prior data on the population when equal costs of sampling from different strata are assumed indicates that more units should be sampled in more variable and in higher populated strata (Neyman 1938). If the strata themselves are domains of study then the size of the strata for most problems becomes irrelevant and only the variability of the attribute under study is important.

Further problems arise when the multivariate nature of the study is recognized. Optimum allocation for univariate samples is well researched and generally fairly easily applicable. Optimum allocation in a multivariate survey requires data on variability of each attribute, which are generally not available. In this study one variable was used as a proxy to measure the variability of all attributes.

Data were available, from a previous study by Samuels and Smyth (1969) on variability of profits of quoted UK companies 1960–5. In this study, ten strata were used, delineated by various levels of capital employed. These seemed reasonable for the present study and were thus used. An average variability measure was produced for each stratum using the variances of profits in each stratum for the five years and the Neyman allocation technique applied yielding the sample allocation, a constraint being imposed: that no stratum should have less than five sample units. In addition, an approach suggested by Cochran, which sets out to minimize the average variance of the difference between profits in all 45 pairs of strata, was tried. The allocations yielded by the two approaches did not differ greatly, though the latter, as expected, allocated fewer units to the lower, more highly populated more variable strata than the former. The first allocation was used as it was realized that data collection difficulties would leave us with more unobtainable data at the lower (that is smaller company) end than at the higher.

Sampling for the top eight strata was carried out using the list in *Company Assets, Income and Finance* 1960 and for the ninth and tenth strata using the *Stock Exchange Official Year Book* 1960, after first finding all companies falling in these strata. Random numbers were obtained from Rand Corporation (1955).

Simple random sampling was carried out in each stratum until the required number of companies was obtained discarding those which had not survived until 1969. An estimate was thus made of the death rate in each stratum. This procedure was checked using, among other sources, *Who Owns Whom, Stock Exchange Official Year Book* 1969 and Moodies Services. Name changes were checked carefully to avoid unnecessary discarding of companies.

Data were then collected on the 200 companies using Moodies Services where possible, though for the smaller companies it was necessary to visit

* See Cochran (1963). For a discussion of stratified sampling in this type of work, see G. R. Fisher (1969).

Company House to obtain all the data. Because of problems of incomplete data the sample was reduced to 183 companies. This was necessary despite the fact that letters were sent to certain companies in an attempt to fill in gaps in the information.

From inspection of calculations on variability of certain key variables within the ten strata it appears that there have been substantial benefits from stratification. Explicit calculations to determine the gain in precision as compared with a simple random sample of the same size are being carried out. The size classes that were used in the study with the size of the sample taken from each class are shown in table 2.

Table 2

Stratum	Boundary (£m)	Sample of the companies that survived over the period 1960–9
1	65>	5
2	35–65	5
3	15–35	6
4	10–15	6
5	5–10	14
6	2.5–5	16
7	1–2.5	39
8	0.5–1	32
9	0.25–0.5	33
10	<0.25	21
Total		183

III. GROWTH RATES BY SIZE OF COMPANY

The law of proportionate growth implies that the probability of a certain percentage growth in a firm over a period of time is independent of the size of the firm at the beginning of the period. For example, a firm with assets of £1 million in 1960 has as much chance of growing at a rate of 10 per cent over the next period as a firm with assets of £100 million in 1960.

It has been observed in a number of studies that the size distribution of companies at any time approximates to a lognormal distribution (see for example, Hart and Prais 1956; Simon and Bornini 1958). This was in fact tested with data for the year 1960 and found still to hold true. A lognormal size distribution for companies could result from a number of small random factors affecting all sizes of companies in a similar manner in a multiplicative fashion. The distribution of companies by size would then at different points of time appear lognormal.

Gibrat developed a model to explain the changing size distribution of companies. This model is based on two assumptions: one is that the law of proportionate growth is valid, the second is that the number of firms is constant. If the law is found to hold, this itself will lead to increasing concentration. The fact that Gibrat's second assumption is not supported by the evidence invalidates his model, it also means that concentration has been increasing at an even faster rate than that predicted by Gibrat because the number of firms has been decreasing (for a discussion of this point, see Hart and Prais 1956).

We start by testing the assumption of Gibrat's model that relates to the law of proportionate effect and then examine one of the implications of his model, namely that concentration will increase over time.

Let x_t equal firm size at the beginning of a period and x_{t+1} equal firm size at the end of the period. The size measure used initially in the study is capital employed. One way of detecting a systematic relationship between firm size at two dates is to fit the following equation to the data

$$\log x_{t+1} = \alpha + \beta \log x_t + \varepsilon \tag{1}$$

If β is found to equal 1, growth is independent of size. If β is found to be less than 1 the smaller firms are growing at the faster proportional rate.

This 'growth equation' was fitted to our data for various sub-periods using the ordinary least squares procedure. The results are recorded in column A of table 3. Starred slope coefficient estimates are significantly different from unity. On examining the 1960–9 regression we observed that the squared residuals increased as the determining variable decreased. If the disturbances in equation 1 are heteroscedastic, a biased estimate will be made of the

Table 3

	A No weight		B $\log x_t$	
	α	β	α	β
$\log C_{69} = \alpha + \beta \log C_{60}$	1.58 (0.45) $R^2 = 0.826$	0.940 (0.032) $d = 2.03$	1.30 (0.43) $R^2 = 0.850$	0.961 (0.030) $d = 2.03$
$\log C_{69} = \alpha + \beta \log C_{68}$	−0.12 (0.09) $R^2 = 0.994$	1.014* (0.006) $d = 1.94$	−0.11 (0.09) $R^2 = 0.994$	1.013* (0.006) $d = 1.94$
$\log C_{69} = \alpha + \beta \log C_{65}$	−0.02 (0.25) $R^2 = 0.952$	1.031 (0.017) $d = 1.97$	−0.28 (0.24) $R^2 = 0.957$	1.036* (0.016) $d = 1.97$
$\log C_{68} = \alpha + \beta \log C_{60}$	1.57 (0.42) $R^2 = 0.845$	0.936* (0.030) $d = 2.01$	1.30 (0.39) $R^2 = 0.867$	0.955 (0.028) $d = 2.02$
$\log C_{68} = \alpha + \beta \log C_{65}$	−0.13 (0.21) $R^2 = 0.965$	1.020 (0.015) $d = 1.95$	−0.21 (0.20) $R^2 = 0.969$	1.026 (0.014) $d = 1.95$
$\log C_{65} = \alpha + \beta \log C_{60}$	1.58 (0.34) $R^2 = 0.889$	0.923* (0.024) $d = 1.99$	1.42 (0.33) $R^2 = 0.902$	0.935* (0.023) $d = 1.99$

Figures in parentheses are standard errors of estimators.
d = Durbin–Watson statistic.
Number of observations = 183.
* Significantly different from unity.

covariance matrix of the coefficient estimators and the usual significance test will yield misleading results. This is a problem in weighted least-squares.

Following the Aitken procedure, equation 1 was transformed in an attempt to obtain a model with homoscedastic disturbances. The transformation involved fitting the line

$$\log x_{t+1} \log x_t = \alpha \log x_t + \beta(\log x_t)^2 + v_t$$

to the transformed data. The resulting estimates are given in column B of table 3; the residuals do not vary systematically with the determining variable.

This transformation gives most weight in the regression to observations corresponding to high values of the determining variable. One observes that in almost all cases $\hat{\alpha}*$ falls, its standard error rising, and $\hat{\beta}$ rises its standard error falling, when the transformation is applied. It is well known that ordinary least squares applied to a model conforming to the Gauss–Markov restrictions, except those concerning the covariance matrix of the disturbances, produces unbiased estimators of the coefficients in the model. The systematic shift in our estimates is thus surprising and could indicate a further mis-specification in the original equation 1.

These movements in the estimates suggest that the true relationship between beginning and end-period company size may be of the form

$$\log x_{(t+1),i} = \alpha + \beta_i \log x_{t,i}$$

where β_i varies systematically with $x_{t,i}$. A model with random coefficients is at present the subject of investigation.

If we do not admit random coefficients then we observe the following. Small companies grew faster than large companies early in the 1960s, there being a reversal later in the decade, the net effect being a similar ten-year growth rate for large and small companies. These results differ from those found in other studies for the decade ending 1960, when β was found to be greater than 1. We find this to be only the case in the latter half of the 1960s.

As has been explained, the sample of companies used to estimate the proportionate rate of growth are taken from those companies that existed in 1960 that still existed in 1969 as independent companies. When results are reported for a sub-period, say 1960 to 1965, it is the growth rate of this particular group of companies that is being referred to, not the growth rate of all the companies that existed over the period from 1960 to 1965. It might be thought that this could introduce a bias into the estimates for the sub-period as the companies that disappeared from the population over the period 1965 to 1969 are being excluded. However, the vast majority of companies that disappeared over this period were taken over and there are theoretical arguments to support the case for fast-growth companies being taken over as well as arguments for the less successful companies being acquired. It is suggested that the evidence is not strong enough to be able to predict the direction in which the bias would work. In fact, results from other research which is being undertaken, in which estimates are obtained from a sample of all companies that existed over the sub-periods, show that the changes from the estimates shown in table 3 are quite small, and do not alter the conclusions.

---

* $\hat{\theta}$ will denote an estimate of a parameter θ.

It can be implied from earlier work of Samuels (1965) and Hart (1962) that large firms grew faster than small firms in the 1950s, and this tendency increased over the latter half of that decade. Singh and Whittington obtained a similar result, when considering four industries over the period 1948–60. They found that the larger companies were growing at a faster proportional rate than small companies in the latter half of the period (1954–60). They found that the difference in the rates of growth of large and small firms was greater in this latter half of the period than in the earlier period (1948–54). The evidence up to 1960 suggests therefore that large companies were taking advantage of any benefits that they had to obtain the higher rates of growth. This study suggests that, contrary to popular belief, this process was reversed in the early 1960s.

Capital employed is, following the usual definition, taken to be total assets minus current liabilities. Thus it represents the long-term investment in the company. A problem arises with certain of the firms in the smallest size group who rely quite heavily on short-term borrowing as a source of finance. They are more dependent on short-term loans than larger companies. As short-term bank borrowing is a current liability, it is not included in capital employed and so is not taken into account in determining the size of the company. This only affects certain of the companies in the smallest size group.

One explanation of the results that has been offered is that the small companies examined are an exceptional group of companies, they are quoted companies. They have therefore gone through some form of examination by the Stock Exchange, which ensures that only good small companies obtain a quotation. 'Bad' small companies are therefore not included in the analysis. In that the vast majority of large companies are quoted on the stock market, our sample of large companies would include both 'good' and 'bad'. This explanation is not, however, satisfactory, for although it may be the case that the small company that is obtaining its first quotation must be 'good', the smallest group contains many companies that obtained a quotation a long time ago and which have not been successful but have remained in the smallest groups. It can even contain companies that have been so unsuccessful they have been reduced in size.

It was possible to obtain statistics on the turnover and employee position of companies for the latter part of the period being studied. This was because the Companies Act of 1967 increased the amount of information that had to be disclosed in the annual report. For the period 1968 to 1969 it was possible therefore to use as alternative measures of company size, employees, employees' remuneration and turnover. As reported when capital employed in 1969 was regressed on capital employed in 1968 it was found that the slope was equal to 1.014, suggesting that large companies were growing at the faster proportional rate. The results of the regression when using the alternative measures of company size are given below:

Employees:

$$\log x_{69} = -0.011 + 1.004 \log x_{68} \quad R^2 = 0.990$$
$$\quad\quad (0.056) \quad (0.008)$$

Employees' remuneration:

$$\log x_{69} = -0.022 + 1.008 \log x_{68} \quad R^2 = 0.991$$
$$(0.103) \quad (0.007)$$

Turnover:

$$\log x_{69} = -0.014 + 1.007 \log x_{68} \quad R^2 = 0.991$$
$$(0.115) \quad (0.007)$$

The results from these three regressions all support the law of proportionate growth. It might be thought that the rate of increase in employment by large firms would be less than the rate of increase in employment by small firms. This is because one of the claims often advanced to justify a merger or acquisition is that it will result in a saving in the labour force. The findings of this study lend some support to this claim, for it was found that although the capital employed of the larger firms grew at the faster rate over the end of the period, this higher rate of growth in capital was not accompanied by a higher rate of growth in employees, or employees' remuneration.

The turnover finding is not so easy to explain. It might be thought that the more rapid increase in capital employed by the larger firms would have been linked with a higher rate of growth in turnover. It is possible, however, that one year is too short a period in which to identify changes in different variables. Capital employed is a stock concept, and the full amount of any acquisition, even if only made one day before the end of a company's financial year, is added to the values in the year-end balance sheet. The employees' remuneration and turnover figures are, however, flow concepts, and only the amounts paid or the sales made after the date of acquisition are included in the final accounts of the acquiring company. The employees figure shown in the accounts is usually based on some average level of employment. It can be seen therefore that it is really not surprising that, in the short run, capital employment as a measure of size, would show a higher rate of growth than any of the three alternative measures of size.

The results that have so far been considered relate to the aggregate data, where all 183 companies are included. It is meaningful to ask if there are any industry differences. Does the law of proportionate growth apply to some industries but not to others? Table 4 shows the results of regressing the logarithm of size in the beginning of the period on the logarithm of size at the end of the period for the companies in the different industry groups, size being measured here by capital employed. As might be expected, for the majority of the groups the small companies have been found to grow at the same proportional rate as the large companies. Three of the groups are, however, found to have a growth pattern which differs from the 'all industry' pattern. The vehicle, shipping and transport group and the non-electrical engineering group have smaller companies growing at a faster proportional rate than the large companies. Only the miscellaneous services sector shows the opposite pattern.

It is perhaps surprising that in the vehicle, shipping and transport group the smaller companies were growing at the faster rate. However, this group contains a number of small successful transport companies and certain large unsuccessful shipping companies.

The miscellaneous service sector includes very few large companies. The biggest at the beginning of the period being Trust Houses with a capital employed in 1960 of £6 236 000. The second largest company in the group is also in the hotel industry. There has been a large amount of merger activity in the hotel industry centred around the large companies. This undoubtedly explains the results for this group of companies. It is not a very successful classification as it is biased by activities in this one industry. We must recognize that these results arise from very small samples.

Table 4. Growth in capital employed: by industry. $\log x_{69} = \alpha + \beta \log x_{60}$

Industry	n	α	β	R^2
1. Food and tobacco	6	0.0552 (0.7763)	1.0252 (0.1155)	0.95
2. Chemicals and textiles	15	−0.1890 (0.7031)	1.0698 (0.1095)	0.88
3. Clothing and footware	15	0.8927 (0.7851)	0.9091 (0.1369)	0.77
4. Retail and wholesale distribution	34	0.3188 (0.4157)	0.9931 (0.0667)	0.87
5. Bricks and construction	13	0.5671 (0.7846)	0.9741 (0.1310)	0.83
6. Timber, paper and printing	15	0.3860 (1.2520)	1.0406 (0.1810)	0.85
7. Vehicles, shipping and transport	16	1.3347 (0.5109)	0.8266 (0.0788)	0.89
8. Other manufacturing and metal goods	20	0.1486 (0.5110)	1.0315 (0.0821)	0.90
9. Electric engineering	12	0.1382 (0.7613)	1.0320 (0.1255)	0.87
10. Non-electrical engineering	24	1.2168 (0.7780)	0.8580 (0.1282)	0.67
11. Miscellaneous services	12	−1.5962 (0.7565)	1.3632 (0.1347)	0.91

The data used in the analysis are taken from the companies' annual financial accounts. They are therefore expressed in monetary terms rather than real terms; and part of the growth rate that is being recorded is not real growth, it is caused simply by inflation forcing up asset values. Part of the growth calculated will be due to the revaluation of assets. Current assets and current liabilities are expressed in monetary values at the date of the balance sheet. Fixed assets are, however, recorded initially at cost and are only occasionally revalued. Some companies revalue more frequently than others, which could give a slightly misleading impression of growth in the years in which the revaluation took place.

If, as is often supposed, large companies revalue assets more frequently than small companies, this would lead to a bias in the results. This different approach to revaluation has been offered in many studies as the explanation for large companies apparently having a faster rate of growth than small companies. The findings of this study are, however, the other way, and if the revaluations by large companies are still more frequent than those by small companies, this would add weight to the findings of this study. We would in fact be under-estimating the extent to which the small companies grow at the faster proportional rate in certain periods.

Only if small companies had not revalued assets immediately prior to 1960, could our results, that differ from expectations, be explained away by revaluations. If this type of revaluation process had taken place, it would mean the observed growth of small companies would be exaggerated relative to the growth of large companies. Unfortunately it was not possible to obtain accurate details on the timing of all revaluations.

We were able to obtain details of revaluations from the accounts of the larger companies, and when such revaluations did occur they were not sufficient to significantly affect our observed average rate of growth for the largest size groups. It is not easy to obtain details of the revaluations of small companies, but because large samples were taken from the smaller groups, it would require revaluations by a substantial number of companies within each group for the average of the group to be moved more than a few points.

The studies of Singh and Whittington (1968; Singh 1971; Whittington 1971) were based on standardized accounting data that had been prepared by the Board of Trade. Such standardized data allowed for the uneven revaluation of assets over time. Unfortunately, such accounts are only available up to the year 1960, and so they are of no use if recent performance is to be studied.

One further point that should be taken into account when calculating growth rates on the basis of net assets is that for yet another reason the true growth rate can be understated. When a company purchases another company it often pays a price which is higher than the value of the net assets. The difference, which can be referred to as 'goodwill' has on many occasions in the past been written off against previous year's profits—that is, against reserves. The effect of this accounting treatment is to not increase the size of the company (as measured by net assets) by the amount of the purchase. The accounting treatment of the premium on the issue of shares in consideration for a purchase—that is, the difference between the price of the shares and the par value of the shares—can also cause an understatement of the 'true' growth of a company. Some companies have not recorded the share premium and so have understated the value of assets acquired. The accounting profession is at present discussing the question of how mergers and acquisitions should in future be recorded.

IV. CONCENTRATION

There are, of course, many different measures of concentration. One measure is provided by the residual variance of the growth equation. The lognormal distribution gives an approximate description of the size distribution of firms. The variance of the distribution provides an indicator of the level of concentration in industry. The greater the dispersion about the mean the more concentrated the structure, the less the dispersion about the mean the less concentrated the structure. A wide dispersion means, of course, that there are some very large companies and some relatively small, hence a high level of concentration. An implication of the logarithmic growth model is that:

$$V \log x_{t+1} = \beta^2 \, V \log x_t + \sigma_\varepsilon^2$$

where $V \log x_t$ is the variance of the logarithm of x at time t, and σ_ε^2 equals the residual variance (see Hart and Prais 1956). If r equals the correlation coefficient, then

$$r^2 = \frac{1 - \sigma_\varepsilon^2}{V \log x_{t+1}}$$

This can be written as

$$\frac{V \log x_{t+1}}{V \log x_t} = \frac{\beta^2}{r^2}$$

If β^2 is greater than r^2, the variance, and so concentration, will increase over time.

If β is found to be greater than unity, the concentration must be increasing over time as $r^2 \leqslant 1$. As was shown earlier in the paper for the last year (1968–9), β was greater than unity and so concentration was increasing. For the period 1960–8, β was estimated at 0.936, and R^2 as 0.829; thus indicating a period of increasing concentration.

It should be remembered that the results so far discussed in this paper relate only to the companies that survived through the 1960s. The conclusion that concentration was increasing related only to those firms that survived through the decade. It would be possible that with a sufficient number of 'births', that is new companies entering the stock market, there need be no increase in overall concentration. This is, however, not the case. There were in fact a greater number of companies dying than being born. The size and number of companies being 'born' were not sufficient to counteract the increase in concentration among the surviving firms. Rather, the birth and death process added to the trend of increasing concentration.

It is possible using the earlier results to measure the exact change in concentration among the companies that survived over the period. The size of the residual variance of the growth equation (σ_ε^2) is a measure of the mobility of firms. Standardized for a ten-year period it is estimated as 1.213 (in logarithms to base 2) which means that for a number of companies of similar size at the beginning of 1960, approximately 35 per cent would be more than double the mean size by the end of 1969 and approximately 35 per cent would be less than half the mean size. For the previous decade, from 1950 to 1960, the residual variance was higher than this, indicating a greater rate of dispersion of firms by size at the end of the period, a greater rate of mobility over the period (Samuels 1965). This means that the rate of increase in concentration was less among surviving firms in the 1960s than in the 1950s. This result is consistent with our finding ($\beta \approx 1$) that the small firms were not growing at a slower proportional rate over the 1960–9 period. This result, however, does not necessarily apply to overall concentration, the change in concentration resulting from births and deaths was more dramatic in the 1960s than in the 1950s.

It should also be remembered that the results for the latter part of the 1960s show clearly that at the end of the decade the large companies were growing at the faster rate. The residual variance standardized for a ten-year period (based on the estimate for 1968–9) was 2.06, which shows that concentration among surviving companies is again increasing at a fast rate.

Hart and Prais, examining an earlier period, 1938–50, obtain an estimated σ_ε^2 of 1.24 (standardized to ten years). This result is similar to that which we have found for the period 1960–9.

V. BIRTH AND DEATH PROCESS

The birth of a company can be defined in a number of different ways. All companies have to be registered with the Registrar of Companies, and statistics are published showing the number of companies that register each year. These new companies are analysed in the official statistics on the basis of their size as measured by nominal capital. This is not a very meaningful measure of company size, for nominal capital is an extremely arbitrary figure, being based on the practically redundant concept of the par value of a share. This measure has nothing to do with the amount of money raised from equity issues, nor anything to do with the net asset value of the company.

This particular study is, however, only concerned with companies that are quoted on the London Stock Exchange. Consequently a birth is defined as a company receiving a quotation on that market for the first time. These 'births' are analysed by size in table 5, where size is defined as capital employed.

The table shows births over the period from 1 April 1963 to 31 March 1970. Three sets of figures are given for each year, one figure being all companies that have been granted a quotation during a year, a second figure shows the overseas companies included in the annual total, and a third figure gives the births in the sector with which we are concerned in this study, namely 'industrial and commercial'. It can be seen that there is considerable variation in the number of companies coming to the market for the first time in any year. The number of births in even the best years is, however, surprisingly small when compared to the number of companies that die in a year either through takeover or liquidation.

On the question of the size of company coming to the market it can be seen from the second part of the table that in 1969 the majority of companies had a capital employed of over £1 000 000; they are therefore already quite large before they seek a quotation. It is more difficult for non-quoted companies to obtain equity finance than it is for quoted companies, yet as can be seen a company is of substantial size before it obtains access to the capital market. Indeed one of the Stock Exchange requirements is that the company must have a minimum market value of at least £250 000 before it can be granted a quotation, although as can be seen from the figures most companies are well above the minimum size before they in fact seek a quotation, or at least before they are granted a quotation. It is this question of finance for the small, developing company that the Bolton Committee discussed.

The London Stock Exchange is of course only one of the stock exchanges operating in the country. Statistics were collected for one of the regional exchanges, the Midland and Western. The number of new issues coming to a

Table 5. Births on London Stock Exchange

A. By Number

Year ending 31 March	Total including overseas	Commercial and industrial	Overseas
1970	135	93	25
1969	192	126	17
1968	106	75	10
1967	89	65	13
1966	80	55	14
1965	201	160	23
1964	152	106	16

B. By Size

(i) Year ending 31 March 1969

Capital employed £000s	Number
0–250	3
251–500	19
501–1000	32
1001–2500	48
2501–5000	17
5000–10000	6
10001–15000	1
Total	126

(ii) Year ending 31 March 1962

Capital employed £000s	Number
0–250	3
251–500	19
501–1000	18
1001–2500	7
2501–5000	6
5001–10000	2
10001–15000	1
Total	56

provincial stock exchange is, however, quite small. The companies that are 'born' on the provincial exchanges are typically smaller than those going to the London market. The regional exchanges can therefore provide a valuable link in attempting to alleviate the difficulties of small companies in obtaining finance. It should be remembered that some of the 'births' on the London Stock Exchange are companies that also have a quotation on a regional exchange; they are merely being introduced to the London market for the first time.

Deaths

A quoted company can die either because it is taken over, because it is liquidated, or because its quotation is withdrawn. Table 1 shows estimates of the probability of the first two events happening to a company over the ten-year period from 1960 to 1969. The third event is so unlikely that it is not worth considering; it did not happen to any of the companies we investigated. These results imply that for any company existing at 1 January 1960 there is only a limited chance of it surviving until 31 December 1969; the chance that it will survive and the chance that it will be taken over or liquidated is reflected in the table. To take size classification 9 as an example, there was only a 0.42 probability that a company in this class at the beginning would survive through the period; there was a 0.48 probability of it being taken over (or merged where it is the weaker company in the association) and a 0.10 probability that it would be liquidated.

In order to obtain accurate estimates of the survival probability in the top four groups, the sample sizes for each group were enlarged to fifteen companies. This was done because it was not thought that many deaths would occur in these larger groups. It must be remembered that the sample sizes were chosen for the earlier part of the study based on a probability sampling procedure that used as its base the variability of profits within a size group. There is no reason to suppose that variability of profits within groups is in any way related to the distribution of takeover by size.

The number of companies sampled was in fact larger for all groups than those shown in table 2. The sample sizes referred to in table 2 are the companies examined that survived during the ten years. In order to find such numbers for any size class it meant considering a far larger number of the companies that existed in 1960. For example, to find 16 companies in size group 6 that survived over the period, meant tracing what happened to 32 companies, for, as table 1 shows, half of these were taken over by other companies during the decade.

Ijiri and Simon (1971) find, on examining the largest 500 companies in the USA, that the survival probability is the same for firms of all sizes. We would agree that the survival probability is the same for companies in the largest size groups, but the survival probability for companies in all the ten groups is far from similar, the probability of survival increases with company size. Survival is a motivation for a large number of mergers and takeovers; although it is not often discussed by the participants. The defensive merger is discussed by the usual jargon about economies of scale and rationalization. The results of this study suggest however, that the probability of survival does not increase once a company has reached group 5, that is once a company has a capital employed greater than £5 million.

This is an interesting result as it is comparable to that found by Singh (1971) for an earlier period. In examining the period from 1948 to 1960 Singh shows that the probability of survival does not increase with size, once a company has a capital employed greater than £4 million. Allowing for the effects of inflation on assets costs and values, it is suggested that these two results are similar, and that the same real size safety barrier has existed over a long period.

A clear distinction can be drawn between groups 1 to 5 and groups 6 to 10; the probability of surviving for the decade for the former being in the region of 0.74, and for the latter in the region of 0.50. The probability of take-over is (with the exception of group 6) a decreasing function of size, with very approximately, the smallest companies having twice the probability of being taken over that the largest companies have.

The really dramatic differences in survival probability can be explained in terms of liquidations. During the decade none of the companies sampled in the largest seven size groups were liquidated. (However, Rolls–Royce was one of the companies sampled in group 2, and it came to its sad end early in the 1970s.) Liquidations did occur in groups 8, 9 and 10, at a rate which decreased with size.

The survival probabilities of companies in the smallest group are surprisingly small. For those quoted companies with a capital employed of less than £250 000 in 1960, the estimated probability of surviving until the end of 1969 was only 0.41, an estimated 42 per cent of such companies were taken over, and 17 per cent went into liquidation.

These figures can be compared with the survival probabilities for small non-quoted companies given in the Bolton Report and shown in table 6.

Table 6. Mortality ratios among small firms

	Manufacturing and construction	Wholesale	Motor trade	Retail
Liquidation	8%	19%	8%	15%
Ceasing to trade	2%	6%	5%	9%
Taken over	13%	8%	5%	4%
Total deaths	23%	33%	19%	28%

Percentage of small firms in existence in 1963 going into liquidation, ceasing to trade or taken over by 1970—that is, estimates, of probabilities for an eight-year period.

The definition of a small firm used in the Bolton study was a firm employing 200 or less people. As explained, such firms are usually too small to be quoted on the Stock Exchange, and are in most cases much smaller than the smallest companies in our sample. It can be seen that the probability of these 'small' firms being taken over is, for each industry group, considerably less than for the small quoted companies. However, the table in the Bolton Report gives estimates of the probability of being taken over during an eight-year period, whereas our table 1 refers to a ten-year period; but even when the Bolton figures are standardized for a ten-year period they still show a much lower probability.

One reason why this probability of death as a result of takeover is greater for small quoted companies than for small non-quoted companies is because a company with shares quoted on the market is easier to acquire. It is sometimes suggested that one reason why certain companies seek a market quotation is so that they can make themselves an easier target for takeover. One result, however, that has emerged from our study of new companies, is that they do not have a higher probabilty of being taken over than companies that already have a quotation.

With regard to death through liquidation, the results for the two types of small companies are not so different. The Bolton Committee's small firms, showed (adjusted to ten years) a 10 per cent chance of being liquidated in the manufacturing and construction and the motor trade groups and a 24 per cent and 19 per cent chance in the wholesale and the retail groups respectively. The small group in our sample (group 10) consisted of a mixture of companies from many industries including wholesaling and retailing; so our finding of a 17 per cent chance of being liquidated at some point over a ten-year period for our heterogeneous group is not different to the finding for the small (under 200 employees) category described in the Bolton Report.

Reduction in the Number of Companies with a Market Quotation

That concentration is increasing in industry is well known. How serious it is can be seen from a finding in a study by Prais (1972), that by the end of the 1970s, if present trends continue, the top companies in the country will control 67 per cent of the net output of the private sector engaged in manufacturing. This compares with a 25 per cent share in 1953.

The stock market or rather those who operate through the market must accept much of the responsibility for this state of affairs. The investment policies of the large institutions have led to an increase in the proportion of the nation's savings being invested in the largest companies. The market has allowed businessmen to play their takeover 'games' and has perhaps actively encouraged this type of development. As Caves (1968) pointed out, a much larger proportion of the growth in US industry can be accounted for by internal expansion than could the growth of UK industry. When a British industrialist wants to expand his typical reaction is to buy up another company.

The stock market itself needs to become worried, for the number of deaths of quoted companies is vastly exceeding the number of births. There are becoming fewer companies available in which the investor can buy an equity interest. The serious situation can be seen in the change in the number of companies with a quotation on the London Stock Exchange. The number of firms with a quotation in the market was about the same in 1960 as in 1948. However, as Singh (1971) has pointed out over the latter part of this period, from 1954 to 1960, the number of deaths greatly exceeded the number of births; the incidence of deaths being double the incidence of births. Singh shows that the death rate over this period was unprecedented in any other observed period (See also Hart and Prais 1956; Ma 1960.) He found that takeover only became the predominant cause of death for quoted companies during the 1950s. Prior to that, as Hart and Prais have shown, liquidation was the most common cause of death.

As at 31 March 1962, there were 2311 companies in the commercial and industrial classification that had equity share quotations. Over the next eight years there were 770 companies in these classifications that received quotations for the first time on the London Market. However, as at 31 March 1970, there were only 2039 such companies with a quotation, which means that 1042 companies in this sector died over this period (they were either taken over, or liquidated). This is a reduction of nearly 300 companies in an eight-year period. Dangers of this trend seem, however, to have been reversed in the early months of 1972 where there is a lengthy queue of new companies seeking a quotation. Whether this is a temporary or longer-term phenomenon cannot yet be determined. The reduction in the number of quoted companies in the 1960s represents a minimal estimate of the increase in concentration in the stock market where concentration is measured by the relationship between the total market value and the number of companies. The reduction in investors' choice has been greater than these figures indicate, for not all mergers and takeovers result in the ending of the quotation for the acquired company. One company can acquire a controlling interest in another company, and yet still keep the shares of the subsidiary quoted on the market. The number of shares available to the public has been reduced, but, more seriously, the potential influence of the market over this subsidiary is practically nothing.

VI. CHARACTERISTICS OF TAKEN OVER COMPANIES

In two earlier studies (Samuels and Tzoannos 1969; Tzoannos and Samuels 1972) the financial characteristics of the companies involved in merger and takeover activity were examined. These were attempts to identify the distinguishing features of both companies that purchase others and of the companies that are themselves acquired.

In one of the studies support was found for the Marris (1964) hypothesis that the companies taken over were those undervalued by the stock market. This analysis was, however, based on a share-valuation model, and the usefulness of such models has recently come under considerable criticism. Keenan (1970) has pointed out that after two decades of empirical research with models of equity valuation only the crudest sorts of generalizations can be made about the factors which explain share prices.

The second study used the statistical technique of discriminant analysis. A number of explanatory variables were examined to see if it was possible to differentiate between a sample of companies that had been acquired and a sample of companies that had not been the subject of attempted acquisition. The study was based on a nine-month period from the beginning of July 1967 to the end of March 1968. The analysis takes the form of estimating a linear probability function, which can be used to select companies most likely to be purchased.

In addition to assigning to companies the probability of being purchased, the results obtained from testing the model also show which variables are significant in determining whether a company is attractive to a would-be purchaser. The capital-gearing variables show that companies purchased have a higher absolute level of capital gearing than those in the control sample, and they have a greater upward trend and greater variability. This offers some support to the theory that the victim companies have already used their borrowing possibilities and are not, therefore, being purchased because they will allow the purchasing company access to new loan funds.

The higher the trend in profits to capital employed the less likely a company is to be purchased. This is what one would predict: the better the growth in profits, the less likely the shareholders are to sell. The effect of volatility in profits is not what one would expect, for the higher the volatility the less likely the purchase. A liquidity variable, the so-called acid test, was found to be significant, but has the opposite effect to that predicted. The higher the ratio of quick assets to current liabilities the more likely it is that a company will be taken over. The companies taken over were not, therefore, on average, in a poor liquidity position.

The effect of the price-earnings ratio is exactly as the theory implies. The higher a company's price-earnings ratio the less the likelihood of its being purchased. This reflects the widespread interest of the stock market in this ratio, and the fact that one of the 'guidelines' in takeover policy is that taking over a company with a lower price-earnings ratio than oneself helps one's own earnings position. The ratio of price to cash flow has less popular appeal and yet it could be argued that it is of equal, if not of greater, significance than the price-earnings ratio. Cash flow represents, in the terminology of the investment analyst, retained earnings plus depreciation. These are the resources generated by the company's own operations that are available for reinvestment. The earnings per share figure is not the amount which is available for reinvestment, it is a figure arrived at after deduction of depreciation. The amount of depreciation, it can be argued, is a management decision and is bound to be flexible within a range. It could be said that it is the cash-flow figure that the acquiring company is interested in buying. The results obtained from testing the model, unfortunately, do not offer support for this hypothesis: the higher a company's price to its cash flow per share, the greater the probability of its being taken over.

The importance of the dividend variables are as would be expected. The higher the trend in dividends in a company, the less likely it is to be taken over. The greater the variability in dividends over time in a company, the more likely it is to be taken over. Both these results reflect the feelings of shareholders: the greater the upward trend in dividends with little variability, the more satisfied are the shareholders and the less inclined they are to sell to a possible purchaser.

CONCLUSION

This paper has reported findings on the growth of surviving companies, on the rate of death due to takeover and liquidations, and upon certain characteristics of taken over companies. Further research is being undertaken into the growth rate and characteristics of new companies, and the performance and characteristics of companies that are liquidated. When this additional work is completed, it should be possible to construct a model representing the process of change in the size distribution of companies, to obtain estimates of the magnitudes of the various parameters and so to enable forecasts to be made on the future level of concentration and the ways in which these levels will come about.

STRATEGY OF THE FIRM AND MARKET STRUCTURE: AN APPLICATION OF OPTIMAL CONTROL THEORY

by

ALEX P. JACQUEMIN and JACQUES THISSE

INTRODUCTION

What is the shortest distance between me and my lady love on the other side of the lake? Not being Byron, I follow a straight line until it touches the lakeshore tangentially. Then I race along the curved shore, until I encounter the tangential straight line that runs into the object of my heart's desire. Bolza and Valentine tell how to handle the inequality. 'Don't go in the water', and the two tangencies are critical to an optimal solution.

          P. A. Samuelson, *Journal of Political Economy*, no. 6, 1970, p. 1376.

The purpose of this paper is to study some topics in industrial organization where optimal control theory has recently been applied and to suggest new lines of attack for developing the dynamics of industrial organization. It is nevertheless clear that this paper cannot explore all the recent research for dynamising the study of industrial organization through the various possible analytical tools nor can it present all the recent applications of control theory to the firm, where no substantial aspects of industrial organization are involved.

Within these limits, we first present a general model of optimal control theory as applied to industrial organization (section I). Then, we analyse and extend specific models: price policy and market share (section II), limit pricing and barriers to entry (section III), advertising and product differentiation (section IV) research and development expenditures and induced technical progress (section V). In our conclusions, we draw common features from the analyzed models and we point out some actual limits of the dynamic theory of industrial organization.

I. TOWARDS A BASIC MODEL

The complaints about the lack of realism of static models for analysing the industrial world are not new. In 1942, J. Schumpeter wrote:

> The fundamental impulse that sets and keeps the capitalist engine in motion comes from the new consumers' goods, the new forms of production or transportation, the new markets, the new forms of industrial organization that capitalist enterprise creates . . . . Now a theoretical construction which neglects this essential element of the case neglects all that is most typically capitalist about it; even if correct in logic as well as in fact, it is like Hamlet without the Danish prince.

Some 13 years later, J. P. Miller had to confess:

> . . . if we are to achieve an understanding of the competitive processes, we must develop a verified theory of market structure and behaviour

The authors would like to thank N. Ireland, H. Jones, A. Minguet and J. Williamson for helpful comments and criticisms.

relevant to an economy in constant change. Such a theory should explain not only the processes by which wants and resources are mutually adapted, but also the constantly changing structure of markets and behaviour by which this mutual adaptation is brought about . . . At present the principal frame of reference is the vision of the static economy or the circular flow, in which change is treated as essentially exogeneous to the system, and market structure and behaviour are taken as structurally determined (National Bureau of Economic Research, 1955, p. 135).

In more recent years, several efforts have been made to overcome such a limitation and to consider the changing contours of business structure and behaviour.* An expression of this research is the book edited by R. Marris and A. Wood, *The Corporate Economy* (1971).

In the models included in Marris and Wood's book, the firm is supposed to actively attempt to affect the rate at which the industrial environment is changing over time. The authors then try to determine 'the size and/or growth of the firm over time in association with major strategic variables such as advertising, diversification rates, price policy and stock market value' (p. 5). The instrumental variables used to shift the demand curve and/or the production function are called 'development expenditures' (R. Marris) or 'promotional expenditures' (R. Solow).

This stimulating research still presents two limits. First, the mathematical tools used are not able to reveal some important implications of a dynamic analysis of the relation between the firm's market behaviour and the market structure. Second, there is a gap between these new theories of the firm and the 'empirical' industrial organization approach. As A. Wood puts it, 'benefits from interchange of ideas may exist for both schools: for example, for theorists of the firm in estimating their models. On the other hand, newer views of the firm may enable researchers in industrial organization to explain phenomena which are ill accounted for in terms of traditional static models of firms and markets' (p. 41).

Concerning the first limit, the nature of the mathematical tool used, it appears that for a dynamic analysis, the classical methods are less powerful than the optimal control theory.

A first characteristic is that the optimal control theory makes a clear distinction between two types of variables. Indeed, this theory assumes that the manner in which the system changes through time can be described by specifying the time behaviour of a finite collection of variables, x, which are referred to as *state variables*. There also exists a set of *control variables*, s, such that if the control variables and the initial conditions are specified, then the time variation of the state variables, and therefore the evolution of the system through time, is determined (see Hadley and Kemp 1971; Arrow and Kurz, 1970). Furthermore, the optimal control theory generalizes the classical calculus of variations by extending the optimality conditions on the boundary of the set of admissible constraints in the case where this set is closed :† the allowed constraints may be inequalities.

Finally, by using the adjoint variables $\lambda(t) = [\lambda^1(t), \ldots, \lambda^n(t)]^T$ in the

---

* We should remember here the pioneering work of Edith Penrose (1959).

† An example is the 'bang–bang' principle.

Hamiltonian, the Pontryagin theory substitutes a sequence of static optimizations to a dynamic optimization. Albouy and Breton (1968) have shown that, along the optimal control path, these adjoint variables can be interpreted as the shadow prices of a unitary increase of the state variables:

$$\frac{\partial V_t^*}{\partial x}, \quad \text{with } V_t^* = \int_t^{t_2} F(x, s^*, t)\, dt$$

This is the origin of fruitful economic interpretations.

The second problem, the bridge between the new models of the firm and the industrial organization viewpoint, may then be approached through the use of optimal control theory. A starting point is to consider $s = s(t)$, an m-vector of control variables, as a set of market behaviours and $x = x(t)$, an n-vector of state variables, as a set of market structure. We know that the changes of the state variables are related by n state equations to the control variables. What is so implied is that *different forms of market conduct have the capacity to produce either directly or as side effects, gradual changes in the structure of industries.*

For a firm acting in an imperfect environment, it is possible and profitable to try to increase or at least to sustain its actual market share through price policy, mergers, absorptions or collusion; to try to maintain or to increase the given degree of product differentiation through advertising investments and the various forms of selling costs; to try to sustain or to develop the barriers to entry, through limit pricing or the acquisition of patents, in order to impede the entry of new firms.

Let $\pi[s(t), x(t), t]$ be the firm's profit function at time t, as a result of having a set of 'inherited' market structure, i.e. a given market share, a given level of product differentiation and a given level of barriers to entry at that particular date, together with the set of current decisions s, aimed at moulding market structure, at time t.

The firm attempts to maximize the present value of the stream of profit:

$$V = \int_0^\infty e^{-\rho t} \pi[s, x, t]\, dt \tag{1}$$

where the discount factor ρ is taken to be positive and constant.

We construct the Hamiltonian function:

$$H = e^{-\rho t}[\pi(s, x, t) + \lambda^T f] \tag{2}$$

The first term of equation (2) is the instantaneous profit and the second term is the effect of the current change of x on future profits, that is

$$\left(\left[\frac{\partial V_i^*}{\partial x} \right]^T \dot{x}^T \right).$$

The n-vector of auxiliary variables $\lambda(t)$ are shadow prices—that is, the value at time t of the marginal unit of imperfect market structure along the optimal control path. They are the implicit prices attached by the firm to its industrial environment.

If the possible constraints are not binding, the necessary conditions for a maximum imply that:

$$\pi'_s = -\lambda^T f'_s \tag{3}$$

and

$$-\dot{\lambda} = \pi'_x + \lambda^T f'_x - \rho\lambda \tag{4}$$

Equation (3) means that the set of market conducts must be selected so that the marginal immediate profit is in balance with the negative of the effect of current decisions on future profits.

Hence, as long as it may be proved that $\lambda^T \neq 0$, the classical result of the static analysis, $\pi'_s = 0$, becomes invalid once the long-run effects are taken into account: *the firm could have to sacrifice some current profits in order to obtain larger profits in the future.*

Equation (4) says that the loss, $-\lambda$, to be incurred if a (unitary) change in market structure were postponed for a short time is the net contribution of the unitary increase in market structure imperfections to the profit realized during the interval.*

By specifying the signs of partial derivatives, it is possible to obtain further results.

First, let us assume that, for a given level of profit, the more imperfect is the given set of market structure the lower will be the level of strategic expenditures: that is, $\pi(x^i_1, s^i_1) = \pi(x^i_2, s^i_2)$ and $x^i_1 > x^i_2$ imply $s^j_1 < s^j_2$. Furthermore, the marginal profit π'_{s^j} is supposed to be a decreasing function of s^j: $\pi''_{s^j s^j} < 0$.†

Then, it may be shown that $\pi'_{x^i} > 0$ and $f'_{s^j} > 0$ imply $\lambda^i(t) > 0$ for almost all t.‡

Assuming that $f^{k'}_{s^j}$ and π'_{x^k} are non-negative for $k = 1, \ldots, n$,§ and rewriting

* Compare with Dorfman (1969).

† If f^k is linear for all k such that $f^{k'}_{s^j} \neq 0$, this condition is equivalent to the necessary condition of optimality of $H: H''_{s^j s^j} < 0$.

‡ Indeed, let us assume $\lambda^i(t) < 0$. If $s^{j*}(t)$ is the optimal policy, we have $\pi'_{s^{j*}(t)} > 0$. For the $\bar{s}^j(t)$ which maximizes π at time t for $x^i = x^{i*}(t)$, we have $\pi'_{\bar{s}^j(t)} = 0$. Then we know that $s^{j*}(t) < \bar{s}^j(t)$. As λ^i is a continuous function with respect to t, the inequalities are verified on a bounded interval $]t_1, t_2[$. Let us build a control $\bar{s}^j$ which gives a higher value of the profit functional.

Let us take $\bar{t} \in]t_1, t_2[$.
For $t < \bar{t}$, let $\bar{s}^j(t) = s^{j*}(t)$. From $\bar{t}$, we take $\bar{s}^j(t) = \bar{s}^j(t)$. According to the state equation, $\tilde{x}^i$ departs gradually from x^{i*}, with $\tilde{x}^i > x^{i*}$. We can then find a Δ_1 sufficiently small such that $\bar{t} + \Delta_1 \in]t_1, t_2[$, and $\pi(x^{i*}, s^{j*})\Delta_1 < \pi(\tilde{x}^i, \bar{s}^j)\Delta_1$. Indeed, on $[\bar{t}, \bar{t} + \Delta_1[, \tilde{x}^i > x^{i*}$ and $\bar{s}^j$ gives the maximum π for $x^i = x^{i*}$.
At $\bar{t} + \Delta_1$, let $\bar{s}^j$ be such that

$$\pi(x^{i*}, s^{j*}) = \pi(\tilde{x}^i, \bar{s}^j)$$

As $\tilde{x}^i(\bar{t} + \Delta_1) > x^{i*}(\bar{t} + \Delta_1)$, $\bar{s}^j(\bar{t} + \Delta_1) < s^{j*}(\bar{t} + \Delta_1)$, the preceding equality is true for all t, until $x^{i*}(t) = \tilde{x}^i(t)$, namely for $t = \bar{t} + \Delta_1 + \Delta_2$.
For $t \geq \bar{t} + \Delta_1 + \Delta_2$, let $\bar{s}^j(t) = s^{j*}(t)$. The contribution of $(\bar{s}^j, \tilde{x}^i)$ would then be higher than that of $s^{j*}, x^{i*})$, and s^{j*} would not be an optimal control. Hence $\lambda^i(t)$ must be non-negative for all t.
If $\lambda^i(t) = 0$, $s^{j*}(t) = \bar{s}^j(t)$. But this result is correct at most for a countable infinity of points of $[0, \infty[$. Indeed, if $\lambda^i(t) = 0$ for all $t \in]t_3, t_4[$, the Hamiltonian equation becomes $\pi'_{x^i} = 0$, which contradicts $\pi'_{x^i} > 0$. Hence the continuity of λ^i forbids the cancellation of λ^i on a non-countable set.

§ Let us notice that these conditions are sufficient, but not necessary, to ensure the positiveness of λ^k for $k = 1, \ldots, n$. It is possible to obtain positive λ^k with other conditions about the signs of derivatives of π and f^k.

$\pi'_{sj} = R'_{sj} - C'_{sj}$ where R and C are respectively the revenue and the cost generated by s^j, we may conclude from equation (3) that along the optimal path of the decision variables, at almost any time, positive shadow prices λ^k, $k = 1, \ldots, n$, associated with imperfect market structure imply that *the marginal revenue generated by s^j is less than the marginal cost equally generated by s^j.* *

This result is typically obtained by various special cases (see the following sections), but in fact does not depend upon the specifications of these models. It offers a very general alternative hypothesis to the 'managerial models', where the arguments included in the objective function are used to explain the departure from maximizing current profits (see Baumol 1959; O. E. Williamson 1964).

Let us now assume the existence of a profits tax rate, $\tau < 1$, the net profit being $(1 - \tau)\pi$. Then equation (3) becomes:

$$\pi'_s = -\left(\frac{1}{1 - \tau}\right) \lambda^T f'_s. \tag{4a}$$

Thus, *unlike the static profit maximizer*, and as in the managerial models, *the long-run profit maximizer's policy may be influenced by the profits tax rate:* increases in τ will extend the level of s.

As a further step, we assume one control and one state variable with $\pi'_x > 0$, $\pi'_{xx} < 0$, $\pi'_s \lessgtr 0$, $\pi''_{ss} < 0$ and constant, $\pi'_{ss} \leqslant 0$ and constant, and we specify a linear state equation with $f'_s > 0$ and $f'_x \leqslant 0$.† Then, the equilibrium state $(\hat{s}, \hat{x})$—that is, the point at which $\dot{x} = 0$, $\dot{s} = 0$—is a saddle.‡ This implies the existence of two trajectories of the system of differential equations which converge to this equilibrium (Pontryagin 1962).

This leads to an interesting result which, again, has been deduced from much more specific models: *the optimal strategy of the firm, for $x_0 < \hat{x}$, is to use most of its power to mould market structure in the initial period and to reduce the effort as x approaches its equilibrium value $\hat{x}$* (see also Jacquemin 1972).

At this level of generality, it is not possible to deduce further results. The purpose of the following sections is then to present more specific applications of control to industrial organization.§

* If there is an upper boundary for s_j, for example if the firm cannot borrow above a given maximum, we may have $H'_{sj} < 0$ at the optimum. As in our preceding analysis, we still deduce $R'_{sj} < C'_{sj}$.

† These conditions are sufficient but not necessary.

‡ We have the following system of differential equations:

$$\dot{x} = f(x, s) \tag{i}$$

$$\dot{s} = -\frac{\pi''_{sx}}{\pi''_{ss}} f(x, s) + \frac{\pi'_x}{\pi''_{ss}} f'_s + \frac{\pi'_s}{\pi''_{ss}} (\rho - f'_x). \tag{ii}$$

Expanding equation (ii) linearly around the equilibrium, we compute the characteristic roots, which are, under the precedent conditions, real and opposite in sign.

§ We have standardized the notation and the presentation of all the following models.

II. PRICE POLICY AND MARKET SHARE

An interesting case of application is the relationship between pricing behaviour (the control variable) and the firm's market share (the state variable).

Several efforts have been made to build long-run demand functions, but
the notion of a long-run demand curve poses theoretical difficulties.

> By tradition, demand curves are represented geometrically as two-
> dimensional schedules relating quantities demanded to the price
> charged. But what does the price dimension mean in a long-run frame-
> work? If the price axis reflects the current price only, the quantity
> variable (presumably some weighted average of quantities demanded
> in various periods) is not fully determined, since future demands depend
> upon future prices as well as the current price. If it represents the price
> charged in every period, reality is flouted, for even the most cautious
> oligopolists revise their prices from time to time. If price is viewed
> merely as an average of current and future values, we are left in the dark
> about the actual price in any specific period, including the current
> period, for which decisions must be taken (Scherer 1971, p. 213).

A recent contribution by E. Phelps and S. Winter (1970) handles this
problem by simply relating the firm's profit-maximization decision to the
rate at which the quantity sold changes over time.

The basic assumption of their model is that because of 'sluggishness in the
diffusion of information', the firm finds itself at every moment having
transient monopoly power.

The problem is then to determine the optimal pricing behaviour 'for a
firm which enjoys, at each instant of time, monopoly power with respect to
its current customers, yet which could not indefinitely maintain a price above
the going market price without losing all its customers' (p. 310). This feature
of non-instantaneous customer response to price changes is the sole element
of economic friction that they admit into the theory.

Their state equation tells us that the variation of the firm's proportion of
the total customers at time t, is a function of the divergence between the
firm's price p and the mean price of the other firms, $\bar{p}$, taken as a constant over
time:

$$\dot{x} = f(x, s) = f(\bar{p}, p)\, x$$

with $f(\bar{p}, \bar{p}) = 0,\ f'(p) < 0,\ f''(p) < 0$.

Then, the firm maximizes:

$$V = \int_0^\infty e^{-\rho t} \pi(x, p)\, dt,$$

where $\pi = p(xq(p)) - c(xq(p))$, $q(p)$ is the quantity demanded from the
industry as a whole and c is the firm's total variable cost function.

A necessary condition for maximizing the Hamiltonian is:

$$xq'(p)\left[p + \frac{q(p)}{q'(p)} - c' \right] = -\lambda f'_x$$

Phelps and Winter show that there is no optimal solution for a negative λ. Then, for $\lambda = 0$, we find the classical monopoly solution, and for $\lambda > 0$, the optimal price policy implies marginal revenue less than marginal cost.*

The conclusion is that the firm produces beyond the point where marginal cost equals instantaneous marginal revenues, 'because it estimates that a temporary rise of price, while bringing a larger cash flow for the immediate future, would cost it some valuable customers and thus some future cash flow' (Phelps 1970, p. 19).

A second result derived by the authors is that 'the firm produces less than that output rate at which its marginal costs would equal the equilibrium goin price' (Phelps 1970, p. 19). These results correspond to what is called a 'non-Walrasian equilibrium'.

Still, according to the authors themselves, the limitations of the model are serious.

First, the model is such that if we assume a constant margin between $\bar{p}$ and p, the market share grows at an exponential rate.

Second, $\bar{p}$ is constant while in fact it must be taken as a function of time.

Third, by assuming the fulfilment of all the conditions of perfect competition, except the 'non-instantaneous customer response to price changes', the authors do not explicitly introduce the variables which determine such an 'economic friction'. Is it related to the large number of firms or of customers? Then there is some internal contradiction among the perfect competition conditions. If not, can $\bar{p}$ be a constant and is it not possible to generalize the analysis to the oligopolistic case: then $\bar{p}$ may become a reaction function depending upon p, so that $\bar{p} = g(p, t)$.†

Finally, it seems that we are confronted with a very small departure from perfect competition and yet the hypotheses are already very restrictive.

III. LIMIT PRICING AND BARRIERS TO ENTRY

Until recently, the limit price has been exclusively concerned with determining how far above costs price can be held without inducing entry. The work of Bain, Sylos-Labini and Modigliani allows us to determine the exact size of the discrepancy between the limit price and the competitive price. In this viewpoint, the nature and the height of the entry barriers (economies of scale, absolute cost advantages, product differentiation) are stressed. But what is not explained is: when should the dominant firm (or the group of joint-profit-maximizing oligopolists) reduce its monopoly price to the limit price to block entry, or, more generally, what is the optimal pricing strategy through time, given the threat of entry?

P. Pashigian (1968) has tried to answer the first aspect of the question. In his model, the industry demand curve and the long-run average cost are assumed constant. The rate of entry is simply a function of the elapsed time

---

* The expression in brackets is clearly marginal revenue minus marginal cost, with x treated as constant.

† Comparing the mean price of the firm's competitors $\bar{p}$ and the firm's price, J. Thisse (1972) suggests a model without 'sluggishness' but with differentiated products. According to the existing type of competition, $\bar{p}$ is a function of p and t, or of t alone.

during which price, p, has been above the limit price p_L. Denoting $x(t)$ the market share of the dominant firm at time t, with $x(0) = 1$, the rate of change of the market share is:*

$$\dot{x} = f(t - t_0) \quad \text{for } p > p_L \text{ and with } f < 0$$

Because $\dot{x}$ is not a function of the price, the dominant firm will fix its price at the monopoly level p_M, as long as $p \neq p_L$. The optimal price policy is then a two-parameters policy, p_M, p_L. The firm maximizes

$$V = \int_{t_0}^{T} \pi_M x \, e^{-\rho t} \, dt + \int_{T}^{\infty} \pi_L x(T) e^{-\rho t} \, dt$$

where π_M is the monopoly profit of the industry for $p = p_M$, and π_L the limit profit of the industry for $p = p_L$; π_L and $x(T)$ are constant because, for $t > T$, the rate of entry is zero and the market share remains constant at $x(T)$.

The corresponding optimal time at which to lower the price to the limit price T is the solution of:

$$\pi_M(T) \, x(T) = \pi_L x(T) - \frac{1}{\rho} \pi_L \dot{x}(T)$$

This theory suggests that the firm has to move abruptly from a 'short-run' monopoly pricing policy which allows entry, to a 'long-run' limit pricing policy which blocks entry.

Such a result depends heavily upon the hypothesis that the rate of entry is not a function of the price. In a footnote, Pashigian suggests a more general model where $\dot{x} = f[p(t) - p_L]$, with $f(0) = 0$, $f < 0$. He asserts that in this case, we have a result similar to what he obtains with his model. Two short-comings affect his approach.

First, the model ignores the possibility of gradually changing the product price. Once the alternative p_M, p_L is disregarded, the optimal trajectory of $p(t)$ between t_0 and T is not determined. Second, when he proposes a more general model, he suggests that T is finite, whereas $T \to \infty$.

By using the optimal control theory, Gaskins (1971) overcomes these difficulties. Defining the state variable $x(t)$ as the competitive fringe and $\dot{x}(t)$ as the rate of entry of rival producers, he assumes that the rate of entry is directly proportional to the difference between the current price $p(t)$ and the limit price p_L:

$\dot{x} = k[p - p_L]$, where k is a constant 'response' coefficient. The difference between p_L and the dominant firm's average total cost c measures the cost advantage enjoyed by the dominant firm. It is assumed that $p_L \geqslant c$. The firm maximizes

$$V = \int_{0}^{\infty} e^{-\rho t}[p - c] \, [f(p) - x] \, dt$$

where $f(p)$ is the market demand curve.

For a stationary market demand curve, Gaskins obtains the simultaneous differential equations:

* This equation is not explicitly given by Pashigian.

$$\dot{x} = k[p(t) - p_L]$$

$$\dot{p} = \frac{k(p_L - c) + \rho[x - f(p) - (p - c)f'(p)]}{-2f'(p) - (p - c)f''(p)}$$

From this system, it appears that, for $x_0 < \hat{x}$, the optimal pricing policy implies that the dominant firm will sacrifice market share by initially pricing substantially above the limit price and gradually lowering product price towards the limit price p_L, p being equal to p_L for $t \to \infty$.* Furthermore, defining $m = (f(p) - x)/f(p)$ as the market share of the dominant firm, the long-run optimal market share is equal to

$$\hat{m} = \frac{\{k(p_L - c)/\rho\} - f'(p_L)(p_L - c)}{f(p_L)}$$

The market share is an increasing function of the cost advantage enjoyed by the dominant firm. For a firm with no cost advantage ($p_L - c = 0$), $\hat{m} = 0$: the dominant firm prices itself out of the market in the long run. But Gaskins also demonstrates that this result is not valid once a growth of the product market, $f(p)\,e^{\gamma t}$, is assumed: then, the long-run product price is above the average cost of production.

These results are of such interest that it is tempting to see what they become once slightly different assumptions are used. In a comment on the *dynamic case*, Ireland (1972) suggests that it is better to assume that increases in market demand are not monopolized by the dominant firm (a hypothesis of Gaskins) but that these increases are shared out according to the current market shares.

The result is then that 'the dominant firm's market share is zero if it has no cost advantage—a result analogous to Gaskin's static demand model'.

We suggest that in the *static case*, once the net rate of entry does not depend exclusively upon price policy but simultaneously on the other policies of the dominant firm, then this latter with no cost advantage will not ultimately leave the market.

Indeed, it is reasonable to assume that the firm will not rely only on its price policy to maintain its position on a market, but on an optimal mix of various strategies. An important case is the firm which tries to control independent firms in the industry by various legal devices: through mergers, T.O.B., interlocking directorates or explicit agreements, the dominant firm is able to raise or at least to sustain the degree of seller concentration.

The gross rate of entry is then given by

$$\dot{y} = k_1(p - p_L)$$

The gross rate of exit is given by

$$\dot{w} = k_2(s)$$

where s is the level of expenditures for buying firms and k_2 is such that $k_2(0) = 0$, $k_2(s) > 0$ for $s > 0$, $k_2' \geqslant 0$, $k_2'' < 0$ and $\lim_{s \to \infty} k_2(s)\,k_2'(s) = 0$.

---

* From the negativeness of λ, we deduce that $\pi_p' > 0$. As the quantity sold by the firm, at time t, is a decreasing function of p, we have $\pi_q' < 0$ where q is the firm's output: then along the optimal price policy, the marginal revenue is less than the marginal cost.

Hence, the net rate of entry becomes:

$$\dot{x} = \dot{y} - \dot{w} = k_1(p - p_L) - k_2(s)$$

The Hamiltonian is:

$$H = \{(p - c)[f(p) - x] - s + \lambda[k_1(p) - p_L) - k_2(s)]\}\, e^{-\rho t}$$

The optimal value s^* which maximizes H is given by:

$$H'_s = -1 - \lambda k'_2(s) \leqslant 0, \quad \text{for } s \geqslant 0$$

If $H'^*_s < 0$, we have $-1/\lambda > k'_2(0)$, given $\lambda < 0$; that is, the shadow cost of an additional unit of rival entry is not sufficiently high to induce a take-over $(s^*(t) = 0)$.

On the other hand, assuming $s^*(t) > 0$, and then $H'^*_s = 0$, we obtain the set of differential equations:

$$\dot{x} = k_1(p - p_L) - k_2(s)$$

$$\dot{p} = \frac{k_1(p_L - c) + k_2(s) + \rho\{x - f(p) - (p - c)f'(p)\}}{-2f'(p) - (p - c)f''(p)}$$

$$\dot{s} = \frac{\{k'_2(s)\}^2(p - c) - \rho k'_2(\hat{s})}{k''_2(s)}$$

At the equilibrium $(\dot{x} = \dot{p} = \dot{s} = 0)$, we obtain:

$$\hat{p} = p_L + \frac{k_2(\hat{s})}{k_1} \tag{5}$$

$$k'_2(\hat{s})(\hat{p} - c) - \rho = 0 \tag{6}$$

Substituting for $\hat{p}$ from equation (5) into equation (6), we find that

$$k'_2(\hat{s})\left\{p_L + \frac{k_2(\hat{s})}{k_1} - c\right\} = \rho$$

By assuming that the dominant firm has no cost advantage, that is $p_L = c$, it becomes:

$$k'_2(\hat{s})\frac{k_2(\hat{s})}{k_1} = \rho$$

Then we have:

$$\hat{s} \neq \infty \text{ because } \lim_{\hat{s} \to \infty} \frac{k'_2(\hat{s})\, k_2(\hat{s})}{k_1} = 0 \neq \rho$$

and

$$\hat{s} > 0, \text{ because } k'_2(0)\frac{k_2(0)}{k_1} = 0 \neq \rho$$

According to equation (5), this implies that the optimal price, p^*, does not tend any more towards the limit price p_L. Hence, the firm with no cost advantage will achieve a positive equilibrium market share thanks to its acquisition policy:

$$\hat{m} = \frac{\{k_2(\hat{s})/\rho\} - (\hat{p} - c)\,f'(\hat{p})}{f(\hat{p})} > 0$$

This conclusion underlines how heavily the results obtained by Gaskins depend upon the assumption that the firm, in order to survive or grow, uses a unique control variable instead of an optimal mix.

Kamien and Schwartz (1971a) suggest what may be considered as a more limited model but which in fact extends the application field of optimal control theory. While the previous models determine the optimal price policy for the whole lifetime of the firm, before and after entry, this model is exclusively concerned with the optimal pre-entry price policy—that is, the price for the period when entry has not yet occurred. Once another firm has entered the industry, the profit that can be earned by the dominant firm (or the cartel) is assumed to be constant.

The extension brought by the model is the passage from a deterministic framework to a probabilistic one: the timing τ of the occurrence of entry is stochastically governed by the dominant firm's price policy. More specifically, the state variable $x(t)$ is the probability that entry has occurred by time t or the distribution function of τ, with $x(0) = 0$. Then, the 'instantaneous' conditional probability of entry,* at time t, is assumed to be a non-decreasing function of the control variable p—that is, the product price at that time:

$$\dot{x}/(1 - x) = f(p)$$

or

$$\dot{x} = f(p)\,(1 - x),$$

with $f(0) = 0$, $f'(p) \geqslant 0$, $f''(p) \geqslant 0$.

The height of the function $f(p)$ is a reflection of the ease of entry into the market:

If $p(t) = p_L$, $f(p_L) = 0$: there is no entry.
If $p_1(t) > p_2(t)$, $f(p_1(t)) > f(p_2(t))$: the risk of entry for p_1 is greater than for p_2.
If $p(t) \to \infty$, $f(p(t)) \to 0$: there is free entry.

The objective functional is the present value of expected future profits:

$$V = \int_0^\infty e^{-\rho t}[\pi_1(p)\,(1 - x) + \pi_2 x]\,dt$$

---

* In fact, Kamien and Schwartz do not realize that the conditional probability of entry at time t is equal to zero. However, one can adopt the following procedure: let $x(t) = \Pr[\tau \leqslant t]$, then

$$[x(t + dt) - x(t)]/dt = (1 - x(t)).\,\Pr[t < \tau \leqslant t + dt|\tau > t]/dt.$$

For $dt \to 0$, we have

$$\frac{\dot{x}}{1 - x} = \lim_{dt \to 0} \frac{\Pr[t < \tau \leqslant t + dt|\tau > t]}{dt}$$

We call this limit the 'instantaneous conditional probability' of entry at time t.

where $\pi_1(p)$ is the pre-entry current profits which depend only upon current price, with $\pi_1'' < 0$, and where π_2 is the post-entry profit which is assumed to be constant, with $0 \leqslant \pi_2 < \max \pi_1(p)$. Then the authors demonstrate that the price which gives the largest value to the objective functional is constant over time, $p^*(t) = p^*$, until the first entry. This price will be set below or equal to the period monopoly profit-maximizing price,

$$p^* \leqslant p_M \text{ with } f'(p^*) \geqslant 0.$$

Three cases are possible:

1 As the function f is convex, $f'(p^*) = 0$ implies that p^* minimizes f. Furthermore, knowing that $f(0) = 0$, we have $f(p^*) = 0$: then, for an increase of p^*, $f(p^*)$ remains equal to zero. The entry is effectively blocked and $p^* = p_M$. The non-price barriers to entry are sufficiently high to keep potential entrants out of the market.
2 If $f'(p^*) > 0$ and $f(p^*) = 0$, we have, because of the convexity of f, $f'(p) = 0$ for all $p < p^*$: then p^* is the limit price p_L and the entry is effectively impeded.
3 If $f'(p^*) > 0$ and $f(p^*) > 0$, the entry is ineffectively impeded and the optimal price policy is such that entry is accepted.

Kamien and Schwartz also show that the optimal pre-entry price tends to fall as the discount rate drops, the post-entry possibilities decline or certain non-price barriers to entry fall. Finally, they include a positive constant market growth rate such that the discount factor becomes $e^{-(\rho - \gamma)t}$; by assuming $f(p, \gamma)$ with $f_\gamma' \geqslant 0$, they conclude that if market demand is growing at a positive rate, the optimal price will be lower than the best price if demand were stationary.

In a subsequent paper (1972b), Kamien and Schwartz introduce an additional control variable: the capital stock of the firm.

The objective functional then becomes:

$$V = -ws + \int_0^\infty e^{-\rho t} [\pi_1(p, s)(1 - x) + \pi_2(s) x] \, dt$$

where ws is the cost of the investment required initially to obtain s units of capital. The state equation is unchanged.

Therefore, the firm has to select optimally both the capital stock and the pre-entry price in order to maximize V.

With the same assumptions as in the preceding model, the authors first show that, in the pre-entry period, the optimal price is constant and second that the marginal cost exceeds the marginal revenue.

In addition, the firm selects a capital stock so that 'unless output is identical in the two periods, there may be excess capacity in one of the periods and inadequate in the other'. The equilibrium condition states that the purchase price of a unit of capital is set equal to a weighted sum of capital's marginal productivity during the two periods. 'The more heavily (smaller) the future is discounted and the longer (sooner) the monopoly is expected to be maintained, the more the plant selected will conform to pre-entry (post-entry) needs.'

In conclusion, the major contribution of Kamien and Schwartz is the introduction of uncertainty into the application of optimal control theory, through an ingenious hypothesis for the state equation.

Among possible further research is the use of nonlinear risk preferences.

IV. ADVERTISING AND PRODUCT DIFFERENTIATION

It is well known that advertising expenditures affect the future demand for the product as well as the present. Therefore an optimal decision rule for this market conduct must take into account the present and future net revenue of the firm which advertises. One of the best contributions to this topic is that of Nerlove and Arrow (1962).

They define a state variable $x(t)$ which summarizes the sole effect of current and past advertising outlays on demand, and they call it 'goodwill'. They assume that, 'The price of a unit of goodwill is supposed to be \$1, so that a dollar of current advertising expenditure increases goodwill by a like amount.' Furthermore, goodwill depreciates over time at a constant proportional rate δ. Hence

$$\dot{x} = f(x, s, t) = s - \delta x$$

where s is the advertising expenditure at time t.

Let $q(t)$ be the output sold at time t, $p(t)$ the price charged and $c(q(t))$ the total production costs, so that the firm's profit is:

$$\pi = pq - c(q) - s$$

where $q = q(p, x)$.

Nerlove and Arrow first determine the optimal price policy p using the Euler equation and substitute it into the profit function. The problem becomes:
Maximize

$$\int_0^\infty e^{-\rho t} [\pi(x, p^*) - s] \, dt$$

subject to $x(0) = x_0$

$$\dot{x} = s - \delta x$$

Through the use of the calculus of variations it is shown that at the optimal point, the ratio of goodwill to sales revenue is directly proportional to goodwill elasticity β and inversely proportional to price elasticity η and the sum of the rate of interest and the rate of depreciation

$$\frac{x^*}{pq} = \frac{\beta}{\eta(\rho + \delta)}$$

Nerlove and Arrow consider that 'this is a dynamic counterpart of Dorfman and Steiner's main result' (p. 134), while in fact Dorfman and Steiner obtain

$$\frac{s^*}{pq} = \frac{\theta}{\eta}$$

where s is current advertising expenditures (and not goodwill), and θ is advertising elasticity.

Furthermore, under certain regularity assumptions, it is shown that the optimal policy is to jump instantaneously from x_0 to $\hat{x}$, for $x_0 < \hat{x}$.

Again, by not using the maximum principle, this model suffers from serious shortcomings. First, the authors ignore the possibility of a continuous evolution in advertising to optimize the level of goodwill and determine only the moment in time for an immediate jump to a level where the firm is then supposed to remain.

Second, the (implicit) price of goodwill is not allowed to vary over time, one unit having a fixed price of $1.

In his extension of the Nerlove–Arrow model, J. Gould (1970) imputes these limits to the hypothesis of a linear cost function for additions to goodwill.

Using the optimal control theory, he instead introduces the twice continuously differentiable cost function $w(s)$, where, for $s \geq 0$, $w(s) > 0$, $w'(s) > 0$, $w''(s) > 0$. The problem becomes:
Maximize:

$$\int_0^\infty e^{-\rho t}[\pi(x) - w(s)]\,dt$$

with $\pi'(x) > 0$, $\pi''(x) \leq 0$.

Gould then obtains the following autonomous system of nonlinear differential equations

$$\dot{s} = \frac{1}{w''(s)}\left[(\rho + \delta)\,w'(s) - \pi'(x)\right]$$

$$\dot{x} = s - \delta x$$

From this, Gould does not deduce an expression which could be compared with the Nerlove–Arrow theorem and does not utilize the economic meaning of the auxiliary variable. Instead, he directly uses the phase diagram and establishes that: 'the optimal policy for $x_0 < \hat{x}$ is to advertise most heavily in the initial periods and continually decrease the level of advertising expenditures as x increases toward the equilibrium level $\hat{x}$.' Hence, the instantaneous jump policy is not optimal if advertising cost are nonlinear.

An alternative model has been proposed by A. Jacquemin (1971). While maintaining the linear cost hypothesis, he assumes that the firm's profit is a function of the level of product differentiation x and also of the current advertising outlays. Then, the firm maximizes

$$\int_0^\infty e^{-\rho t}[\pi(s, x) - s]\,dt$$

with $\pi(s, x) = (p - c)\,q(x, s)$ and $q'_s > 0$, $q'_x > 0$.

The concept of product differentiation is distinct from the concept of goodwill. Product differentiation not only summarizes the effect of past advertising outlays on current profit but depends also upon the given opportunity within the industry for introducing significantly different physical designs and qualities of the good in question. By maximizing the

Hamiltonian with respect to s, Jacquemin obtains, for the same state equation as before:

$$\pi'_s + \lambda' = (p - c)\, q'_s + \lambda = 1$$

When the optimal programme of advertising is being deployed, the positive shadow price λ, associated with the stock of goodwill (or product differentiation) implies that the current marginal revenue generated by advertising is less than the marginal cost equally generated by advertising. This result offers an alternative hypothesis to the sales-maximization theory of Baumol which implies that the level of advertising will extend beyond the point at which its marginal cost equals its marginal revenue.

The equation of optimality may be restated in elasticity terms:*

$$\frac{s^*}{pq} = \frac{\theta}{\eta(1 - \lambda)}$$

In this expression, $\theta/1 - \lambda$ may be considered as the long-run advertising elasticity of demand which is greater than the short-run elasticity θ. This is a more direct dynamic counterpart of the Dorfman–Steiner result than the Nerlove–Arrow theorem because the optimal ratio of current advertising expenditure (and not of goodwill) to sales revenue is derived. Furthermore, by using the same model and the other necessary condition, a distinct generalization of the Nerlove–Arrow theorem itself is obtained:

$$\lambda = \lambda(\rho + \delta) - (p - c)\, q'_x$$

or

$$\frac{x^*}{pq} = \frac{\beta}{\eta[\lambda(\rho + \delta) - \lambda]}$$

It is only if we assume a constant unitary price of a unit of goodwill, that is $\lambda = 1$, $\lambda = 0$, that we get the Nerlove–Arrow result. Hence, it is not necessary to assume a nonlinear cost function to show that the price of goodwill changes over time. Even when cost of adding to goodwill, elasticities, interest and depreciation rates are constant, the optimal stock of goodwill does not stand in constant ratio to current sales.† This result is precisely one of the virtues of optimal control theory. Furthermore, by assuming $q''_{ss} < 0$ and constant, $q''_{xs} \leqslant 0$ and constant, $q''_{xx} < 0$, it may be shown, as in our general model of section I, that the optimal policy for $x_0 < \hat{x}$ is to advertise most heavily in the initial periods: we find a result identical to the one of Gould even if we assume a linear cost function.‡

* If a nonlinear cost function for addition to product differentiation is assumed, $w(s) > 0$, $w'(s) > 0$, $w''(s) > 0$, we have:

$$\frac{s^*}{pq} = \frac{\theta}{\eta(w' - \lambda)}$$

† In other words, when Nerlove and Arrow assume that the price of a unit of goodwill is \$1, there is in fact a double hypothesis implied. First the monetary cost of adding to goodwill is always one, an assumption relaxed by Gould, and second the shadow price of a unit of goodwill is also \$1, an assumption explicitly relaxed by the last model.

‡ Note that while we assume π''_{ss} constant, Gould implicitly makes a similar hypothesis, that is $w''(s)$ constant.

V. R & D EXPENDITURES AND INDUCED
TECHNICAL PROGRESS

In this last section, we explore models where technical progress is not entirely exogenous but can be influenced by deliberate market conduct of the firm, namely expenditure on research. Indeed firms are able, to a certain extent, to modify their technology by the purchase of appropriate inputs. Several authors have applied optimal control theory to this problem.

Kamien and Schwartz (1971b) define the objective functional to be maximized as

$$V = \int_0^\infty e^{-\rho t} [\pi(x_1, x_2, x_3) - \sum_{i=1}^3 s_i] \, dt$$

By devoting resources to research, the current technological level x can be changed according to the state equations:

$$\dot{x}_1 = \frac{s_1^k x_1}{R_1}, \qquad \dot{x}_2 = \frac{s_2^k (1 - x_2) x_2}{R_2}, \qquad \dot{x}_3 = \frac{s_3^k x_3}{R_3}$$

with $x_1 \geqslant 0, 0 \leqslant x_2 \leqslant 1, x_3 \geqslant 0$.

The symbols are defined as follows:

x_i, the current state of technology, corresponds to the parameters of the production function, $\phi[x_1 f(z_1, z_2; x_2, x_3)]$:* the shape of the isoquants will be determined by the values of the parameters x_2, x_3 (non-neutral technical change), while neutral technical advance is realized through increase in the positive parameter x_1;

s_i is the amount of expenditure for achieving technical changes at the rate $\dot{x}_i$ when the technology is at a level x_i;

R_i is a positive constant reflecting the relative cost of the ith type of technical change;

k is a parameter $(0 < k \leqslant 1)$ indicating the degree to which technical change is subject to decreasing returns $(0 < k < 1)$ or to constant returns to research effort $(k = 1)$.

Note that the state equations are obtained from specific equations relating the cost of achieving technical change at the rate $\dot{x}$ when the technology is at level x: $s_i = s_i(\dot{x}_i; x_i)$.

Among the results obtained, it is shown that the relative effort devoted to each type of technical change varies inversely with the relative cost R_i, directly with the elasticity of the production cost function to that type of change,† and directly with the size of the firm.

Furthermore, when the static rules of maximization are compared with the dynamic one, it appears, for the case in which technical change leads to an expansion of firm size, that if there are decreasing returns to research effort, 'myopic policy' tends to under-invest in technical change and to allocate the

---

* Given the assumptions on x_2, the range of admissible production functions is limited but includes the CES case.

† This result may be compared with the one obtained for advertising, see p. 79.

given funds among the various types of technical advance in non-optimal proportions.

Again, by neglecting the non-instantaneous reduction in the cost function due to expenditures on research, the allocation of funds is insufficient. But if the returns are constant, myopic and dynamic rules coincide.

A first limitation of this model is that the firm is considered as so insignificant that its actions have no effect on its own environment other than its technology'. Furthermore, there is no recognized interdependence of sellers* and, more generally, no public-good aspect of knowledge. Nevertheless, the important questions in this field seem related to these two problems.

First, is the 'Schumpeterian hypothesis' that large, monopolistic firms will undertake more research than will smaller firms, theoretically valid?

Second, does the 'public-good' nature of basic knowledge make private research, by competitive or monopolistic firms, socially non-optimal?

A specific aspect of the first question has been analyzed by Kamien and Schwartz (1972c). These prolific authors examine the impact of alternative market structure on the timing of innovations. More specifically, they compare the introduction time selected by a firm operating under conditions of rivalry with the timing that would be selected by a firm or cartel operating without any rivals. As they do not use the optimal control theory to derive their results,† we shall simply state the main conclusions: 'if the firm has no rivals at the innovation stage but cannot prevent imitation, then the firm's introduction date will always be related with the cartel date', and 'intensive rivalry will cause the firm to postpone development indefinitely, or equivalently to drop the project' (p. 26).

In a previous article, Ruff (1969) also explored the 'Schumpeterian hypothesis',‡ but at the same time has taken into account the 'public-good' nature of knowledge, within the frame of an N-firm Cournot equilibrium. The more complete and more complex nature of this model explains why we will develop it here.

The Socially Optimal Programme

It is assumed that there is a single input, labour, L, which is fixed in total

---

* At the other extreme, Kamien and Schwartz, in another paper (1972a) have assumed the existence of a dominant firm, a 'technical leader firm' which initiates technical advance, while rivals behave in a purely passive manner. The rivals' reaction is described by an exponential lag:

$$\dot{x}_2 = \delta(x_1 - x_2)$$

where the state variables x_1, x_2 are respectively the quality index of the firm's product and the quality index of the rival goods, and where $\delta \geq 0$ is a response coefficient similar to the one in Gaskin's limit pricing model. Within the context of their model, it is shown that a slow response by rivals (a low δ) to the firm's product improvements increases the duration of the penetration by the leader into the rivals' markets and so stimulates technical progress by the leader. In a different context, Gaskin concludes that a more rapid rival response to price signals would lead to a larger equilibrium market share for the dominant firm.

† However, they devote one section to development of a specific illustrative cost function where optimal control theory is used. But the subsequent sections do not depend upon this formulation.

‡ Using optimal control theory, J. H. Williamson, in an unpublished paper (1967), has also compared the effect of the degree of competition upon technical progress. He concludes that in an industry in which technology has to be separately acquired by each firm, perfect competition is unlikely to be viable, while the emergence of imperfect competition is likely to stabilize the system.

supply, and a single consumption good which may be considered as a numeraire.

The social planner has to optimally allocate labour between the modern sector (s_2), the traditional sector (s_3) and the research sector (s_1). By assuming full employment, we have

$$s_1 + s_2 + s_3 = L_0$$

so that we determine s_3^*, once we know s_1^* and s_2^*.

Let x denote the current technology level, and q_2 and q_3, the production in the modern and in the traditional sector, according to the production function:

$$q_2 = xs_2$$

$$q_3 = \Phi(s_3),$$

with $\Phi' > 0$, $\Phi'' < 0$, $\Phi(0) = 0$ and $\Phi(L_0) < \infty$.

The social objective functional to be maximized is:

$$V = \int_0^\infty e^{-\rho t}[x.s_2 + \Phi(s_3)]\, dt$$

By devoting labour to research, the technological level x can be increased according to the state equation:

$$\dot{x} = f(x, s) = x[h(s_1) - \delta]$$

with $h(0) = 0$, $h'(s_1) > 0$, $h''(s_1) < 0$, $\delta > 0$ and

$$h(s_1^0) = \delta \quad \text{for } 0 \leqslant s_1^0 \leqslant L_0$$

Finally, the unitary wage w is determined by the marginal product in the traditional sector:

$$w(s_1 + s_2) = \Phi'(s_3)$$

With x as the state variable and s_1, s_2 as the control variables ($0 \leqslant s_1$; $s_2 \leqslant L_0$), Ruff obtains the following system of equations for an optimum:

$$x \leqslant w(s_1 + s_2), \quad \text{with equality if } s_2^* > 0 \text{ and inequality if } s_2^* = 0 \tag{7}$$

$$\lambda x h'(s_1) \leqslant w(s_1 + s_2), \quad \text{with equality if } s_1^* > 0 \tag{8}$$

$$\dot{x} = x[h(s_1) - \delta] \tag{9}$$

$$\dot{\lambda} = [\rho + \delta - h(s_1)]\lambda - s_2 \tag{10}$$

A Non-co-operative Multiform Economy

Ruff assumes that the modern sector consists of a number N of firms. Each firm pays the same wage and has the same production function.

$$q_1^{(i)}(t) = x^{(i)}(t).s_2^{(i)}(t), \quad \text{with } x^{(i)}(0) = x_0$$

If firm i were in total isolation, the rate of change of its technological level is determined by the state equation

$$\dot{x}^{(i)} = x^{(i)}[h(s_1^{(i)}) - \delta]$$

But the firm i is not in total isolation and may obtain information from competitors. Then the 'effective research effort' of firm i, $E^{(i)}$, is 'the number of research workers firm i would have to employ in order to generate in isolation the rate of technological progress it actually has' (Ruff 1969, p. 402).

$$E^{(i)} = s_1^{(i)} + \bar{G}(s_1^{(1)}, \ldots, s_1^{(i-1)}, s_1^{(i+1)}, \ldots, s_1^{(N)})$$

with $\bar{G}(0,\ldots,0) = 0$ and $\bar{G}(s_1^{(1)}, \ldots, s_1^{(N)}) \leqslant \sum_{j=1}^{N} s_1^{(j)}$.

If $\bar{s}_1^{(i)} = \sum_{\substack{j=1 \\ j \neq i}}^{N} s_1^{(j)}$ and $\bar{s}_2^{(i)} = \sum_{\substack{j=1 \\ j \neq i}}^{N} s_2^{(j)}$, the firm maximizes:

$$\int_0^\infty e^{-\rho t}[x^{(i)}.s_2^{(i)} - (s_1^{(i)} + s_2^{(i)}).w(s_1^{(i)} + \bar{s}_1^{(i)} + s_2^{(i)} + \bar{s}_2^{(i)})]\, dt$$

subject to $\dot{x}^{(i)} = x^{(i)}[h(E^{(i)}) - \delta]$, $x^{(i)}(0) = x_0$
with $E^{(i)} = s_1^{(i)} + \bar{G}(s_1^{(1)}, \ldots, s_1^{(N)})$.

To determine $s_1^{(i)*}(t)$ and $s_2^{(i)*}(t)$, the firm must know the plans of competitors as well as their reactions, since their research efforts affect $E^{(i)}$ and the cost of labour.

Ruff assumes a 'generalized Cournot behaviour': each firm 'knows the plans of all other firms and assumes these plans are independent of its own decisions' (p. 404). This implies that $\bar{G}$, $\bar{s}_1^{(i)}$, $\bar{s}_2^{(i)}$ are parameters, independent of $s_1^{(i)}$, $s_2^{(i)}$. Furthermore, he assumes that all the firms have identical plans. Having suggested various adjustment mechanisms (indicative planning, recognition of the symmetric nature of the problem) for reaching this result, he obtains:

$$s_1^{(1)} = \ldots = s_1^{(N)} = \frac{S_1}{N}, \quad \text{with } s_1 = \sum_{j=1}^{N} s_1^{(j)}$$

$$s_2^{(1)} = \ldots = s_2^{(N)} = \frac{S_2}{N}, \quad \text{with } s_2 = \sum_{j=1}^{N} s_2^{(j)}$$

Then it becomes:

$$\bar{G} = \beta(N - 1)\frac{S_1}{N}$$

where β is the transmission coefficient and measures the ease with which research results are transmitted among firms ($0 \leqslant \beta \leqslant 1$).

It follows that

$$E^{(1)} = \ldots = E^{(N)} = E = [1 + \beta(N - 1)]s_1/N$$

and

$$x^{(1)} = \ldots x^{(N)} = x$$

Ruff then defines $\gamma = E(t)/s_1 = [1 + \beta(N - 1)]/N$ as the research efficiency coefficient: γ is less than unity—that is, research is inefficient—unless there is either perfect transmission of knowledge between firms ($\beta = 1$), or a single firm ($N = 1$). Writing $E = \gamma s_1$, Ruff obtains the new set of equations describing the motion of the N-firm economy:

$$x \leqslant w(s_1 + s_2) + \frac{s_1 + s_2}{N} w'(s_1 + s_2) \tag{7a}$$

$$N\gamma\lambda h'(\gamma s_1) \leqslant w(s_1 + s_2) + \frac{s_1 + s_2}{N} w'(s_1 + s_2) \tag{8a}$$

$$\dot{x} = x[h(\gamma s_1) - \delta] \tag{9a}$$

$$\dot{\lambda} = [\rho + \delta - h(\gamma s_1)]\lambda - \frac{s_2}{N} \tag{10a}$$

If $N > 1$, 'there are two logically distinct forces acting to make the N-firm economy less progressive than is socially optimal. The first is the inefficiency due to separate research effort; imperfect communication between firms ($\beta < 1$ and hence $\gamma < 1$) raises the cost of achieving any given rate of progress. The second force is more fundamental, and is present even when there is perfect communication ($\beta = \gamma = 1$). It is due to the problems of indivisibility and inappropriability in research' (p. 406). Indeed as the number of firms increases, the size of each decreases as well as the attractiveness of research:

1   For N sufficiently large, no research is undertaken.
2   For $N \to \infty$, the dynamic equations (9a) and (10a) diverge from the corresponding dynamic equations in the social maximization conditions (9) and (10); but we have the static efficiency because equation (8a) implies (8) for $\gamma N > 1$;
3   For $N = 1$, the dynamic equations are identical, but the static relations (7) and (8), (7a) and (8a) are different, because of the monopsonistic restricted demand for labour. Hence in the 'laissez-faire' economy, there is a trade-off between static efficiency with dynamic inefficiency for a large N, and dynamic efficiency with static inefficiency for a small N.
4   For N 'not too large' and X_0 sufficiently large, V^* is a decreasing function of N.

Social Intervention

Ruff assumes that the N firms set up a joint research laboratory and share its costs equally. The social intervention is a subsidy $Z(t)$ for each research worker.
    Then firm i maximizes:

$$V = \int_0^\infty e^{-\rho t}\left[x^{(i)} \cdot s_2^{(i)} - \left(s_2^{(i)} + \frac{s_1}{N}\right)w(s_1 + s_2) + Z\frac{s_1}{N}\right]dt$$

Assuming a symmetric 'Cournot equilibrium', we have the equations:

$$x \leqslant w(s_1 + s_2) + \frac{s_1 + s_2}{N} w'(s_1 + s_2) \qquad (7b)$$

$$\lambda x h'(s_1) \leqslant w(s_1 + s_2) + (s_1 + s_2) w'(s_1 + s_2) - Z \qquad (8b)$$

$$\dot{x} = x[h(s_1) - \delta] \qquad (9b)$$

$$\dot{\lambda} = (\rho + \delta - h(s_1)\lambda - s_2 \qquad (10b)$$

If the subsidy rate is equal to

$$Z^*(t) = (s_1^*(t) + s_2^*(t)) w'(s_1^*(t) + s_2^*(t))$$

and if $N \rightarrow \infty$, equations (7b), (8b), (9b) and (10b) are identical to the equations in the social maximization conditions.

Ruff concludes his analysis by saying that 'full optimality can be achieved only by social intervention, such as a subsidy paid to a joint cooperative research lab'. But if strict *laissez-faire* is required, 'it may be better to have fewer firms, because Schumpeter's contention that dynamic performance is more important than static efficiency receives support from this model' (p. 411).

These stimulating conclusions are weakened once the specificity of the hypotheses is underlined.

Social utility is identified with consumption; the capital input is neglected and the full-employment of labour is assumed; technological progress is disembodied, while it is actually considered that new capital accumulation is the vehicle of technological progress; the production functions are very specific; it would be useful to relax the hypothesis of a 'Cournot behaviour', perhaps by assuming that the functions $\bar{G}$, $\bar{s}_1^{(i)}$, $\bar{s}_2^{(i)}$ are reaction functions. Nevertheless, this original paper opens the way for fruitful studies on the relationship between the rate of technological progress in an economy and the corporate behaviour.

CONCLUSIONS

Recent applications of optimal control theory to the strategies of the firm in relation to its industrial environment have overcome several limits of the static models commonly used in industrial organization.

Among the most general results, two are especially striking. First, it appears that along the optimal control paths of the decision variable, at any time t, the firm has to accept that the current marginal revenue generated by its policy is less than its marginal cost, because of some non-instantaneous beneficial effects of such a policy. This is a general alternative hypothesis to 'managerial theories' to explain failure to maximize instantaneous profits.

Second, whatever market conduct is assumed (price policy, advertising policy, R & D policy), the optimal strategy for the firm, given a state variable $x_0 < \hat{x}$, is to use its policy most heavily in the initial periods and continually decrease the effort as x approaches $\hat{x}$.

Yet some of the results depend, to a varying extent, upon the nature of the models used and the assumptions adopted. Two assumptions are especially limiting. First, the optimized functional is an indefinite integral. A definite planning period may be preferred to the fiction of an infinite horizon: the value of the finite horizon T may be a function of the size of the firm, its industry and the existing degree of competition.* Then a scrap value for the state variable (market structure) must be defined: for example, the end-of-period value of goodwill, market share or technological progress, may be required to be non-negative $(x_T \geqslant 0)$ or non-inferior to its initial value $(x_T \geqslant x_0)$. In each case, the transversality conditions on the auxiliary variables $\lambda(t)$ will be different.

A second limit is the deterministic framework of the models. In fact, uncertainty affects the evolution of market structure and the impact of market conducts on market structure.

It is then possible to assume a probability distribution of the rate of change of the state variable (market structure) where the distribution itself is a function of the control variable (market conduct).

More fundamentally, a 'replanning' procedure may be set up. According to Hadley and Kemp, 'it is desirable that a control system be able to observe, at least occasionally the actual state of the system and, if the system has deviated from the initially determined optimal path, to determine a new path appropriate to the current state of the system' (1971, p. 272). But with this procedure, serious errors may develop before a check on the state of the system is made.

An alternative is to determine a function 'which gives optimal values of the control variables for each possible state of the system' (Hadley and Kemp 1971, p. 272). This synthesizing function is especially useful in industrial organization. Indeed, we have considered that market conducts influence the evolution of market structure through the state equation:

$$\dot{x} = f(x, s, t).$$

But according to the traditional approach, market conducts are taken as structurally determined: 'market structure is important because the structure determines the behaviour of firms in the industry' (Caves 1967, p. 17).

By introducing a synthesizing function which gives the optimal values of the market conduct for each possible set of market structures, for example $s = s(x)$, we integrate the two points of view: over time, there are influences flowing from market conduct toward market structure as well as influences flowing from market structure toward market conduct. But in fact, the synthesizing of an optimal control is still in its infancy.

More generally, even within the limits of the previous simple models, the analysis quickly leads to tedious mathematical complications and to results without economic meaning.

What would be the situation if it were necessary to take into account the main aspects of the firm's growth process? That is why the role of empirical and case studies remains essential in this field. Our hope is that the optimal trajectories of the various methodologies are convergent.

* Note also that there are problems involved in optimizing with an infinite horizon. First, the functional might not converge at all. With a constant rate of discount, the necessary (but not sufficient) convergence condition is $\rho > 0$. Second, most existence theorems have been proved only for optimization with a finite horizon. Third the transversality conditions are often mis-specified.

OPTIMALITY IN FIRMS' ADVERTISING POLICIES: AN EMPIRICAL ANALYSIS

by

KEITH COWLING

This paper is concerned with examining the behaviour of firms and consumers in a series of markets for durable and non-durable goods. The actual behaviour of firms in these markets is then compared with the predictions of various optimizing models, in order to establish what sort of rules firms appear to follow in determining their competitive strategies. The results will also provide evidence on the degree of monopoly power existing in a variety of markets and on the significance of the barrier to entry into the market created via advertising.

The paper will consist of three parts. First, a theoretical exploration will be made of optimal advertising behaviour in a variety of market situations. Results will be obtained for monopoly and oligopoly situations where advertising is alternatively viewed as a current input or a capital good, and both profit-maximizing and more general managerial utility maximizing behaviour will be examined. The second part of the paper will be concerned with the construction and estimation of a model of market behaviour, where both market share and advertising appropriations are endogenous to the model. The markets to which the model is applied consist of two durables: cars and tractors, and three non-durables: toothpaste, margarine and instant coffee. Section III of the paper will involve an interpretation of the empirical results. Evidence will be collated on advertising as a capital good, inter-dependence in advertising and advertising and price elasticities of demand. More generally, the results will be examined in the light of the alternative models of optimal behaviour advanced in section I.

I.   OPTIMAL ADVERTISING BEHAVIOUR

Monopoly

(1) *Advertising as a current input*

As a first approximation, let us take the case of a firm in a monopoly situation where price and advertising are decision variables.* We can then write down the demand function facing the firm as,

$$X = X(p, A) \tag{1}$$

where X is the rate of sales, p is price and A is current advertising expenditure. The profit equation is,

$$\Pi = pX - C - A \tag{2}$$

where C is total production costs. Then first-order conditions for a profit maximum are

$$\frac{\partial \Pi}{\partial A} = p \frac{\partial X}{\partial A} - \frac{dC}{dX} \cdot \frac{\partial X}{\partial A} - 1 = 0 \tag{3}$$

The research reported here represents part of a project on the economics of advertising, sponsored by the Department of Trade and Industry.

* The way quality is handled later in the empirical work would allow us to integrate quality in the form of quality corrected prices in this analysis. In this case there is little point in considering quality separately.

which can be rewritten as,

$$\frac{\partial X}{\partial A} \cdot \frac{A}{X} \left(pX - \frac{dC}{dX} \cdot X \right) = A \tag{3a}$$

$$\frac{\partial \Pi}{\partial p} = p \frac{\partial X}{\partial p} + X - \frac{dC}{dX} \cdot \frac{\partial X}{\partial p} = 0 \tag{4}$$

which can be rewritten as,

$$\frac{\partial X}{\partial p} \cdot \frac{p}{X} \left(pX - \frac{dC}{dX} \cdot X \right) = -pX \tag{4a}$$

Dividing equation 3a by equation 4a gives us our equilibrium condition, which is simply a restatement of the Dorfman–Steiner (1954) result:

$$\frac{A}{R} = \frac{-\partial X/\partial A \cdot A/X}{\partial X/\partial p \cdot p/X} = \frac{\eta_A}{\eta_p} \tag{5}$$

where A/R is the ratio of advertising expenditure to sales revenue and η_A/η_p is the ratio of the advertising elasticity of demand to the price elasticity of demand. Second-order conditions for a maximum require $\partial(\eta_p - \mu)/\partial A > 0$, where $\mu = p\partial X/\partial A$. Equilibrium, where price is fixed, is given by equation 3. It should be noted that in the case of a Cobb–Douglas demand function and constant production costs the optimal advertising to sales revenue ratio is a constant.

(2) Advertising as a capital good

Up to this point, we have regarded the impact of advertising as completely dissipated within the current period. More generally, we want to examine the dynamics of advertising. Advertising may have an impact on future periods for several reasons. First, it may have a cumulative effect in moulding consumer behaviour. Second, consumer behaviour may show bandwagon effects, such that one set of consumers reacts to current advertising with others later following this behaviour. This interdependency among consumers may be interpreted as an indirect response to changes in current advertising. Last, consumers influenced by current advertising may not immediately enter the market. Thus, theoretically, we are interested in determining optimal behaviour where advertising is a capital good.

Nerlove and Arrow (1962) have determined the optimal stock of 'goodwill', K (advertising capital), under the same conditions as described above (that is, assuming monopoly with price and advertising as decision variables) and have come up with a dynamic analogue to the Dorfman–Steiner condition (assuming the firm is interested in maximizing a discounted stream of profits over time):

$$\frac{K}{R} = \frac{\eta_K}{\eta_p(r + \delta)} \tag{6}$$

where r is the discount rate and δ is the depreciation rate. We note that

$$A = \dot{K} + \delta K \tag{7}$$

$$\frac{K}{R}\frac{A}{K} = \frac{\eta_K}{\eta_p(r+\delta)}\frac{K+\delta K}{K} \qquad \eta_K = \frac{\partial Q}{\partial K}\left(\frac{K}{Q}\right)$$

$$\frac{A}{R} = \frac{K\frac{\partial Q}{\partial K}}{Q\,\eta_p(r+\delta)} \qquad \frac{A}{K} = \frac{\frac{\partial Q}{\partial A}Q}{\eta_p(r+\delta)} \qquad \eta_A = \frac{\partial Q}{\partial A}\left(\frac{A}{Q}\right)$$

that is, current advertising (gross investment) equals the change in the capital stock $(\dot{K})$ plus depreciation. We can, therefore, put equation 6 in terms of A/R by multiplying through by A/K,

$$\frac{A}{R} = \frac{\eta_A}{\eta_p(r + \delta)} \qquad (8)$$

since $\partial X/\partial K = \partial X/\partial A$.

If we assume a geometrically declining lag structure, relating sales to advertising, of the form

$$\log X_t = B + \beta \sum_{n=0}^{\infty} \lambda^n \log A_{t-n} \text{ (where } 0 < \lambda < 1)$$

which happens to have some useful properties from an estimational viewpoint, then we can define β as the short-run elasticity of sales with respect to advertising expenditures and $\beta/(1 - \lambda)$ is the long-run elasticity, the sum to infinity of the coefficients on advertising. Thus, provided $\lambda > 0$, that is provided advertising is a capital good, then the long-run elasticity with respect to advertising will exceed the short-run elasticity. For this form of lag structure, δ, the rate of depreciation, equals $1 - \lambda$ and we can rewrite equation 8 in terms of the long-run elasticity η_A^L,

$$\frac{A}{R} = \frac{\eta_A^L}{\eta_p(1 + r/\delta)} \qquad (8a)$$

The problem with this dynamic analogue of the Dorfman–Steiner conditions for optimal price and advertising is that there is a basic assymetry in the treatment of the two decision variables. We are allowing for possible dynamic effects of advertising but we are not doing so for price. We may advance similar reasons to those already discussed for advertising to explain lagged effects associated with price changes. In addition, there may be consumer uncertainty about the price (and quality) of a product. The price (and quality) 'image' may be derived from observations in earlier time periods.*

The dynamic effects of pricing decisions may also be examined in the context of entry by other firms into the market. It is reasonable to suppose that the rate of entry to the market varies directly with the price-unit cost margin. Thus for the same future price structure higher prices today will mean lower sales tomorrow. Advertising, of course, has similar dynamic effects, but these are exerted via the heightened barrier to the entry of new firms due to brand loyalty created by the cumulative effect of past advertising expenditures.

In the case of both advertising and price variables we can incorporate the various dynamic effects into the definition of long-run elasticities of sales with respect to these variables and in both cases we would expect the long-run elasticities to exceed the short-run elasticities. In aggregate demand studies,

---

* There will also, of course, be consumer uncertainty about the utility to be derived from any change in quality-corrected price brought about via a change in specifications which may be quite complicated. Only with time, allowing for experience and observation, will the consumer move to a new equilibrium.

where total market sales of the commodity is related to the average price of the commodity and other variables, there is bounteous evidence that long-run price elasticities are indeed much more elastic than their short-run equivalents. In the more limited studies of the demand function facing the firm similar evidence is accumulating (Cowling and Cubbin 1971, 1972; Cowling and Rayner 1970; Lambin 1970a; Peles 1971).* For our purposes, the important outcome of the discussion is that the adjustment to the Dorfman–Steiner rule to allow for dynamic effects need not be as great, in terms of the ratio of advertising to sales revenue, as is suggested by Nerlove and Arrow. Their rule would suggest higher ratios of advertising to sales revenue, the magnitude of the change being dependent on the difference between the short-run and long-run advertising elasticities and the discount rate. Treating the pricing decision symmetrically gives us a variant of the Nerlove–Arrow rule.

$$\frac{A}{R} = \frac{\eta_A(r + \zeta)}{\eta_p(r + \delta)} \qquad (9)$$

where ζ is the depreciation rate on the stock of 'goodwill' created by price-cutting. More familiarly, this equilibrium condition can be written in terms of the long-run elasticities with respect to advertising and price:

$$\frac{A}{R} = \frac{\eta_A^L(1 + r/\zeta)}{\eta_p^L(1 + r/\delta)} \qquad (10)$$

This dynamic variant of the Dorfman–Steiner condition can lead to the prediction of higher, lower, or the same ratios of advertising to sales revenue, depending on the ratio of short-run to long-run elasticities for the two variables. Thus, if the lag structure in the demand equation is the same for both variables, then we end up back at the Dorfman–Steiner condition

$$\frac{A}{R} = \frac{\eta_A^L}{\eta_p^L} = \frac{\eta_A^S(1 - \lambda)}{\eta_p^S(1 - \lambda)} = \frac{\eta_A^S}{\eta_p^S} \qquad (11)$$

where η_A^S, η_p^S are the short-run elasticities, equivalent to the elasticities in the static model.

Oligopoly

In the previous section we have assumed that each firm can proceed independently in manipulating price and advertising expenditures without having any significant impact on any other firm. Thus the realistic situation of a high degree of interdependence within a group of firms has been ignored. The rational approach to decision-making in such an environment involves an exploration of the costs and benefits accruing to the firm from collusion. Assuming costless collusion, the industry will adopt advertising and price policies so that equations 3 and 4 are satisfied, where each variable is measured at the industry level. These equations simply state that industry advertising is taken up to the point at which the marginal revenue productivity of

---

* The extent to which the empirical estimates of the long-run elasticities capture the entry-limiting effects of changes in the decision variables is debatable. It will obviously depend importantly on the length of the time-period of observation.

advertising for the industry is equated with the extra costs incurred (production and selling costs) and price is set where industry marginal revenue equals industry marginal costs. Thus the Dorfman–Steiner conditions (ignoring dynamic effects for simplicity) will be

$$\frac{A_i}{R_i} = \frac{\eta_A}{\eta_p} \tag{12}$$

where the ratio of advertising to sales revenue for the average firm will be equated with the ratio of the industry advertising elasticity to the industry price elasticity. Thus joint profits will be maximized. Compared with a non-collusive solution, advertising will obviously be lower and prices higher, since at the industry level the relevant elasticities will be smaller than at the firm level. However, this need not mean that the ratio of advertising to sales revenue will be different with collusion. This depends on the ratio of industry to firm elasticities for the two variables. On the basis of the behaviour of demand analysts, working essentially at the industry level, we would be forced to the conclusion that advertising is irrelevant to consumer behaviour at this level of aggregation. Certainly many results have demonstrated non-zero industry price elasticities,* whereas few observations have been made of non-zero industry advertising elasticities.† If these empirical relationships give a reasonable approximation to the true relationships, then we can infer that ratios of advertising to sales revenue will be lower under collusion. Another argument strengthens this conclusion. We have assumed until now that collusion is costless and equally possible for both advertising and pricing decisions. However, it is in each firm's interest to break the collusion, so long as it is possible to do so undetected. Thus the costs of maintaining a collusion become the costs of effectively policing it. These costs are likely to be lower for advertising collusions than for pricing collusions (since actual transactions prices may deviate markedly from quoted prices) so that it is likely that oligopoly groups will approximate more closely to joint-profit maximizing advertising than to joint-profit maximizing price.

There may be cases in which collusion is difficult. In this case we can reformulate the first-order Dorfman–Steiner conditions, this time allowing for interaction between firms:

$$\frac{A_i}{R_i} = -\frac{(\partial X_i/\partial A_i + \partial X_i/\partial A_j \cdot \mathrm{d}A_j/\mathrm{d}A_i)A_i/X_i}{(\partial X_i/\partial p_i + \partial X_i/\partial p_j \cdot \mathrm{d}p_j/\mathrm{d}p_i)p_i/X_i} \qquad (i = 1, 2, \dots, N) \tag{13}$$

This defines an equilibrium for a firm where A_j is competitive advertising and p_j is competitive price: equilibrium for the group is obtained by solving the N equations. Recognizing the existence of reaction functions obviously has a depressing effect on the firm's expectations of the gain in sales from either increasing advertising or reducing price. If we assume that there will be no adjustment in competitive price, at least in the short term, as own price is varied, then the effect of recognizing interdependence in advertising

---

* Although the recent classic in the area by Houthakker and Taylor (1970) puts a question mark on this statement.

† Some of the few are provided in a recent study by Peles (1971). This may of course indicate that other models of consumer demand have been mis-specified.

will be to reduce the ratio of advertising to sales revenue, since $\partial X_i/\partial A_j < 0$ and $dA_j/dA_i > 0$. If we assume Cournot behaviour, then we return to the Dorfman–Steiner result. Each firm assumes there will be no reaction to changes in its own decision variables (that is $dA_j/dA_i = dp_j/dp_i = 0$), the second term in the brackets falls out and we are left with:

$$\frac{A_i}{R_i} = - \frac{\partial X_i/\partial A_i . A_i/X_i}{\partial X_i/\partial p_i . p_i/X_i} \tag{14}$$

We have, in fact, been rather restrictive about the form of competitive interactions among firms. More generally, we could define reaction functions for each decision variable where all competitive variables entered each equation. However, it is empirically more convenient, and may be more realistic, to simply allow for a reaction (in terms of advertising or price) to variations in sales which reflect the various competitive variables.

Advertising and Utility-Maximizing Firms

It can be demonstrated (Peel 1972) that if the managerial utility function includes profits and unit sales as arguments, then the Dorfman–Steiner condition remains unviolated, although of course the firm will be operating at a higher level of sales and therefore of advertising. If, however, the managerial utility function includes advertising, sales revenue, or price as arguments then the Dorfman–Steiner conditions will be violated. Take the case of a utility function where profits and revenue are arguments. Then the first-order condition for maximization is:

$$\frac{\eta_A}{\eta_p} = \frac{A}{R} \left(\frac{U'(\Pi)}{U'(R) + U'(\Pi)} \right) \tag{15}$$

where $U'(\Pi)$ is the marginal utility of profits and $U'(R)$ is the marginal utility of sales revenue. This result means that the ratio of advertising to sales revenue for this sort of utility-maximizing firm will be greater than for a profit-maxizing firm, since $U'(R)$ is assumed positive. We would obviously get a qualitatively similar result if the firm had an expense preference for advertising. Then the firm would take advertising expenditure beyond the point at which advertising maximized its contribution to profits. This is rather similar to O. E. Williamson's notion (1964) of expense preference for staff, defined as selling and administrative expenses. It depends whether the labour element in advertising is internal or external to the firm.

Another facet of the firm's objective function we might briefly explore is the firm's attitude toward risk. If we assume that the firm faces a stochastic demand function, then it follows that, *at any fixed price*, risk aversion will lead to an increase in advertising expenditures to reduce the variance in revenues and costs (Horowitz 1970). If we allow advertising and price to be jointly determined then no unambiguous predictions can be made about changes in the equilibrium conditions where demand is stochastic and firms are risk-averse. Obviously, for firms linear in risk, faced with uncertain demand, the Dorfman–Steiner conditions remain, we simply interpret the elasticities as expected values. Empirically we need a ratio of unbiased estimators to test this hypothesis.

II. EMPIRICAL ANALYSIS

To test hypotheses about firms' behaviour in pricing and advertising decisions, as developed in the previous section, we need estimates of the price and advertising elasticities facing the firm in each of the markets to be analyzed. To examine the dynamics of the situation we will need to generate both short-run and long-run elasticities, and we will also need estimates of reaction coefficients defining retaliation by other firms to changes in any particular firm's competitive strategies.

We have, therefore, set up a model consisting essentially of an equation defining the demand function facing the firm, or division of the firm, and an equation defining the advertising appropriations relation for the firm. The advertising appropriations relation must be defined in such a way that it allows consistency with optimal behaviour as defined by the form of the demand function. Thus, if the demand function is Cobb–Douglas, then the Dorfman–Steiner condition would dictate a linear relationship between advertising and sales revenue. The system is obviously potentially simultaneous, since sales are determined by advertising via advertising's impact on consumer behaviour, and advertising may be determined by sales via an appropriations mechanism within the firm. This problem will be examined in the process of parameter estimation within each of the five markets.

We are assuming price (and quality) is predetermined in this analysis, which seems reasonable on the basis of observed behaviour.* To complete the model, we would need to specify a price (quality) equation where current price (quality) is determined by exogenous and lagged endogenous variables, but this is unnecessary as far as this paper is concerned.

The Model

Initially, we will specify the model in a form which has been found to be empirically useful and which has some attractive theoretical properties. The details of the construction of this model are discussed in a previous paper (Cowling and Cubbin 1971). Having got the basic specification down, we will then examine some variants of the model which may be somewhat less restrictive in terms of the constraints on the parameters.

The separate relationships in the model, the demand function facing the firm (equation 16), the equation explaining quality-adjusted price (equation 17) and the advertising appropriations equation (18), are specified below. We will, at this stage, ignore the stochastic properties of the model.

$$X_{it}/X_t = S_{it} = \exp\{\beta_0 + \beta_1 U_{it}\} A_{it}^{\beta_2} S_{it-1}^{\lambda} \tag{16}$$

* Obviously, this assumption becomes less valid as the time-period over which each observation is made is increased. The empirical analysis, in fact, uses mainly annual observations and, in some cases, quarterly. If we were to take longer periods for each observation then price (and quality) must be considered endogenous.

where X_{it} is sales by the ith firm in year t, X_t is total industry sales in that year and thus S_{it} is the market share of this ith firm, U_{it} is quality-adjusted price of the ith firm's product in that year relative to the other products available at that time, A_{it} is the ith firm's share of total industry advertising in the same year. The βs and λ are parameters with expected signs: $\beta_0 > 0$, $\beta_1 < 0$, $\beta_2 > 0$, $\lambda > 0$.

$$U_{it} = \log P_{it} - \{\alpha_{0(t)} + \alpha_{1(t)}V_{1i(t)} + \alpha_{2(t)}V_{2i(t)} + \ldots\} \qquad (17)$$

where P_{it} is the average list price of the ith firm's product and $V_{ji(t)}$ is the level of the jth characteristic in the ith firm's product—that is, the V_{ji}'s define the specification of the ith firm's product, the α's are parameters with expected signs: $\alpha_0 > 0$, $\alpha_j > 0$.

$$A_{it} = \gamma_0(X_{it}/X_t)^{\gamma_1}(X_{it-1}/X_{t-1})^{\gamma_2}A_{it-1}^{(1-\rho)} \qquad (18)$$

where the γ's and $(1 - \rho)$ are parameters with $\gamma_0 > 0$, $\gamma_1 < 0$, $\gamma_2 > 0$ and $0 < \rho < 1$.

Equation 16 is written down in market-share form simply for convenience in estimation. Equation 17, the price-quality relationship, is discussed in the next section. Where no separate quality-corrected price is estimated, then the actual price replaces U_{it} in equation 16. In the last equation, 18, we are allowing the ith firm's share of current industry advertising to be linked to its market-share behaviour in two ways. First we will allow for a direct relationship between advertising and sales consistent with the optimality rules, and also consistent with rule-of-thumb behaviour, as described by Kuehn (1961) and Taplin (1959). Working at the same time, we allow for a compensatory mechanism by which a current decline in market share will generate more intensive advertising efforts in the short run. We may then approximate the advertising appropriations equation with $A_{it} = a_0 + \frac{1}{2}a_1$ $(S_{it} - S_{it-1}) + a_2(S_{it} - S_{it-1})$, assuming the 'rule of thumb' is applied to the average of this period's and last period's market share, with $a_1 > 0$ (the 'rule of thumb' parameter) and $a_2 < 0$ (the compensatory parameter). Equation 18 simply involves rewriting this equation in nonlinear form, and allowing for partial adjustment in any one period to the desired advertising level, where ρ is the coefficient of adjustment.

The specification of this model is in some ways rather restrictive and we will look at variants of the model to allow for (a) non-constant advertising and price elasticities and (b) differential lag structures on price and advertising in the market-share equations. Linear and semi-logarithmic versions of the market-share equation will be examined, to allow for non-constant elasticities. To allow for differential lag structures, we will estimate a version of the Koyck distributed-lag model proposed by Peles (1971) of the form:

$$S_{it} = \beta_0 + \beta_1 \sum_{n=0}^{\infty} \lambda_1^n A_{t-n} + \beta_2 \sum_{m=0}^{\infty} \lambda_2^m P_{t-m} \qquad (19)$$

By the Koyck transformation this gives a working equation with S_{it-1}, S_{it-2}, A_{it}, A_{it-1}, P_{it}, P_{it-1} on the right-hand side.

Price-Quality Relationships among Brands or Models

Following Ironmonger (1960) and Lancaster (1966), we recognize commodities as bundles of characteristics. Different varieties of the commodity (brands or models) possess differing amounts of these characteristics. Given that we can measure, directly or indirectly, the relevant characteristics, and assuming that we have more varieties than characteristics, then we can generate implicit prices on the various characteristics by relating the variation in prices of specific varieties to the variation in the set of characteristics associated with the different varieties. We are interpreting the results as consumer valuations of the qualitative characteristics of different varieties. However, price-quality relationships estimated in this way may be interpreted as cost functions, but cost functions derived from a range of models which have survived the competitive environment at that point in time. The price-quality relationships become more obviously demand-oriented when we weight each observation by the market share captured by that model. Using weighted regression, we get estimates of the average prices paid for the different attributes at a particular point in time.

Our selection of characteristics to be included in the cross-section regressions between prices of specific varieties of a commodity and their quality was based on a postulated stable relationship over time between the characteristics and the services which, in combination, they provide. For example, it is not sufficient that in any one year a particular variable can explain a significant amount of the price variation among automobiles. Thus, brake horse-power has a fairly constant relation to requirements like speed and comfort, whereas weight has not. Therefore, although each of them is capable of explaining a large proportion of the variation in price within any year, horse-power is a candidate for inclusion as a relevant attribute, whereas weight is not.

We ran price-quality regressions for both the durable goods, automobiles and tractors, and generated estimates of quality-adjusted prices for all models over the sample period—1956 to 1968 in the case of automobiles and 1948 to 1965 in the case of tractors (see Cowling and Cubbin 1972; Cowling and Rayner 1970). These two commodities are technically quite complicated, with many differences in specification across models. In the case of the non-durable commodities—toothpaste, instant coffee and margarine— qualitative differences are relatively unimportant except subjectively through advertising. Where differences are apparent, they can often be allowed for by simply including brand dummies in the demand equations.

In the case of automobiles, we ran single-year regressions of the price of the basic model on brake horse-power, passenger area, fuel consumption, length, power-assisted brakes or not, four forward gears or not, and luxury (quality of trim) or not. The number of models included in the cross-sections tended to increase over time, ranging from 25 in 1956 to 40 in 1965. The explanatory power of the equations was always very high.

In the case of tractors, the price of the basic model was adjusted, so that all models were defined to include self-starter, simple hydraulics and power take-off. These adjusted prices were then related to the belt horse-power ratings of the different models and to whether they had a diesel engine or not.

Again, the explanatory power of the equations was high in all single-year, cross-section regressions.

III. RESULTS

The reporting of results will basically centre on the simple log linear form of the market-share equation, assuming dynamic adjustment, as this has given generally good results. The model allowing for a differential lag adjustment to advertising and price has generally suffered from problems of collinearity, including as it does both current and lagged values of the same explanatory variables. Results are only reported when the parameters are reasonably well determined (*t*-statistics are included in parentheses). Similarly, alternative algebraic specifications appear to offer no improvement over the basic formulation. Only the interesting results are reported.

In many cases, simultaneous estimation techniques would appear to be theoretically appropriate and we have generated two-stage least squares (TSLS) estimates in each such case. However, in some cases the effect of collinearity among the set of variables has been magnified using this technique and resort has had to be made to ordinary least squares (OLS) regression.

Cars

The results reported here relate to the period 1957–68 and the observations are for the major British manufacturers: British Motor Corporation (BMC), Ford, Standard–Triumph, Vauxhall and Rootes* and the major importer Volkswagen. Rover and Jaguar have been excluded, since they are assumed to compete in a separate market.† We are, therefore, trying to explain 66 observations on market-share performance,‡ although of course the observa-

---

* Over the period of observation, British Motor Corporation has been merged with Standard–Triumph, along with Rover and Jaguar, to form the only major, British-owned motor car manufacturer. Ford and Vauxhall (General Motors Corporation) are both US-owned subsidiaries and Rootes has recently been taken over by Chrysler.

† This assumption is obviously only approximately true but, typically, these firms are producing a high-valued package which will be a feasible alternative for only a small segment of consumers. Thus, we are saying that despite the fact that the quality-adjusted price for Rovers or Jaguars may indicate a good buy, they will still not attain an important market share, because the bundle of characteristics is 'too big' for most consumers. This might suggest the use of uncorrected list-prices in the market-share equation, in addition to quality-adjusted price. However, we would suspect that, in this case, some significant problems would remain. We note that Rover has had a persistently positive residual in the price-quality regression, which may indicate specification error in the equation, since Rover has a substantial reputation for safety and durability: characteristics which are not captured in our specification of quality. Jaguar, on the other hand, has had persistently negative residuals, indicating 'good value for money', which is not reflected in Jaguar's market share. This observation is, in fact, entirely consistent with the persistent excess demand for Jaguars, currently exemplified by a considerable excess of second-hand price over list price for certain models. We therefore consider Rover and Jaguar as special cases and exclude them from the present study.

‡ We are grateful to all the firms involved for providing sales data. Advertising data was drawn from *Statistical Review of Press and T.V. Advertising* (Legion Publishing Co.). Price and specification (characteristics) data are from *Motor* and *Autocar*.

tions for any one year *are* subject to the restriction that the sum of the market shares must equal unity. To incorporate our information on quality-adjusted prices, we have to average our estimated residuals across the array of models offered by the firm in question. The level of disaggregation chosen is the one most relevant to the type of advertising in this market—for example, most of Ford advertising over the period was not specific to a particular model, but rather covered the range of models on offer at that time.

$$\widehat{\log S_{it}} = -0.0233 - 1.9497 \, \hat{U}_{it} + 0.1889 \log A_{it} + 0.7237 \log S_{it-1}$$
$$\quad\quad (-0.5882) \quad (-3.802) \quad\quad (2.400) \quad\quad\quad\quad (9.836)$$
$$R^2 = 0.936$$

We see that about 94 per cent of the variation in market shares across six firms, over the period 1957–68, can be explained by price, advertising and lagged market share. The coefficients on the explanatory variables are significant and of expected sign and magnitude. The coefficients on U_{it} and $\log A_{it}$ are, respectively, our estimates of the *short-run* elasticities with respect to price and advertising.*

The long-run elasticities, defining the full impact over time of changes in price and advertising, are obtained by dividing the short-run elasticities by $(1 - 0.7237)$. The price elasticity, so calculated, is -7.06 and the advertising elasticity is 0.684.

Market share and advertising appropriation: TSLS estimates
We report below results obtained when we assume market share and advertising appropriations to be simultaneously determined. The predetermined variables are U_{it}, $\log S_{it-1}$ and $\log A_{it-1}$. The estimating techniques used was two-stage least squares.

$$\log S_{it} = 0.0173 + 0.3087 \, (\widehat{\log A_{it}}) - 1.915 \, \hat{U}_{it} + 0.6621 \log S_{it-1} + W_{it}^1$$
$$\quad\quad (-0.402) \quad (1.949) \quad\quad (-3.311) \quad (4.886)$$

$$\log A_{it} = -0.1496 - 1.3396 \, (\widehat{\log S_{it}}) + 1.5351 \log S_{it-1}$$
$$\quad\quad (-2.044) \quad (-1.791) \quad\quad (2.278)$$

$$+ 0.6267 \log A_{it-1} + W_{it}^2$$
$$(3.620)$$

The signs of the parameter estimates were as expected, and they were all significant, if we accept this interpretation of the t statistic when applied to the second-round estimators, except for the coefficients on current market share in the advertising appropriations relationships. This situation may be explained by the substantial sample correlations existing between the estimated value of market share from the first round $(\widehat{S_{it}})$ and its lagged value, S_{it-1}. Compared with the OLS estimates, the price elasticities are smaller and the advertising elasticities are substantially bigger in the market-share equations. The long-run price elasticity is now estimated to be -5.67, whereas the OLS estimate was -7.06 and the long-run advertising elasticity

---

* Recall that $U_{i(t)} = \log P_{i(t)} - [\hat{\alpha}_{0(t)} + \sum_j \hat{\alpha}_{j(t)} V_{ij(t)}]$, so that, holding quality and its implicit price constant, our estimate of $\partial \log S_{it}/\partial \log P_{it}$ is provided by the coefficient on U_{it}.

now turns out to be 0.914, whereas the OLS estimate was 0.684. The reason for this disparity in the estimates of the elasticity of market share with respect to advertising share is easy to find, if we refer to the results for the advertising appropriations relation. There, we find a negative relationship existing between current advertising appropriations and current market share, which means that OLS estimates of the market-share relation will give advertising parameters which are biased down.

The advertising appropriations relations, as estimated, also tend to confirm our hypotheses of a short-term compensatory mechanism, coupled to longer term rule-of-thumb behaviour. The rule-of-thumb parameter (α_1) which we predict to be positive, equals $\hat{\gamma}_1 + \hat{\gamma}_2$, and since $\hat{\gamma}_2 > -\hat{\gamma}_1$, then $\hat{\alpha}_1 > 0$. The compensatory parameter α_2, which we predict to be negative, equals $\frac{1}{2}(\hat{\gamma}_1 - \hat{\gamma}_2)$ and, since $\hat{\gamma}_1 < 0$ and $\hat{\gamma}_2 < 0$, then $\hat{\alpha}_2 < 0$. The rule-of-thumb parameter estimates also suggest a less than proportionate increase in advertising expenditure as market share increases.

Tractors

The results reported here refer to the period 1948–65 and the observations are for major British manufacturers—David Brown, Ford, International Harvester, Massey-Ferguson and Nuffield (BMC).* Again, the level of disaggregation is the most relevant to the type of advertising over the period. We do not report any two-stage least squares results for this market, since there is good reason to doubt the presence of important simultaneity in market share and advertising behaviour. The market is highly seasonal, peaking in autumn at the beginning of the model year. There is thus little opportunity for retaliatory advertising within the model year.

Market-share equation: OLS estimates

$$\widehat{\log S_{it}} = 0.9988 - 0.0055 \, \hat{U}_{it} + 0.4859 \log A_{it} + 0.4743 \log S_{it-1}$$
$$\qquad\qquad (-5.2) \qquad (4.0) \qquad\qquad (10.5)$$

$$R^2 = 0.88$$

Again, the explanatory power is good and the coefficients are significant and of expected sign. The coefficient on the advertising variable gives us directly our estimate of the short-run advertising elasticity, but the coefficient on quality-corrected price does not, since this variable is derived from a *linear* price-quality relationship for tractor models. The average price elasticity over the period 1947–65 turns out to be -3.29 in the short run and -6.25 in the long run. The long-run advertising elasticity is 0.92. The price elasticity is in fact increasing over time, so that in 1965, at the end of the sample period, we estimate the short-run price elasticity to be -4.63 with the long-run elasticity being -3.81.

* We are, again, grateful to all the firms involved for providing sales data. Advertising data was, again, drawn from *Statistical Review of Press and T.V. Advertising* and price and specification (characteristics) data are from *Farmer and Stockbreeder Year Books*. A more complete analysis of the tractor market can be found in Cowling and Rayner (1970).

Toothpaste

In this market, our sample relates to a cross-section of major brands over the period 1960 through 1968, giving a total of 49 annual observations. In this case, we have chosen the brand as the level of disaggregation, since advertising is usually brand specific. The brands included are Macleans' Regular, Gibbs' S.R., Gibbs' Spearmint and Colgate Dental Cream, for the whole period, together with Macleans' Spearmint and Colgate Ultrabrite— introduced in 1967. All brands, other than the major brands specified, were included in 'others'.*

Market share equation: OLS estimates

$$\widehat{\log S_{it}} = -0.2260 + 0.2375 \log A_{it} - 1.9767 \log P_{it} + 0.4549 \log S_{it-1}$$
$$(-4.056)\ (3.574) \qquad\qquad (-2.056) \qquad\quad (22.721)$$

$$R^2 = 0.934$$

We, again, get good explanatory power and significant coefficients of expected sign. The price variable in this case is the price of a family-size tube of the ith brand, relative to the average price of the other $n - 1$ brands in year t. No adjustment was made for quality differences among brands which are probably unimportant.† The long-run advertising elasticity is 0.436 and the long-run price elasticity is 3.626.

The introduction of a dummy variable for year of new brand introduction has no important impact on the above result. However, this dummy variable is important where lagged advertising is not allowed to exert an effect. It appears with a significant negative coefficient, as might be expected, since all brands are treated as if they are new brands, from an advertising view-point, except that the new brands have this dummy variable associated with them which illustrates the goodwill/brand loyalty that has been created for established brands. The coefficient on the new brand variable was -0.2885 with a t value of -5.354, a substantial barrier to entry for new brands!

We also ran some experiments using two-stage least squares, but these gave unsatisfactory results with exploding standard errors—the problem posed by multi-collinearity has been intensified, as we might expect.

Margarine

In this market we have 100 quarterly observations on brands over the period 1964–9. Again, our unit of observation is a brand rather than a firm, since this is the name identified by advertising in this market. The brands included are Echo, Stork, Blueband, Summer County and Kraft Superfine.‡ In fact,

---

* Sales data were made available by a market research organization. Advertising data were from *Statistical Review*. Prices (manufacturers' recommended retail prices) were from *Shaws' Price Guides*.

† Some brands are, of course, distinguished by additives of various types, such as fluoride and chlorophyll, but these brands never obtained a large market share over the sample period, and were not included as separate observations.

‡ Market share data and actual transactions prices at retail, were kindly provided by manufacturers. Advertising data were from *Statistical Review*.

the first four brands are all produced by Van Den Bergh, but probably few consumers are aware of this.

Market share equations: OLS estimates (quarterly observations)

$$\widehat{\log S_{it}} = -0.0605 + 0.0391 \log A_{it} - 0.1933 \log P_{it} + 0.9295 \log S_{it-1}$$

$$(-1.817) \ (2.382) \qquad\qquad (-3.112) \qquad\quad (35.639)$$

$$R^2 = 0.979 \tag{20}$$

Again, we get reasonably satisfactory results. However, there is a bigger question mark in this case about excluding any adjustment for quality differences among brands. There are quality differences among margarine brands, such as whether they are manufactured from animal fats or vegetable oils, and whether they have 10 per cent butter or not. The omitted variable, 'quality', is expected to be positively correlated with market share and with price. Thus our estimated price elasticity above will appear less elastic than it really is. In an attempt to allow for quality differences we divided the brands into three classes, low (Echo), medium (Stork) and high quality (Blueband, Summer County and Kraft Superfine) and then by using classificatory dummies we allowed the intercept to vary between classes. In addition, we tried to allow for a trend to quality over time, by means of interaction variables. The result reported below refers to annual data and omits lagged share:

$$\widehat{\log S_{it}} = -0.5262 + 0.5915 \log A_{it} - 4.3022 \log P_{it} - 1.616 B_0 \tag{21}$$

$$(-2.088) \ (7.787) \qquad\qquad (-4.901) \qquad\quad (-2.942)$$

$$- 2.559 B_1 + 0.0520 T - 0.1234 B_0 T - 0.1049 B_1 T$$

$$(-0.679) \quad (1.671) \quad (-1.912) \qquad (-1.687)$$

$$R^2 = 0.967$$

where $B_0 = 1$ for Echo, $B_1 = 1$ for Stork and $T =$ time trend.

The coefficients all have the expected signs and the estimated price elasticity is now much bigger relative to the advertising elasticity. Of course, part of the change in the size of the estimate is due to the fact that the observations are annual. However, using annual data but omitting the quality variables gave a much lower estimate of price elasticity (-2.1). Experimentations with the Peles-type model, allowing for a differential lag on advertising and price, gave the tentative result that the lag structures were not significantly different—only tentative as there were problems of collinearity.

Experiments with two-stage least squares procedures gave market share equations qualitatively very similar to the OLS estimates but the advertising appropriations relation suffered from high standard errors associated with the parameters.

*Instant Coffee**

In this market our observations are on two manufacturers: Nestle's and

---

* Market share data were provided by manufacturers. Advertising data was from the *Statistical Review*. Prices (manufacturers' recommended retail prices) were from *Shaws' Price Guide*.

General Foods (Maxwell House), whose brands dominate the market, and the rest which are grouped into 'mixes' (such as Ricory, Chico, etc.) and 'others'. We use quarterly observations over the period 1958 to 1968.

Market share equation: TSLS quarterly observations

$$\log S_{it} = 0.0825 + 0.1372 \widehat{\log A}_{it} - 0.2020 \log P_{it} + 0.8940 \log S_{it-1} + W_{it}$$

$$(1.167) \quad (4.023) \qquad\qquad (1.613) \qquad\qquad (28.113)$$

This result is not very satisfactory, since the price coefficient is not well determined. This is no doubt due to the lack of recognition of quality in the relation, but we have not been able to integrate this variable because the necessary data is unavailable. The other problem with price is that it is manufacturers' recommended price and not actual transactions price. For reasons of both quality and the definition of price, it seems certain that our estimate of the price elasticity has a downward bias. The advertising appropriations relation was poorly determined because of collinearity. OLS estimates of the market share equation were worse than the TSLS results.

Testing for Optimality

The estimates of advertising elasticities and price elasticities are collected in table 1 and their ratio in each market is compared with an estimate of the ratio of advertising expenditure to sales revenue.* The elasticities reported in the table are short-run elasticities and, based on our estimated equations, they are much smaller than the corresponding long-run elasticities. However, they are from equations where the lag distributions for advertising and price are the same, so that the ratio of long-run elasticities equals the ratio of the short-run elasticities.† The reported elasticities are also exclusively derived from loglinear relationships except in the case of the tractor market, where a semi-logarithmic version of the market-share/price relation was used and elasticities were calculated at the means and for the last year, 1965.

At first glance the elasticities seem reasonable and consistent with *a priori* expectations. The advertising elasticities are of expected sign and less than unity, in both short run and long run, implying that advertisers are working within the range of diminishing marginal effectiveness of advertising, which should be consistent with most managerial utility functions. The price elasticities are of the correct sign and lie within the elastic range,* again consistent with profit-maximizing behaviour.‡

* Total advertising expenditures were from the *Statistical Review*. Sales estimates were made as follows:

Cars ⎫ derived from data provided by manufacturers
Tractors ⎬

Toothpaste ⎫ derived from Census of Production data adjusted
Margarine ⎬ to same sample as advertising data, using information on
Coffee ⎭ market shares as defined previously.

† In experiments in which we have attempted to relax this restriction we have been unable to discriminate between the lag distributions on the two variables.

* Except in the case of instant coffee which was explained previously.

‡ It should be noted that the elasticity estimates are of market-share elasticities rather than quantity (sales) elasticities. However, it can easily be shown that these are equivalent, given the specification of the demand equation.

Table 1. Estimated price and advertising elasticities and advertising to sales ratios

		η_{Ai}	η_{pi}	$\dfrac{\eta_{Ai}}{\eta_{pi}}$	$\dfrac{A_i}{R_i}$	$\dfrac{-\eta_{Ai}/\eta_{pi}}{A_i/R_i}$
Cars	(OLS)	0.189	−1.950	0.096	0.007	13.7
	(TSLS)	0·300	−1.915	0.161		23.0
Tractors	Mean	0.486	−3.290	0.148	0.0136	10.88
(OLS)	1965	0.486	−4.630	0.105		7.72
Margarine	(OLS) Annual	0.592	−4.302	0.138	0.098	1.41
Coffee	(TSLS)	0.137	−0.202	0.678	0.162	4.15
Toothpaste (OLS)		0.238	−1.977	0.120	0.153	0.78

The most outstanding characteristic of the array of advertising to sales revenue ratios is the marked difference between the value for the two durables and the three non-durables. The A/R estimate for tractors is roughly double the one for cars, but it is only about one-seventh of the lowest A/R estimate for non-durables—that for margarine.

The final column of table 1 may be interpreted as a measure of the degree of apparent departure from optimizing behaviour, where such behaviour is assumed to be defined by $\eta_{Ai}/\eta_{pi} = A_i/R_i$, where A_i/R_i is measured for the average firm. There is obviously a considerable departure from optimality in the case of the durable goods, whereas for non-durables the departures are rather small, especially considering the fact that the advertising–sales ratios are subject to errors of measurement. The case of instant coffee is the least satisfactory because of the poor definition of the price and quality variables in the market-share equation. Because of this our view must be that the price elasticity is biased down. Thus, the elasticity ratio is an over estimate and the apparent departure from optimality is less than it appears.

There remains the problem of explaining the results for durables and several possibilities emerge. First, it may be the case that in durable goods markets the essential impact of advertising is to determine the timing of consumer purchases rather than the volume. Thus, an advertising campaign this year may raise current sales of cars but depress next year's sales via the stock effect. This possibility is supported by some results of Peles (1971) for cars and also by some previous work we did on the *aggregate* demand for tractors, where it was found that advertising influenced the speed of adjustment but not the equilibrium stock. A second possibility is that for cars and tractors $\hat{\eta}_{Ai}$ has a upward bias because big changes in advertising share are linked to new model introductions and the associated array of promotional activities. Relative to the non-durables market new introductions have been much more important for cars and tractors. Third, firms in the car and tractor markets may anticipate retaliatory advertising, whereas they may assume no retaliatory pricing, at least in the short run. The evidence from the advertising appropriations relation estimated for cars suggests that if this is the case the relevant advertising elasticity is only half the estimated one.* This will considerably reduce the observed discrepancy between actual and optimal behaviour.

More generally, in both durable and non-durable goods markets we may posit the existence of collusive behaviour. If we assume, as argued earlier, that it is easier to collude over advertising than over price, then we can offer further explanation of the apparent departures from optimality. The result for toothpaste, where actual advertising is greater than predicted, is then explained by the difficulties of collusion due to relatively low concentration—the toothpaste market has the lowest value of the Herfindahl measure of concentration of the five markets considered. Of course, we cannot ascribe departures from optimality purely in terms of advertising expenditures, price may also be suboptimal. To examine this possibility we would have to collect data on price-cost margins for these industries and compare the implied elasticity for firms in the industry, assuming profit maximizing behaviour, with the elasticities as estimated in this paper.† Advertising behaviour could then be examined, assuming actual rather than optimal price-cost margins.

CONCLUSIONS

This paper has examined optimal price and advertising policies under a variety of market assumptions. Empirical estimates have been made of the advertising and price elasticities in five markets for durable and non-durable goods.

For non-durables the predictions of advertising to sales revenue ratios are in reasonable accord with actual observations. For durables the results suggest that advertising and/or price are below the optimal levels. Various possible explanations are conjectured.

---

* Based on the estimated compensatory parameter, we estimate the retaliatory elasticity $(\partial A_j/\partial A_i . A_i/A_j)$ to be 0.447. Then the adjustment to our measured elasticity is $\eta_{Aj} \times 0.447$, where $\eta_{Aj} = -\eta_{Ai}$.

† The implied elasticity, of course, equals $(P_i - C_i)/P_i$ where C_i is marginal cost. If we assume constant-cost industries then estimates of the price-cost margin would indicate the appropriate elasticity.

MARKET STRUCTURE, ADVERTISING POLICY AND INTERMARKET DIFFERENCES IN ADVERTISING INTENSITY

by

JOHN CABLE

I. INTRODUCTION

The relationship between seller concentration and advertising intensity has figured large in previous discussion of the determinants of advertising intensity. However, existing empirical results are highly contradictory. Kaldor and Silverman's early study (1948) suggested an increase in advertising intensity with concentration up to the oligopoly level and a subsequent decline up to pure monopoly. Results consistent with a positive association were obtained by Mann *et al.* (1967) and by Else (1966). On the other hand Schnabel (1970) has recently questioned the Kaldor and Silverman result, while Telser (1964), Doyle (1968), Reekie (1970), Vernon (1971) and the Economists' Advisory Group (1967) failed to find any significant relationship.

A feature of these empirical studies, taken together, is that there has been relatively little formal attention to the underlying theory. From this stem several consequences. In the first place, the concentration-advertising relation has only rarely been viewed as one plane in a multivariate analysis developed from a model of optimizing behaviour by firms and by consumers. Most of the results are from simple regression or correlation analysis, with no attempt to exclude extraneous influences or to examine the impact of concentration in the presence of other variables suggested by the theory. Second, inadequate reasons have been given for explaining advertising intensity (the ratio of advertising to sales) rather than, say, advertising per form or absolute advertising expenditures. Third, all of the studies cited except Kaldor and Silverman have tested for a monotonic relationship between concentration and advertising. This is somewhat surprising, partly because it is not what naive theory suggests (in so far as non-price competition is typically regarded as oligopoly phenomenon) and partly because of the very nature of Kaldor and Silverman's early result. Fourth, the measure of concentration adopted has not been decided by theoretical considerations as it was, for instance, by Stigler (1964) in another context. At best, three- or four-firm seller concentration ratios have been used, which are arguably inferior to alternatives such as the Herfindahl index and the entropy measure in certain general respects (Adelman 1969; Stigler 1968, pp. 29–38), though they have proved significant explanatory variables in studies of other structure–performance relationships. In fact, about half the studies cited have resorted to measures of advertiser-concentration (such as the minimum number of firms responsible for, say, 80 per cent of total advertising) which is a good proxy only under the strong assumption that the advertising to sales ratio tends to be constant across firms within a given market. Finally, the two-way causal relationship between concentration and advertising has been noted, but not directly tackled, except in so far as simple correlation analysis avoids the issue.

This paper re-examines the theoretical hypotheses about advertising and concentration with the aid of the rules for optimal advertising behaviour given by Dorfman and Steiner (1954) and by Nerlove and Arrow (1962). In

I should like to thank Keith Cowling, Norman Ireland, Peter Law, Scott Moreland, Almarin Phillips and Len Waverman for their helpful comments and suggestions.

The research reported here represents part of a project on the economics of advertising, sponsored by the Department of Trade and Industry.

considering the aggregation problem a theoretical justification for explaining advertising intensity emerges. The paper then goes on to report preliminary empirical results for a sample of 26 UK non-durable consumer goods markets. These results are subject to certain reservations, but a significant relationship emerges between concentration and advertising intensity. This is of the general shape found by Kaldor and Silverman when concentration is measured by the Herfindahl index.

II. OPTIMAL ADVERTISING POLICY AND MARKET STRUCTURE

The Dorfman–Steiner (1954) condition for optimal advertising under profit-maximizing monopoly requires:

$$\mu = |\eta_p|$$

where μ is the marginal value product of advertising and η_p is the ordinary own price elasticity of demand. In terms of advertising intensity the requirement is:*

$$\frac{A}{S} = \frac{\eta_a}{|\eta_p|}$$

Incorporation of an interaction term (Lambin 1970a) extends the condition to oligopoly situations:

$$\eta_{a1} = \left\{ \frac{A_1}{q_1} \left(\frac{\delta q_1}{\delta A_1} + \frac{\delta q_1}{\delta A_2} \cdot \frac{\mathrm{d}A_2}{\mathrm{d}A_1} \right) \right\}$$

$$\eta_{p1} = \left\{ \frac{P_1}{q_1} \left(\frac{\delta q_1}{\delta p_1} + \frac{\delta q_1}{\delta p_2} \cdot \frac{\mathrm{d}p_2}{\mathrm{d}p_1} \right) \right\}$$

where the subscripts 1 and 2 refer to oligopolistic firms.

The Dorfman–Steiner theorem takes no account of the capital-good nature of advertising outlays, since advertising is treated as a current input. The condition for optimal advertising set out by Nerlove and Arrow (1962) for the dynamic case, where advertising exerts both current and lagged effects, requires:

*

$$\eta_a = \frac{A}{q} \cdot \frac{\delta q}{\delta A} = \frac{A}{pq} \mu = \frac{A}{S} \mu$$

In equilibrium

$$\mu = \eta_a \frac{S}{A} = |\eta_p|$$

Therefore

$$\frac{\eta_a}{|\eta_p|} = \frac{A}{S}$$

$$\frac{G^*}{S} = \frac{\beta}{\eta_p(\lambda + r)}$$

where G^* is the optimal stock of 'goodwill' created by advertising; λ is a (constant proportional) rate of decay of goodwill; r is the rate of interest; and β is the goodwill elasticity of demand.* This result also can be extended to oligopoly in the same way as the Dorfman–Steiner condition.

While optimal advertising behaviour is assumed, it is clear that any relationship between market structure and advertising intensity must operate through the advertising (or goodwill) and price elasticities. The following discussion refers to the advertising and price elasticities, but may equally well be applied to the goodwill and price elasticities. Under competition, monopoly and Cournot oligopoly the interaction terms for the ith firm, $(\delta q_i/\delta A_j)$. $(\mathrm{d}A_j/\mathrm{d}A_i)$ and $(\delta q_i/\delta p_j)$. $(\mathrm{d}p_j/\mathrm{d}p_i)$, in the advertising and price elasticities are both zero. Hence on Cournot assumptions the relationships between the elasticities and seller concentration depend on the behaviour of the terms $\delta q_i/\delta A_i$ and $\delta q_i/\delta p_i$ as concentration varies.

These terms capture the 'initial' response to own advertising and price, respectively, before retaliation takes place, or the total response if there is no retaliation.

In monopoly the term $\delta q_i/\delta A_i$ registers the advertising responsiveness of total market sales. As between a monopolist and an oligopolist facing the same industry demand conditions, $\delta q_i/\delta A_i$ will typically be higher for the oligopolist, since it registers consumers switching brands as well as the total market response. There seems little *a priori* reason to suppose that $\delta q_i/\delta A_i$ will be any higher or lower at lower concentration levels than in the oligopolistic range, as long as there is sufficient product differentiation for individual brands to be identified by consumers. The absolute value of the term $\delta q_i/\delta p_i$ in the price elasticity will decrease monotonically as concentration increases, from infinity under perfect competition to a level given by industry demand conditions under monopoly. In the special case where firms are of equal size at all levels of concentration,

$$\eta_{pi} = \frac{E}{H}$$

where E is the industry elasticity and H is the Herfindahl index of concentration.†

* Under certain circumstances the two conditions are equivalent. In the Nerlove–Arrow model a dollar of advertising outlay creates a dollar's worth of goodwill, so that by definition $\delta q/\delta A \equiv \delta q/\delta G$ and hence $\beta = \eta_a(G^*/A)$.

If price cuts also have lagged as well as current effects on sales, via the creation of goodwill, and if the rate of decay is the same as for advertising goodwill, then (long-run) price elasticity is $\eta_p/(\lambda + r)$ and the Nerlove-Arrow condition becomes $G^*/S = \beta/\eta_p$, which is clearly the Dorfman–Steiner condition multiplied through by G^*/A.

† The Herfindahl index is given by $\sum_{i=1}^{n}(s_i^2)$ where s is the market share of the ith firm in a market of n sellers. Among its properties is the fact that its reciprocal gives the number of equal-sized firms consistent with the observed degree of seller concentration (Adelman 1969). Stigler (1968) shows that under Cournot assumptions $(p - c)/p = 1/nE$, where n is the number of firms, c is marginal cost and, of course, $\{(p - c)/p\}_i = 1/\eta_{pb}$ assuming profit-maximising price behaviour.

110

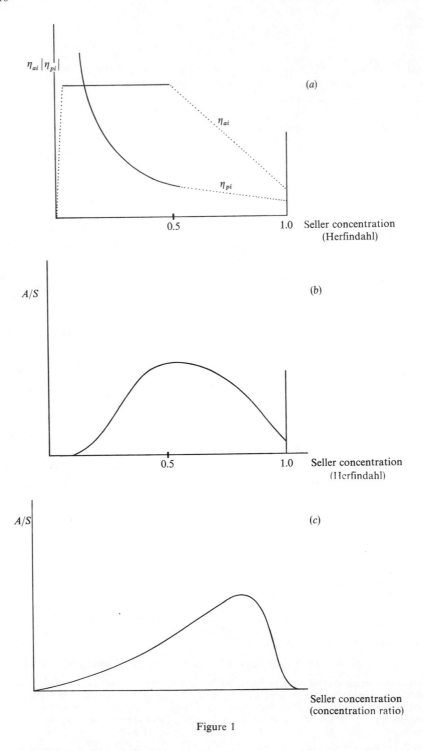

Figure 1

These relationships are sketched in figure 1(*a*). Strictly the curves are not defined in the concentration range $0.5 < H < 1.0$. However, in practice we might expect to observe some intermediate positions between duopoly and pure monopoly, these being price- (and advertising-) leadership situations. At some low level of concentration $\eta_{ai} < \eta_{pi}$ and so no advertising takes place. η_{ai} need not exceed η_{pi} under pure monopoly, and in this respect figure 1(*a*) is illustrative only. The relationship between advertising intensity and seller concentration suggested by figure 1(*a*) is broadly a quadratic one as sketched in figure 1(*b*), reaching a maximum at around $H = 0.5$. The Herfindahl index is a log-linear measure of concentration. If the function in figure 1(*b*) is thought to be approximately lognormal, the relationship we should expect between advertising intensity and some linear measure of concentration, such as the concentration ratio, would resemble that sketched in figure 1(*c*). This strongly resembles the relationship found by Kaldor and Silverman (1948).

The relationships sketched in figure 1 have to be modified if there is recognized interdependence or collusion in the oligopolistic range. With recognized interdependence, the terms dA_j/dA_i and dp_j/dp_i arguably increase with concentration. The argument is that the values perceived by the oligopolists will depend on the degree of awareness of rivals' behaviour. For complete awareness in a market of n firms, each firm must evaluate the $\frac{1}{2}n(n-1)$ interaction terms between firms (since the total effect of, for example, i's advertising on j's sales in a market of three or more firms includes the indirect effects via $(\delta q_j/\delta A_k)\,(dA_k/dA_i)$, etc.) Hence there will be an exponential fall in the costs of maintaining awareness as seller concentration (measured by the Herfindahl index) increases and, presumably, a consequent increase in the optimal level of awareness of rivals, up to $H = 0.5$.

At the same time the costs of surveillance of product differences among sellers will behave in a similar way to the costs of evaluating interaction terms. This could make for increasing homogeneity among competing brands, up to the duopoly concentration level.* The tendency would then be for the terms $(\delta A_j/\delta q_i)$ and $(\delta q_i/\delta p_j)$ to become larger as concentration increases, due to reduced brand loyalty for less differentiated brands.

Thus the overall result is for the absolute values of the interaction terms to become larger as seller concentration increases up to $H = 0.5$. If figure 1(*a*) were redrawn on the assumption of recognized interdependence, the general effect would be for both curves to be pulled down towards the monopoly levels of the elasticities in the oligopolistic range.† Clearly the advertising intensity-concentration relationships characterized in figure 1(*b*) and (*c*) could be eliminated or suppressed in the process, but for this to happen the effect of interaction would have to be relatively more pronounced for advertising than for price. If the reverse were true, the tendency would be for the relationship shown to be more pronounced as a result of interaction.

Colluding oligopolists would experience the elasticities faced by a single seller. For any particular industry the curves relating the elasticities to seller

---

* This result may also be obtained from an analysis in terms of firms locating in multi-dimensional product-characteristics space (Hotelling 1929).

† The extreme situation where the interaction term is (absolutely) larger than the difference between the oligopolists' and the monopolists' 'initial' responsiveness to price and advertising can, perhaps, be ignored since it seems eminently ripe for collusion.

concentration would show a discrete drop to the relevant monopoly levels at some point. Stigler (1964) has argued that the probability of collusion is an increasing function of seller concentration, on account of falling costs of maintaining the agreement. To allow for the possibility of collusion, figure 1(*a*) could be redrawn such that the values of η_{ai} and η_{pi} at any concentration level are the weighted average of the monopoly values and the values at present indicated for that concentration level. The appropriate weights would be P and $(1 - P)$ respectively, where P is the probability of collusion occurring. The general effect would again be to pull down the elasticities in the oligopolistic range. In this case, collusion over both price and advertising or over advertising alone could effectively suppress the 'basic' relationship between advertising and concentration previously discussed. But collusion over price only would tend to emphasize it.

In short there is strictly no unequivocal theoretical prediction about the relationship between advertising and concentration. It depends on firms' behavioural reactions and, in particular, on the patterns of interacting behaviour over price and advertising and on whether collusion takes place. On foregoing arguments there seem to be two main possibilities: either no systematic relationship, or an inverted-U shaped relationship, when concentration is measured by the Herfindahl index. The latter of the two is the more to be expected if the possibility of rivals' retaliation figures larger in the firm's perception of price elasticity rather than of advertising elasticity, or if collusion occurs mainly over price rather than advertising.

It has so far been assumed that firms pursue short-run profit-maximizing policies with respect to price. However, price may in some situations be limited—for example to forestall the entry of new competition.* In this case we require the optimal advertising rules for *any* price. Substituting from the relation $c = p(1 - 1/|\eta_p|)$, where c is marginal cost, the Nerlove–Arrow condition becomes:

$$\frac{G^*}{S} = \frac{\rho\beta}{(\lambda + r)}$$

where $\rho = (1 - c/p)$, i.e. the profit margin. Similarly the Dorfman–Steiner condition becomes:

$$\frac{A}{S} = \rho\eta_a$$

These reformulations can be given an intuitive explanation. Departures from short-run profit-maximizing prices clearly will be registered in the actual profit margin earned, but not in the ruling price elasticity. Hence the actual profit margin will diverge from the one implied by the price elasticity (that is, its reciprocal). Obviously, if short-run profit-maximizing prices *are* charged, the original and reformulated versions of the Dorfman–Steiner and Nerlove–Arrow equations are identical. The possibility of departures from short-run profit-maximizing prices leaves the expected relationship between market structure and advertising intensity previously discussed

---

* There would tend not to be such a restraint on advertising expenditure, since this tends to raise entry barriers (and, incidentally, the entry forestalling price).

broadly unaltered, as long as the profit margin is a monotonically increasing function of seller concentration.

Empirical models

For reliable empirical evidence on the seller concentration to advertising relation it is necessary to specify fully and estimate an appropriate advertising determinants model. The Dorfman–Steiner and Nerlove–Arrow theorems provide a basis for models explaining inter-firm differences in advertising. In specifying intermarket models an aggregation problem has somehow to be dealt with. One approach is to rely on the concept of a 'representative' or average firm in each market. There are then two available alternatives. One is to explain intermarket differences in absolute advertising outlays in terms of the determinants of interfirm differences and also intermarket differences in the number of representative firms. Thus from the Dorfman–Steiner theorem (and ignoring stochastic elements) we might write either:

$$A_{it} = f(\mathbf{Z}_{it}, \mathbf{X}_{it}, n_{it}) \tag{1}$$

or

$$\frac{A_{it}}{n_{it}} = g(\mathbf{Z}_{it}, \mathbf{X}_{it}) \tag{2}$$

where A_{it} = level of advertising in the ith market

$\mathbf{Z}_{it}$ = vector of determinants of μ for the representative firm in the ith market at time t

$\mathbf{X}_{it}$ = vector of determinants of η_p for the representative firm in the ith market at time t

n_{it} = number of representative firms in the ith market

and the subscript t refers to the time period.

In practice, the relevant number of firms in each market would be hard to observe. Many markets have a group of leading firms and also a tail of small sellers who (a) may not be strictly comparable if they supply corners of the market not catered for by the leaders and (b) will be difficult to identify and count. One expedient would be to rely on the numbers-equivalent property of the Herfindahl concentration index, where this is available, and approximate the number of firms by the reciprocal of this index. This would be to set the number of representative firms equal to the number of equal-sized firms consistent with the observed degree of seller concentration in the market, which has some intuitive appeal. However, it would then be difficult to unscramble from the empirical results the separate effects of seller concentration in its various roles in the models.

The second alternative is to work from the optimality conditions written in terms of advertising or goodwill intensities. By definition these intensities will be the same for the representative firms as for the market as a whole. Where both price and advertising have current impact only *and* where both create goodwill which decays at the same rate, we then have:

$$\left(\frac{A}{S}\right)_{it} = g(Y_{it}, \mathbf{X}_{it}) \tag{3}$$

where $(A/S)_{it}$ is the advertising intensity for both the ith market as a whole at time t *and* for the representative firm; Y_{it} it is a vector of determinants of η_{ait}; and X_{it} is as previously defined.

Where advertising is a capital good but price cuts are not, the appropriate model is:

$$\left(\frac{G^*}{S}\right)_{it} = j(B_{it}, X_{it}, L_{it}, r_{it}) \tag{4}$$

where B_{it} is a vector of determinants of β_{it} and L_{it} is a vector of determinants of λ_{it}. In practice, intermarket differences in r might be fairly safely relegated to the error term. If departures from short-run profit-maximizing prices are to be allowed for, the profit margin ρ would replace X_{it} in this model. Introducing the variable G^* raises some measurement problems. The variable can be approximated from current and past advertising levels, for example:

$$G^* = \sum_{i=0}^{m} (1 - \lambda)^i A_{t-i}$$

This involves arbitrary decisions over the length of period m and also the value of λ, which is not directly observable. These difficulties can be circumvented. Since* $\beta_i = \eta_{ai} G^*_i / A_i$ the Nerlove–Arrow optimality condition can be seen as the Dorfman–Steiner condition with the long-run advertising elasticity $\eta_{ai}/(\lambda + r)$ substituted for the short run elasticity η_{ai}. As a result, the advertising to sales ratio may be retained as the dependent variable in a dynamic intermarket model, simply by the addition of the variables L_{it} and r_{it} to the right-hand side of equation 3:

$$\left(\frac{A}{S}\right)_{it} = k(Y_{it}, X_{it}, L_{it}, r_{it}) \tag{5}$$

Equations 1 to 5 are, then, the advertising-determinants models under various assumptions about firms' behaviour and the effects of advertising and price policy. To complete the specification of testable models it is necessary to identify at least the more important elements in the vectors Y, X, B and L. It is convenient to structure the discussion by grouping these elements into three categories: market structural characteristics including seller concentration as previously discussed, factors affecting consumer search, and characteristics of the product. Advertising is assumed to operate through the transmission of market information.† It is received by potential consumers along with information from other sources such as newspapers, retailers and consumers' information services. Consumers are assumed to maximize expected utility, with less than perfect knowledge of the characteristics of

---

* See footnote on page 109.

† The distinction between informative and persuasive advertising is indeed 'purely metaphysical' (Johnson 1967) *unless* the consumer's utility function is specified in terms of product characteristics (Lancaster 1966) rather than goods. Under Lancaster's new approach advertising would be informational but non-persuasive if it merely indicated what characteristics certain goods possessed, but in so doing did not alter the consumer's preference structure for product characteristics and *vice versa*. To regard advertising as informational does not necessarily signify approval; 'purely informational' advertising would obviously be 'excessive' if at the margin the social gain fell short of the social opportunity cost.

different goods (including price) and of the relationship between these product characteristics and their own utility. Typically, consumers will commit some non-zero level of resources to acquiring market information, purchasing information media and sacrificing leisure. The transmission of market information and consumer search affect consumer behaviour in so far as more complete information alters the expected utility from consuming particular goods and services, and hence consumer preferences.*

It will be assumed in subsequent discussion that the effectiveness of advertising and hence advertising intensity vary inversely with the level of search activity (and also the level of supply of other market information). In fact, the reverse could be argued, that higher search activity raises the effectiveness of advertising by increasing the degree of market penetration of advertising messages. But consumer search will presumably extend over other sources of information; the ability for advertisers to affect sales by emphasizing only the more attractive features of products, suppressing other information, will be reduced; and, in general, consumers' choices will be based on a broader array of information than the claims of advertisers alone.

Market Structure

The earlier discussion of seller concentration and advertising intensity was concerned with the elasticities facing firms as concentration varies, given the price and advertising elasticities for the market as a whole. These market elasticities are evidently themselves market structural characteristics which should be included as determinants of advertising intensities. The growth of market demand is another. In a static market any change in market share by one firm is wholly at the expense of its rivals (ignoring entry and exit from the market): in a duopoly, dq_i comes wholly from j's sales. In a market where demand is growing due to exogenous factors such as rising real income, $\delta q_i/\delta A_i$ may be only partially at the expense of q_j, or may even leave q_j unaffected. Thus, where demand is growing, dA_j/dA_i would tend to be smaller than where demand is static, if rival firms react less strongly to foregone expansion of their own sales than to erosion of existing sales. This reaction pattern could be consistent with profit-maximizing behaviour, since there are positive transaction costs in reducing output, but 'negative' transaction costs in not raising output. For a given cutback in output the firm loses the foregone revenue plus the costs of making the change; for the same amount of expansion in sales which is prevented, the firm loses the foregone revenue *less* the transaction cost it would have incurred in raising output. Hence, we might expect dA_j/dA_i, dA_i/dA_j to vary inversely, and η_{ai}, η_{aj} directly, with the growth of market demand, so long as this is positive. For negative growth rates the sign of the demand growth to dA_j/dA_i association is ambiguous. Essentially, this is because firms in declining markets may choose to diversify into other areas, rather than compete for a larger share of the declining total sales.

* The social product of advertising could be thought of as the difference between consumers' collective expected utility gained from the pattern of goods and services actually consumed (including leisure) and the expected utility of the (different) goods and services that would be consumed in the absence of advertising.

The remaining salient characteristics of market structure are the numbers and rate of turnover of buyers,* and the brand structure in the market. The larger the number of potential buyers, the larger is the potential audience for advertising messages, and the less early are diminishing returns to advertising to be expected. Hence the advertising elasticity will be higher where buyers are many, *ceteris paribus*. High turnover of buyers (for example, in markets like infant foods) will make for more rapid decay of advertising goodwill. The theoretical models indicate that this implies a smaller advertising (goodwill) intensity. However, it is arguable that the larger is the stock of market information carried over from previous periods, the less marked will be consumers' response to new or repeated information conveyed by current advertising. Hence the effect of higher buyer turnover would be to raise the short-run advertising elasticity, but the effect on the long-run elasticity is ambiguous.

The greater the total number of brands in the market, the greater the competition among advertising messages for consumers' attention, and the less their effect. The effect on η_{ai} and on advertising intensity is, therefore, negative. But search costs to consumers increase exponentially with the number of brands to be cross-evaluated. This will tend to reduce search and, on previous arguments, raise η_{ai}, giving an ambiguous overall effect. Where firms market several brands, any spillover of advertising effectiveness from one brand to another, bearing a common name, trade mark, etc., would reduce the advertising cost of obtaining a given level of consumers' response for a given brand—that is, increase the effectiveness of advertising for that brand. Advertising effectiveness and intensity would therefore tend to be higher in markets where the average number of brands per firm is high. The effects of the rate of turnover of brands are somewhat similar to those of buyer turnover. On the one hand information about existing brands is made obsolete so that 'goodwill' decays faster where turnover is high. But the effectiveness of advertising for new brands will be higher than for old, by virtue of the absence of an existing stock of information about new brands.† Once again, the short-run elasticity will be higher in markets characterized by a high proportion of new brands, but the effect on the long-run elasticity is ambiguous.

Consumer Search

In general, the consumer's optimal search level in any market area will depend on the balance of search costs and benefits. The nature of costs will depend largely on product characteristics, considered below. The socio-economic composition of buyers might also have some bearing, but with uncertain net effects. Higher educational levels and wider reading habits among AB groups would tend to reduce search costs, but on the other hand

---

* Buyer concentration is not separately included, but would to some extent be captured in an empirical model incorporating both the number of buyers and sales per buyer.

† The typical pattern of behaviour over the product life cycle (an initial rapid build-up to a high level, followed by a levelling-off or decline) could be explained in terms of the advertising elasticity being high in the early stages, because of the lack of existing information about the brand, and then falling off as the stock of information increases.

these groups would tend to place a higher opportunity cost on time devoted to search activity.

The returns to consumers' search (the increase in expected utility resulting from better-informed choices) could be proxied either by unit price (Stigler 1961) or the value of average purchases per consumer per period. For the size of benefits from making shrewd choices will be related to the proportion of income or consumption expenditure involved. Unit price might be preferred for infrequently purchased durable goods and sales per consumer for low-price non-durables, as in the present case, since these may still account for a high proportion of income if frequently purchased. On previous arguments consumer search will reduce advertising effectiveness, and it may also raise price elasticity if it results in consumers becoming more price conscious. The proxies for consumers' search may also pick up to some extent the supply level of information from independent channels (consumer protection publications, newspaper fashion and property columns, book reviews, used car price guides, etc.) in so far as the existence of these channels is sensitive to consumer search and demand for market information.

Product Characteristics

The proximity of a product to sensitive psychological drives—products associated with sex, children, health, beauty, status, etc.—has received some attention as a factor tending to make for advertising effectiveness (Borden 1942). Advertisers' behaviour may well be designed to minimize differences between products in this respect, in that much advertising apparently attempts to link drives such as these with apparently unconnected products. But the scope for making such links will not be everywhere the same, and products like drugs and children's encyclopaedias probably do remain rather special.

Other important product characteristics are product testability and complexity. Product testability would raise the potential return to search effort by consumers or, more exactly, the marginal utility of search. It might also tend to encourage the growth of independent information services. Product complexity implies complexity in use or by virtue of a large number of important user attributes (for example, for cars and hi-fi equipment). Some products may be complex to make, or in chemical composition, but relatively straightforward for appraisal in use. Complexity increases consumers' search costs, but probably encourages the growth of independent consumer information services. Thus, both testability and complexity are important for their effects on levels of consumer search and independent information supply. Testability arguably increases both, while with complexity there are opposing forces. In practice, the two may often go together.

There is one potentially important determinant of advertising intensities which is not easily fitted into the three groups so far considered. This has to do with the existence of specialized media and the general efficiency of advertising media. The audience or readership of different media will tend to coincide more closely with the potential market for some products than others. Unless the media-owners can operate discriminatory pricing policies this means that advertising media will be more cost-effective for some markets.

Finally, the preceding discussion and the Dorfman–Steiner and Nerlove–

Arrow optimality rules relate to 'promotional' activity in the widest sense. In practice, data problems only permit analysis of media advertising expenditures. If the effects of each category of selling expense are separate and independent of each other, no problem arises: the optimality rules and models derived from them may be applied to each expense category in isolation. In practice such independence cannot be assumed. Non-media expenditures, such as below-the-line expenditures and production expenses associated with the actual advertising process (and hence, perhaps, the 'quality' of advertising), may reinforce the effect of media expenditures. Or it could be that, as in the view of some practitioners, below-the-line sales promoting activities work to the detriment of media advertising, which seeks to work via the creation of brand images. Either way, non-media spending should strictly be included in the dependent variable or else as an additional explanatory variable.

III. EMPIRICAL ANALYSIS

Empirical analysis based on the foregoing discussion faces problems over the large number of explanatory variables and difficulties in observing and quantifying several of them. There is also a fairly large number of ambiguous sign expectations. To reduce these difficulties in the present study, a sample was chosen so as to minimize intermarket differences in the more troublesome variables, which were then relegated to the error term. The sample consisted of 26 narrowly-defined UK markets. Products were all low-priced, frequently-purchased consumer goods, mainly food items but with some other household non-durables and some chemists' goods (Appendix A).

Excluding household furnishing, consumer durables and non-consumer goods markets does away with a good deal of intermarket differences across the sample in several variables. The number of potential buyers for all markets is total UK households (with the possible exception of the chemists' goods markets—that is, products more for personal use). This being the case, intermarket differences in the efficiency of advertising media should not be large. Differences in buyer turnover also are hopefully small, since the sample excludes goods like durables, furnishings, and also special food items like infant foods, where individual households are not continuously in the market. Exclusion of durables, in particular, also goes a long way towards removing differences in complexity and testability of product; product appraisal across the sample is essentially subjective—in many cases literally a matter of taste. Finally, since the products in the sample are sold mainly through the same retail outlets (again, with the exception of chemists' goods), we might expect similarities in point-of-sale display advertising; in opportunities for manufacturers' promotional activity, such as dealer margins; and in the supply of market information from retailers. We might also expect broadly similar levels of supply of independent market information, from newspapers, women's pages and from magazines, etc.

The explanatory variables included in the analysis were total manufacturers' sales, seller concentration (measured either by the Herfindahl index or the three-firm concentration ratio), the total number of brands in each market, the ratio of new to existing brands, sales growth, income elasticity of market demand, and a dummy variable taking on a value of one for four products 'close to sensitive psychological drives' and zero otherwise. In so far as the number of buyers is the same across markets, total manufacturers' sales proxies the benefit of consumer search, since it captures the proportion of consumption expenditure committed to each product area. The ratio of new brands is included as a measure of brand turnover. Sales growth and income elasticity are alternatives, the latter being preferable as a measure of *exogenous* demand shifts but involving data problems discussed later. The 'sensitive' products are toothpaste, lipstick, face powder and toilet soap. Their selection is necessarily somewhat arbitrary. Sources of data are set out in Appendix B.

Empirical Results

A selection of regression results appears in table 1. Various functional forms were tried, but consistently superior results were obtained with linear relationships between the variables, except for the quadratic relationship in the case of the Herfindahl index. In terms of both explanatory power and significance levels of individual coefficients the results were better with goodwill intensity rather than current advertising intensity (that is, the ratio of 1963 advertising and sales) as the dependent variable.* This is not of itself to be taken as evidence of the capital-goods nature of advertising expenditures. Except for the difference in the dependent variable, regressions (ii) and (iii) are specified identically, and there is little reason to suppose this specification fits model 5 any less well than model 4, *both* of which relate to the dynamic case. It could be simply that the goodwill variable, being a six-year (weighted) average, more nearly captures current equilibrium advertising level than does current-year advertising itself. On the other hand, when a three-year unweighted average of advertising was used,† specifically to allow for 1963 advertising levels being off equilibrium levels, overall explanatory power was lower than in regression (iii), though the results were otherwise similar.‡ Regression models explaining absolute advertising per representative firm were very much less successful than those reported. Typically the relationship as a whole was insignificant at the 95 per cent confidence level, and explanatory power was very low.

The postulated inverse-U relation between advertising intensity and the Herfindahl index emerges strongly in the results. The quadratic specification proved superior to alternative nonlinear relationships, and also to linear approximations using slope dummies. In view of a simple correlation of 0.97 between H and H^2, the t values for the two coefficients suggest a very highly significant relationship. Solving from equation (ii), goodwill intensity reaches a maximum when the Herfindahl index is 0.3931 (from equation (i)

---

* G^* was measured as $\sum_{i=0}^{5} (1 - \lambda)^i A_{t-i}$. Values of λ from 0.2 to 1.0 were tried. Only the magnitude of the coefficients were affected, R^2 and the F and t values proving highly insensitive to changes in the value of λ. In all reported regressions $\lambda = 0.3$.

† That is $(A_{1962} + A_{1963} + A_{1964})/3S_{1963}$.

‡ The number of brands and ratio of new to total brands were also three-year averages in these regressions.

Table 1. OLS estimate for 26 UK

Regression number	Dependent	Constant	Herfindahl index for 1963	Herfindahl index squared	Concentration ratio 1963	Total sales 1963 £'000
(i)	G^*/S	−0.1939 (−1.4632)	2.0581 (2.5523)†	−2.5310 (−2.0560)†		−0.3976 (−0.5270)
(ii)	G^*/S	−0.2308 (−2.0929)†	2.3036 (3.5694)†	−2.9300 (−3.0774)†		
(iii)	A/S	−0.0789 (−1.6947)	0.7721 (2.8346)†	−0.9572 (−2.3821)†		
(iv)	G^*/S	−0.3457 (−2.4918)†			0.5427 (3.6435)†	
(v)	G^*/S	−0.1668 (−1.5108)	1.5442 (2.6313)†	−1.8750 (−2.1371)†		

t values in parentheses.
† Denotes significance at 95 per cent or better.
‡ Denotes significance at 90 per cent or better.

when $H = 0.4066$). Equation (iii) indicates a very similar result, with advertising intensity reaching a maximum at $H = 0.4033$. These values are very much what would be expected for duopoly in practice—for example, where there are two dominant firms plus a tail of very small sellers. According to equation (iii), the impact of seller concentration on advertising intensity is substantial. Ignoring other variables,* the predicted value of the A/S ratio for a 'competitive' market with 20 equal-sized sellers ($H = 0.05$) is about 3.62 per cent compared with 15.57 for a 'duopoly' ($H = 0.4033$), a difference of some 11.95 percentage points.

In contrast with the results of some previous studies, equation (iv) shows a highly significant monotonic relation between goodwill intensity and seller concentration as measured by the more commonly used (three-firm) concentration ratio. When a quadratic relation was tried both coefficients were insignificantly different from zero, and the squared term was of the wrong (that is, positive) sign. In the light of figure 1(c), and bearing in mind that the sample contained few observations of seller concentration above the duopoly level (the maximum observed value of the Herfindahl index was 0.627), this result is not unexpected. As a further test for curvature in the advertising/concentration ratio relationship, a beta-function formulation was tried:

$$Y = X^\alpha(1 - X)^\beta$$

where Y would be goodwill or advertising intensity and X the concentration ratio. This would generate the negative-skew situation in figure 1(c) if

* The simple correlation matrix for the included variables is:

	H	H^2	D	N	I/N
H^2	−0.974				
D	−0.441	−0.408			
N	−0.421	−0.422	−0.016		
I/N	−0.175	−0.216	−0.134	−0.035	
G	0.101	0.022	0.197	0.045	−0.281

non-durable consumer goods markets

D	Number of brands	Ratio of new brands 1963	Sales growth 1958–63	Income elasticity 1963	$\bar{R}^2$	F
0.3389	0.0036	−0.1306	−0.0775		0.4819	4.5977†
(4.3840)†	(2.5796)†	(−0.7944)	(−1.3875)			
0.3498	0.0035	−0.1201	−0.0812		0.5016	5.5279†
(4.7903)†	(2.5766)†	(−0.7505)	(−1.4934)			
0.1258	0.0013	0.0448	0.0023		0.3932	3.9749†
(4.0819)†	(2.2299)†	(−0.6630)	(−1.0239)			
0.3479	0.3920	0.0898	−0.0040		0.4955	6.3080†
(5.0135)†	(3.0280)†	(0.5826)	(−0.7963)			
0.2500	0.0023	−0.1320		0.1309	0.5165	5.7963†
(3.1420)†	(1.6226)	(−0.8342)		(1.6988)‡		

$\alpha > \beta$ and is appropriate for the case where $0 < X < 1$. Results were very poor:

$$\log(A/S) = -1.3453 + 1.1558 \log(CR) - 0.0279 \log(1 - CR)$$
$$(-0.3773) \quad (0.6440) \qquad (-1.0213)$$

$$+0.1097D + 0.0332 \log N - 0.0008 \log I/N$$
$$(3.93613)† \quad (2.3618)† \qquad (-0.4047)$$

$$-0.6054 \log S$$
$$(-0.3050)$$

$R^2 = 0.3457$

$F = 4.2828‡$

The high simple correlation between $\log(CR)$ and $\log(1 - CR)$ would tend to cause the variables to lose significance, but, of course, this is also true of the quadratic relation in H.

The negative signs attracted by the total sales coefficients are as expected if total sales is interpreted as a proxy for the return to consumer search. But the sales coefficients were consistently nonsignificant. This outcome is not altogether surprising: the markets chosen accounted for less than one per cent of consumers' expenditure, and intermarket differences in the search benefits proxy of this magnitude could scarcely be expected to have much effect.

The 'sensitive areas' dummy variable proved very important in the full 26-market sample. The positive signs are as expected and significance levels very high. With the dummy omitted, results for the full sample of 26 markets were much less good in terms both of explanatory power and the significance levels of other included variables. Omission of the dummy variable and the four markets concerned produced results very similar to those for the full sample with the dummy included. In interpreting these results it is important to note that the dummy may have picked up other effects as well as the one for which it was introduced. The markets concerned were toilet preparations and beauty aids. For this group of products retail outlets would tend to be different from those for the remainder, with possible differences in point-of-sale advertising and promotional activity in general. Arguably, the number of potential buyers and also the average age of consumers would tend to be less. Sign expectations for the first and third of these effects are ambiguous; for the second, previous arguments in fact indicate a negative influence.

In almost all regressions run the total number of brands variable attracted a positive sign and was highly significant. On previous arguments, this would be interpreted as showing that the effect of brand numbers on consumers' search costs more than ‘outweighs any tendency for advertising messages to lose their effectiveness because of competition for consumers' attention. All but one of the ratio of new brands coefficients reported are negative, but other positive coefficients were obtained in other regressions run. However, significance levels nowhere approached the 10 per cent confidence level. With ambiguous *a priori* sign expectations, it could be that the various effects are cancelling out. On the other hand, the measure adopted (usually the ratio of new to total brands in 1963) is somewhat imperfect, especially with the goodwill intensity as the dependent variable. The marginally better results obtained in unreported regressions with the ratio averaged over more than one year lend some support to this interpretation, and suggest that further experimentation with a more refined measure might be worthwhile.

The sales growth coefficients were generally negative and sometimes significant, whereas the theoretical arguments suggested that the advertising elasticity would vary directly with growth.* However, the theoretical arguments are strictly related to exogenous demand shifts, which might be better captured by income elasticity than by sales growth. So far, limited exploration of the behaviour of an income elasticity variable has, in fact, resulted in positive coefficients. In equation (v), the income elasticity coefficient is significant at 10 per cent and appears to have taken over some of the work previously done by the D variable, with which it is correlated ($r = 0.422$). In another regression, not reported, with D omitted, the income elasticity coefficient was again positive and significant at the 0.3 per cent level. But this result is to be treated with caution, since the non-food observations giving rise to the correlation with D had to be taken from US estimates (see Appendix B).

CONCLUSIONS

Although the theoretical arguments about the relationship between advertising and seller concentration proved ambiguous, the empirical results reported in this paper suggest that a systematic relationship does exist, and that the form this relationship takes is at least theoretically plausible. The present estimates suggest that market structure exerts a large influence over the allocation of resources to advertising. Since there is little reason to suppose that market structure responds closely to consumers' wishes there are obvious and important implications for public policy.

* Very similar results were obtained with the absolute value of the growth rate, introduced because of the ambiguous expectations for negative growth rates, as indicated earlier.

However, these conclusions must be preliminary and tentative ones, pending extension of the empirical analysis in at least three important ways. In the first place, the specification of the advertising determinants relation, and of the variables included, is capable of further refinement. In particular it would be desirable to include some presently omitted variables (notably the profit margin and, if possible, the level of promotional activity) and to seek improved variables for the rate of brand turnover and also consumer search costs.

Second, a rather rigid and oversimplified pattern of causal flows has so far been imposed. The effect of advertising on price elasticity may be conjectural (Borden 1942; Dorfman and Steiner 1954) but it cannot be safely ignored, while there is every reason to believe there is also a causal flow from advertising to the profit margin, given the evidence on the importance of advertising as a barrier to entry (Bain 1968) and on the relationship between advertising and profit rates (Comanor and Wilson 1967). A further important causal relationship may be expected to flow from advertising to seller concentration, either because advertising raises the minimum efficient scale of operation (Comanor and Wilson 1967) or for other reasons (Kaldor 1950). Ideally, therefore, empirical analysis of the advertising/market structure relationship should take place within a simultaneous equation framework, in which advertising intensity, price elasticity or the profit margin and seller concentration are endogenous variables. Thus the OLS results reported for the advertising determinants relation are strictly biased and inconsistent, though in their defence it is fair to point out that with only 26 observations the consistency of, for example, TSLS estimates is of doubtful value, while the OLS estimates do have the minimum variance property.

Third, resort to the concept of the representative firm imposes the implicit assumption that oligopolistic firms in different markets respond similarly to given market structural conditions. Even under profit-maximizing assumptions this is a fairly strong assumption. A way of avoiding it in empirical work would be to make the firm the unit of observation, and explain firms' advertising intensities within and across markets in terms of market variables capturing the determinants of the relevant elasticities, variables indicating the position of the firm within the market (such as market share), and a set of market dummy variables. The results, correctly interpreted, would still speak about determinants of intermarket differences in advertising, which have tended to be the prime focus of interest. The market dummies would allow for behavioural differences in the way the competitive game is played in given structural conditions, though they would not of course, reveal what these behavioural differences were. There would be data problems arising from the fact that individual firms' activities often spread over more than one market. On the other hand it would probably be easier to generate larger sample sizes of firms than of markets.

It is hoped to present the results of further studies along these lines in the near future. Returning, meanwhile, to previously published results, it seems likely that their contradictory nature could be due partly to the fact that, according to the theory, a systematic advertising/seller concentration relationship may but will not always exist and partly to the fact that, with so many factors at work, any relationship which does exist will be seen only if these factors are allowed for either explicitly or by an appropriate choice of sample.

APPENDIX A. THE 26-MARKET SAMPLE

Food
Margarine
Instant coffee
Salt
Baked beans
Biscuits
Canned soup
Evaporated and condensed milk
Flour
Jam
Table jelly
Packeted cheese
Breakfast cereals
Sausages
Canned fish

Cake mix
Meat extracts
Sugar

Other
Toothpaste
Lipstick
Face powder
Soap and Detergents
Shoe polish
Toilet soap
Disinfectants
Household bleach
Household polish

APPENDIX B. DATA SOURCES

Advertising: *Statistical Reviews of Press and TV Advertising* (Legion Publishing Co.).

Sales: *Census of Production 1963* (adjusted for imports and exports, where possible); *Retail Business* (packeted cheese); *Neilson* (toothpaste).

Concentration: *Odhams' Branded Food Survey; Odhams' Cosmetic Survey 1967; Retail Business; Market Research; Neilson;* Monopolies Commission, *Report on Soap and Detergents; IPC Marketing Manual* (brand shares adjusted to firms' shares by reference to *Statistical Review* and *Who Owns Whom*).

Number of brands: *Statistical Review.*

Unit price: *Shaw's Price Guide* and *Retail Business.*

Income elasticity: *National Food Survey* and H. S. Houthakker and D. Taylor, *Consumer Demand in the United States: Analyses and Projections* (Harvard University Press, 1970).

ASSESSING AND CLASSIFYING THE INTERNAL STRUCTURE AND CONTROL APPARATUS OF THE MODERN CORPORATION

by

OLIVER E. WILLIAMSON†

and

NAROTTAM BHARGAVA†

† Research on this paper has been supported in part by a grant from the National Science Foundation.

The evolution and economic properties of what Chandler (1966) refers to as the multidivision enterprise have been described by Chandler and by O. E. Williamson (1970). Among the properties that have been imputed to the multidivision (or M-form) structure are that it permits the firm simultaneously to realize strategic responsiveness and operating efficiency and in the process internalizes certain failures in the capital market with net beneficial consequences.* In order for these effects to be realized, however, attention to more than mere divisionalization is required. It is also necessary that a separation of operating from strategic responsibilities be provided. The former are assigned to the operating divisions while the latter are made the focus of the general management. Moreover, such a partitioning does not by itself assure strategic effectiveness; for this to obtain requires that the general management develop an internal control apparatus, to assess the performance of the operating divisions, and an internal resource allocation capability which favours the assignment of resources to high-yield uses. That divisionalized enterprises sometimes, and perhaps often, fail to meet these stipulations is suggested by Ansoff and Brandenburg, who observe that the performance potential in divisionalized firms frequently goes unrealized because general managements 'either continue to be overly responsive to operating problems [that is, non-strategic but interventionist] or reduce the size of the corporate office to a minimum level at which no capacity exists for strategic and structural decision-making' (1971, p. B-722). The results reported in the Appendix are consistent with these propositions.†

A major problem thus is posed for testing the 'M-form hypothesis' (O. E. Williamson 1970, p. 134) in that, if all divisionalized firms are classified as M-form firms, without regard for the related internal decision-making and control apparatus, an over-assignment to the M-form category will result. Some divisionalized firms are essentially holding companies, in that they lack the requisite control machinery, while others are only nominally divisionalized with the general office maintaining extensive involvement in operating affairs. If indeed the M-form designation is to be reserved for those firms that *combine* the appropriate structural and internal operating attributes, as we believe it should, information on both aspects is required.

The difficulty with this is three-fold. First, information on internal operating procedures is less easy to come by than is that on divisionalization. That this can be overcome, however, is at least suggested by the classification efforts reported in the Appendix. Secondly, the appropriate degree of involvement by the general office in the affairs of the operating divisions varies with the nature of the factor or product market interdependencies that exist within the firm and thus need to be 'harmonized'. Divisions that are involved in the exchange of intermediate products (vertical integration) typically face different control needs than those in which such internal, cross-divisional transactions are absent. Similarly, the requisite product

* For a somewhat similar discussion of the internal resource allocation effects, see Drucker (1970). Also of relevance in this connection are the treatments by Heflebower (1960) and Weston (1970). Certain work at the Harvard Business School also relates to these issues (see Bower (1971) and the references therein; also Allen 1970).

† More generally, the results of Bhargava's PhD dissertation, on which the Appendix is mainly based, support the argument that divisionalization is merely a necessary but not a sufficient condition to classify a firm as an M-form structure.

market controls are more extensive if operating divisions produce common products than when, by reason of product diversification, such interdependencies are absent.

The third problem is that reaching the M-form structure may require the firm to pass through a transitional stage during which the 'optimum' control relationship, expressed in equilibrium terms, is violated. An appreciation for the natural life-cycle in the M-form enterprise is necessary if these transitional conditions are to be detected and an appropriate classification made. (The issue is addressed in II.3 below. The sample of firms reported in the Appendix, and the related discussion of the assignments made, go into this as well.)

Although these are the principal difficulties, three further problems ought also to be noted. First, whether or not divisionalization is at all indicated depends on firm size. The most efficient way to organize the small, specialized firm is normally along functional lines. Only as the firm expands in size and/or product variety is divisionalization likely to be appropriate. Since, initially, the classification effort will be restricted to the largest 500 industrials in the United States, which firms generally meet the requisite size and variety conditions to support divisionalization, this is not an immediate issue.

Second, the nature of the environment (market structure, demand uncertainty, information technology, etc.) is of critical importance in determining whether activities are more usefully transacted within firms than across markets, whether the divisionalization of those activities which have been internalized is indicated, and the degree to which internal controls in a divisionalized enterprise ought to be extended. These issues have been examined elsewhere (O. E. Williamson 1971a, 1971b). Suffice it to observe here that (1) whether the exchange of intermediate product between technologically separable activities ought to occur within firms or across markets needs to be assessed in terms of the effects of each mode on incentives and, relatedly, the economizing of transaction costs;* (2) a low-variety environment makes the choice between firm and market transactions less critical—especially in so far as the optimal degree of vertical integration is concerned;† and (3) improvements in the information technology commonly favour internalization and more extensive internal auditing and controls—at least in the short run.‡

Third, even in a divisionalized enterprise with the appropriate control

---

* It is important that these assessments be made in a multiperiod rather than a single-period context. This is the recurrent-behaviour issue discussed in the text below.

† Even in a low-variety environment, internalization may be favoured by incentive advantages of internal in relation to market organization. Thus capital market failures may be internalized to advantage on this account. The extent to which this advantage exists will, however, vary directly with market uncertainties.

‡ New market institutions may develop in the long run, which institutions may permit product market transactions to be consummated more efficiently, in which event vertical integration may be unnecessary, or permit outsiders (mainly stockholders or their agents) more effectively to monitor the affairs of the firm and thus reduce incentives for conglomerate organization.

Note that our use of internalization, both here and elsewhere in the paper, refers to the shift of a market transaction to an internal transaction. This is a somewhat more narrow use of the term than is common. Others use internalization to refer to any efficient adaptation, market or otherwise, with respect to an externality.

apparatus, it is possible that the firm will not be operated in a strictly profit-maximizing fashion. The issue is separable into two parts: first, to what goals does the general management aspire; second, in what degree are the goals of the general management shared. Although we feel that the general management is likely to naturally adopt what is essentially a profit-maximizing attitude (O. E. Williamson 1970, chapter 8), we would concede that shifting from a unitary or holding company structure to adopt an M-form organization mainly assures that (more nearly) least-cost behaviour and a better assignment of resources to high-yield internal uses will be realized. That earnings retention or acquisition biases in support of growth goals may exist cannot be disallowed. Relevant to such an assessment is the efficacy of competition in the capital market. Noteworthy in this connection is that, once a sufficient number of firms have adopted the M-form structure, the *system* can be expected to display superior self-policing properties. Competition in the capital-market forces will better serve to check non-profit-maximizing behaviour under these circumstances (O. E. Williamson 1970, pp. 138–41).

Even if a general management adopts a fully profit-maximizing attitude, however, there is still a problem of internal implementation to be faced. Some compromises with the operating divisions may, as a matter of political reality, have to be made; what Allen refers to as 'conditional autonomy' (1970, p. 26), whereby divisions with favourable performance records develop a degree of internal insularity, obtains. We agree but would suggest that the degree of actual divisional autonomy is less, in an M-form firm, than is commonly supposed. The recurring nature of the bargaining relationship between the general office and the operating divisions generally rebounds to the advantage of the headquarters unit in both informational and effective control senses. As a result, the general management that is disposed to be assertive can expect its preferences to be realized more fully than a short-run focus on 'apparent' divisional autonomy would suggest.

Thus, although the conventional economic theory of the firm may be regarded as defective in that it simply imputes a profit goal and assumes, implicitly, that the firm is staffed by dedicated stewards who accept higher level goals without exception (thereby eliminating any need for an internal auditing apparatus), a more self-conscious examination of internal organization and an assessment of the efficiency properties and systems consequences of the M-form structure lead, from the standpoint of neoclassical analysis, to a somewhat reassuring result.*

A brief review of alternative divisionalized types of firms, expressed in terms of technological and market characteristics, is given in section I. Alternative internal control procedures are treated in section II. A classification scheme is proposed in section III. A sketch of some of the research uses to which a classification of the 500 largest industrials by organization form can be put is given in section IV. The Appendix illustrates the applica-

---

* A problem not discussed above but which nevertheless warrants acknowledgment is that of limits to firm size. One way of putting this is as follows: Why cannot the large firm do everything the small firm can do and more? If it can, the need for markets vanishes. The issues here have been examined elsewhere (O. E. Williamson 1971b). That large size and diversification experience limits will simply be taken as given for the purposes of this paper.

tion of the resulting classification scheme to a sample of 8 companies. The types of documents that have been found useful for such classification purposes and the assignment techniques are discussed.

I. ALTERNATIVE DIVISIONALIZED FIRMS DESCRIBED

It will be convenient in this section to develop the argument in two parts. First, the integrated (mainly single-product) enterprise is described. A discussion of the diversified firm then follows.

1. The Integrated Enterprise

Three general issues are posed within the integrated firm: (1) interstage exchange relationships; (2) replication of production units (the multiplant issue); and (3) marketing. Given that successive processes are *technologically* separable, which even in sequential processes that follow immediately in time and place is commonly satisfied, the question is: What sort of exchange relations ought to obtain between stages? At a minimum, the physical transfer of product ought normally to be metered. Whether indeed the product is separately priced and if so according to what standard need also to be considered. The importance of coordinating the responses of successive stages in reaction to unanticipated changes in the condition of the environment likewise deserves attention.

Aspects of the interstage exchange relation problem have been addressed elsewhere (O. E. Williamson 1971a, 1971b). Of relevance to us here are the following two propositions: (1) vertical integration potentially overcomes the incentives to haggle, posture, distort information, etc. that a small-numbers market-exchange relationship predictably poses, but (2) common ownership, without more, merely creates a bilateral internal exchange with the result that, were the respective stages given semi-autonomous divisional standing, antagonistic bargaining would not be relieved greatly. As a consequence, if successive stages of production are to be accorded divisional standing, extensive interstage (cross-divisional) rules may need to be devised.

Divisionalization by successive stages, however, is not the only possibility. More attractive, frequently, is divisionalization by *replication*—whereby several individually integrated plants are set up and operated in a semi-autonomous fashion. (This assumes, of course, that technological economies of scale are exhausted* at modest plant size—at least for most stages.)

The degree of autonomy to be accorded to each of the divisions in the single-product firm that employs replication as the divisionalizing strategy is nevertheless limited by considerations of possible factor-market economies and product-market interactions. Some centralization may be indicated so as to realize factor-purchasing and inventory economies. Often apt to be more crucial, however, is the need to mitigate antagonistic (competitive) marketing activities between the several divisions. Centralized marketing of the com-

---

* This is somewhat overstrong. Transportation or other factor-cost considerations may even dictate that certain single-plant technological economies be sacrificed in favour of multi-plant operations so as to realize least-cost supply at point of delivery.

bined output of the various plants may be arranged on this account. Alternatively, if the marketing function is not centralized but instead is delegated to the separate divisions, rules to limit competition at the market interfaces presumably need to be designed. Territorialization is frequently resorted to for this purpose.

2. *The Diversified Firm*

Product diversification, mainly because it avoids or at least mitigates product-market interaction effects in the firm's marketing activities, facilitates diversification. Common early stages of production, however, are consistent with a diversified end-product mix. Thus common materials may be involved, as in many metal-refining and processing industries before the fabrication stage, or common processes may be employed for different materials that then go to distinct end uses. Also, there may be a common scientific base on which a variety of quite different end-products rely. Early production stages of these kinds may more appropriately be organized as cost than as profit centres, with profit centre divisionalization being reserved for the divergent end-product activities.

To illustrate, suppose there are three activity stages: an early production stage, an intermediate stage in which production is completed, and marketing. Assume that all products originate in a common first stage, that there are four distinct intermediate-stage processes, and that there are five distinct final products. That there 'ought' under these circumstances to be five

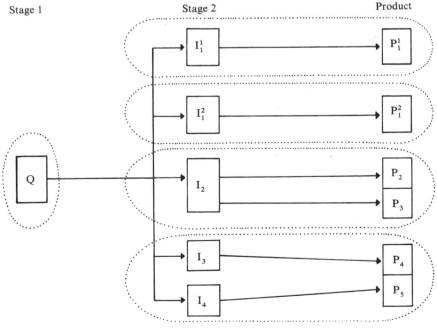

Figure 1

divisions, one associated with each final product, is uncertain. For one thing, the economies of scale at (say) the first stage may be sufficient to warrant that all production originates in a single, indecomposable plant. Second, if for some products economies of scale at the second stage are slight in relation to the size of the market, parallel divisionalization may be feasible. Third, even though products may be distinct, there may be interaction effects to consider. (For example, products may be complements.)

Consider the situation shown in figure 1. Here Q refers to first-stage activity, I_i^j refers to intermediate stage processing, P_l^m refers to the final product, and the subscript refers to the process (product) type while the superscript (if any) denotes replication. The proposed divisions are shown by the dotted lines.

That it is generally inefficient for the early stage of a production process to transfer product to a later stage at a price that maximizes the profit of the early stage is well known. Rather, so as to discourage the use of inefficient factor proportions in the later stages and avoid the restriction of production, product should be transferred at its marginal cost. But then the early-stage production divisions cannot normally* be evaluated in profit centre terms. Rather, Q becomes a cost centre and its performance is assessed in least-cost rather than net-revenue terms.

Plants I_1^1 and I_1^2 are assumed to be identical and produce a common product (designated P_1^1 and P_1^2, respectively). Plant I_2 produces two distinct products, P_2 and P_3, while plants I_3 and I_4 produce the distinct products P_4 and P_5 respectively. Products P_4 and P_5, while manufactured by separate processes, are assumed to be complements.

The rationale for the divisionalization shown is as follows. First, Q is split off as a cost centre since, for the reasons given above, it cannot efficiently be operated as a profit centre, while to assign it to one of the later stages would place unaffiliated stages at a disadvantage† and to combine several later stages leads to over-aggregation (in that such aggregation impairs accountability with the result that internal control is sacrificed in the process) in relation to underlying 'natural' decomposability conditions. Rules to ensure efficient transactional relations between stages one and two are assumed to be feasible, whence the divisional standing according to Q.

A high degree of coordination between each intermediate stage and its corresponding marketing stage is assumed to exist and warrant the joining of each such pair of stages within a division.‡ As indicated, I_1^1 and I_1^2 are replicated production facilities producing the common product P_1. A territorial market is set up for each plant, with the result that $I_1^1 - P_1^1$ and $I_1^2 - P_1^2$ are both profit centres. Territorialization serves to mitigate intra-firm competition in the product market, but interdivisional 'com-

---

* An exception is if the production stage in question is competitively organized by outside suppliers. In such an event, however, there is little incentive to internalize the activity from the outset.

† This assumes that the later stages are about on a parity in terms of the volume and variety of demands placed on the early stage. If one stage were to be much larger than all of the others and to have special needs for coordinating with the early stage, a combination of these two stages might be warranted.

‡ This is clearly arbitrary; a divisional separation between marketing and the prior production stage may sometimes be warranted.

petition', for performance comparison purposes, in other respects is possible.

Technological scale economies are assumed to be such that separate production facilities for P_2 and P_3 are uneconomical. Also, I_2 is assumed to bear a sole source relation to both P_2 and P_3. Since to split I_2 off as a separate division would require that it be operated as a cost centre (given the sole source assumption) with the attendant difficulties that this poses, and as interstage coordination would be impaired in the process, a single profit centre spanning I_2, P_2 and P_3 is set up instead.

I_3 and I_4 are separate plants between which there is no direct exchange relationship. They supply products P_4 and P_5 respectively. These products are assumed to be complements, however, for which a joint marketing effort is warranted. The resulting profit centre spans I_3, I_4, P_4 and P_5.*

II. INTERNAL CONTROLS DESCRIBED

The discussion of internal controls begins with a description of the very limited controls associated with the holding-company form of organization. Strategic controls of the sort appropriate to an M-form organization are considered next. Transitional adjustment problems are then examined, after which the involvement of the general office in operating affairs is briefly discussed.

1. Holding Company

What we refer to here as a holding-company form of organization is a loosely divisionalized structure in which the controls between the headquarters unit and the separate operating parts are limited and often unsystematic. The divisions thus enjoy a high degree of autonomy under a weak executive structure.†

Perhaps the least ambitious type of divisionalization to consider within the holding company classification is that in which the general office is essentially reduced to a clerical agency for the assembly and aggregation of earnings and other financial reports. The holding company in these circumstances serves as a risk-pooling agency, but in this respect is likely to be inferior to a mutual fund. The transaction costs associated with altering the composition of the 'portfolio' of the holding company, by selling off existing divisions and acquiring new operating companies, will ordinarily exceed the costs that a mutual fund of comparable assets would incur by its trading of common stocks (or other securities) so as to adjust its portfolio. Little wonder that those academics who interpret the conglomerate as being a substitute mutual fund report that it has inferior diversification characteristics to mutual funds themselves.‡

---

* That the exercise is hypothetical and oversimple ought to be emphasized. If, however, it serves to better expose the issues, its purpose will have been realized.

† That this is a somewhat special use of the term 'holding company' ought to be appreciated. (We considered referring to this as the federal form of organization, but decided that this posed at least as many problems.) Essentially what we are after is a category which, for reference purposes, represents divisionalization of a very limited sort.

‡ See in this connection Smith and Schreiner (1969) and Westerfield (1970).

Moreover, it is not clear that just a 'little bit' of additional control from the general office will lead to results that are superior to those that would obtain were the various divisions of the holding company to be free-standing firms in their own right. Being part of a holding company rather than an independent business entity easily has umbrella effects. If the holding company serves as a collection agency for unabsorbed cash flows and uses these to shore up the ailing parts of the enterprise, the resulting insularity may encourage systematic distortions (of a managerial discretion sort) among the divisional managements.* Being shielded from the effects of adversity in their individual product markets, slack behaviour sets in.

This is not, of course, a necessary consequence. The general management might consciously refuse to reinvest earnings but mainly pay these out as dividends. Alternatively, it might scrutinize reinvestment decisions every bit as well as the unassisted capital market could. Indeed, because it enjoys an *internal* relationship to the divisions, with all of the constitutional powers that this affords, the general management might be prepared to assume risks that an *external* investor ought properly to decline. (Thus the general management can ordinarily detect distortions and replace the divisional management at lower cost than can an external control agent similarly detect and change the management of a comparable, free-standing business entity. The holding company, in this respect, is less vulnerable to the risks of what might be referred to as managerial moral hazard.) Given, however, that the holding company is *defined* to be a divisionalized form in which the general office does not involve itself in strategic controls of the sort described below, it is unclear that the holding company form of organization is socially to be preferred to an arrangement in which the various divisions are each set up as fully independent enterprises instead. Holding companies certainly cannot be expected reliably to yield results that compare favourably with those which we impute to the M-form structure.

2. Strategic Controls

If indeed the firm is to serve effectively as a miniature capital market, which in many respects is what the M-form structure ought to be regarded,† a more extensive internal control apparatus than the holding-company form of organization possesses is required. The argument here has been stated elsewhere (O. E. Williamson 1970). For purposes of making this paper internally more complete, however, the main points bear repeating.

2.1 Manipulation of the incentive machinery
Closer adherence to the goals of the general management can be secured if the special incentive machinery to which internal organization uniquely has access is consciously exercised to favour operating behaviour that is consistent with the general management's objectives. Both pecuniary and non-pecuniary awards may be employed for this purpose.

That salaries and bonuses can be adjusted to reflect differential operating

---

* For a dynamic-stochastic model that is consistent with this prediction, see O. E. Williamson (1970), chapter 5.

† The argument is developed more extensively in O. E. Williamson (1970), pp. 138–50, 176–77. For a somewhat similar view, see Alchian and Demsetz (1972), Drucker (1970).

performances, assuming that such differentials exist and can be discerned, is a familiar application of the incentive machinery. That nonpecuniary rewards, especially status, can also be adjusted for this purpose is less widely recognized but is scarcely novel. Several points might usefully be emphasized, however, in this connection.

First is the trivial proposition that pecuniary and nonpecuniary incentives are substitutes to some degree. This takes on significance mainly in conjunction with the further proposition that the efficacy of nonpecuniary incentives varies with the manner in which economic activity is organized. To the extent that internal organization is better able to confer status than is the market, which in some respects it presumably is, internal organization is favoured in relation to the market because of the substitution of nonpecuniary for pecuniary rewards that it permits. More generally, organizing modes that *economize on pecuniary outlays*—whether by realizing technological economies, mitigating transactional frictions, tax avoidance, substituting nonpecuniary for pecuniary rewards, etc.—will tend to be adopted in a regime where survival is governed mainly by the test of profits.

That nonpecuniary incentives are not costless, however, ought also to be appreciated. In particular, nonpecuniary incentives are commonly less flexible reward and penalty instruments than are pecuniary incentives. As Barnard (1946) observes, 'Loss of status is more than loss of its emoluments; it is more than loss of prestige. It is a serious injury to the personality' (p. 69). Since typically nonpecuniary rewards are efficacious only to the extent that they are visible, while this is less true of pecuniary rewards, the attitudes of attachment toward each differ. Presumably the loss of status symbols has announcement effects that 'expose' the individual more severely than would a salary cut. Thus Barnard reports that 'the fear of losing status is what leads some to refuse advancement of status' (p. 69) and notes that once status has been conferred, strong resistance to loss of status is to be anticipated (p. 78). Although some types of efforts to maintain status presumably have favourable productivity effects, those that take the form of politicizing or anguish are apt to drain energies. Net productivity losses easily result.

Of course, sometimes a change of employment, or at least of position, may be altogether necessary. The division manager may not have the management capacities initially ascribed to him, conditions may change in ways that warrant the appointment of a manager with different qualities, or he may be managerially competent but uncooperative (given, for example, to aggressive subgoal pursuit in ways that impair overall performance). Changes made for either of the first two reasons reflect simple functional assessments of job requirements in relation to managerial skills. By contrast, to replace a division manager for the third reason involves the deliberate manipulation of the incentive machinery to produce more satisfactory results. The occasion to intervene in this way will presumably be rare, however, if the conditional nature of the appointment is recognized from the outset. Rather, the system becomes self-enforcing in this respect once it is clear that the general management is prepared to replace division managers who regularly defect from general management's goals.*

* This assumes that there are no property rights (of an academic tenure, civil service, etc. sort) associated with positions.

Although the general office does not ordinarily become directly involved in the exercise of the incentive machinery within the operating divisions, its indirect influence can be great. The decision to change (replace, rotate) a division manager is often made for the incentive effects this has on lower-level participants. Employment policies—including criteria for selection, internal training procedures, promotions, etc.—can likewise be specified by the general office in ways that serve to ensure closer congruence between higher-level goals and the behaviour of the operating parts. A more pervasive incentive impact on lower-level participants who are not directly subject to review by the general office can in these ways be effected.

2.2 Internal audits

Adjusting the incentive machinery in any fine-tuning sense to achieve reliable results requires that the changes be made in an informed way. A back-up internal audit that reviews divisional performance and attempts to attribute effects to the several possible causes—distinguishing especially as between those outcomes that are due to changes in the condition of the environment from those that result from managerial decision-making—is useful for this purpose. As Churchill, Cooper, and Sainsbury (1964) observe, 'to be effective, an audit of historical actions should have, or at least be perceived as having, the power to go beneath the apparent evidence to determine what in fact did happen' (p. 258). Of particular importance in this connection is the recurrent nature of this auditing process. Thus although current variations of actual from projected may sometimes be 'acounted for' in plausible but inaccurate ways, a persistent pattern of performance failure can be explained only with difficulty.

The superior inference capability of an internal audit, as compared with the relatively crude powers of the capital market in this respect, commends internal organization as a substitute for the capital market not merely because discretionary behaviour may thereby be attenuated but also because division managers may be induced to accept risks which in a free-standing firm would be declined.* Too often, as Luce and Raiffa (1958) observe, 'the strategist is evaluated in terms of the outcome of the adopted choice rather than in terms of the strategic desirability of the whole risky situation' (p. 76). This tendency to rely on outcomes rather than assess the complex situation more completely is especially to be expected of systems with low powers of inference. Managers of free-standing firms, realizing that outcomes rather than decision processes will be evaluated, are naturally reluctant to expose themselves to high-variance undertakings. *Ceteris paribus,* the low-cost access of internal organization to a wider range of sophisticated inference techniques encourages more aggressive risk-taking.

Even if the incentive machinery is not employed in a systematic way so as to give effect to internal audits, the auditing process may by itself serve to induce self-regulatory behaviour of a sort. Moral suasion reinforced by group compliance pressures can, if the results of the audits are internally publicized, have beneficial control consequences. Still, to rely on informal

---

* If the firm is not merely divisionalized but is also diversified, risk-pooling effects will obtain as well. These, however, are not at issue here.

procedures is unnecessarily casual; mobilizing the incentive machinery as a follow-on to the internal audit will more reliably produce intended effects.

A further use to which audits might be put is as a basis for determining when operating divisions could benefit from outside help. The general management may include on its staff what amounts to an internal management consulting unit—to be loaned or assigned to the operating divisions as the need arises. Partly the occasion for such an assignment may be revealed by the internal audit. Thus, although the general management ought not routinely to become involved in operating affairs,* having the capability to intervene prescriptively in an informed way under exceptional circumstances serves to augment its credibility as an internal control agent.† Again, self-regulatory behaviour by the operating divisions is encouraged.

2.3 Cash flow allocation

In addition to policing on internal efficiency matters, and thereby securing a higher level of adherence to profit maximization than the unassisted capital market could realize (at comparable cost), the general management and its support staff can perform a further capital market function: assigning cash flows to high-yield uses. Thus cash flows in the M-form are not automatically returned to their sources but instead are exposed to an internal competition. Investment proposals from the several divisions are solicited and evaluated by the general management. The usual criterion is rate of return on invested capital. As a recent article in *Business Week* (8 April 1972, pp. 54–7) puts it, the keys to management in the 1970s are 'analysis' and 'control'. Many corporations, accordingly, are assigning financial controllers to the division managers to assist them in assessing and proposing new projects. Again, the recurrent nature of the budgeting relationship serves to assure integrity in the process.

Moreover, because the costs of communicating internally are normally lower than would be incurred in making an investment proposal to the external capital market,‡ it may be practicable to decompose the internal investment process into stages. A sequential decision process (in which additional financing is conditional on prior stage results) may thus be both feasible and efficient as an internal investment strategy. The transaction costs of reproducing such a process through the capital market, by contrast, are likely to be prohibitive.

In many respects, this assignment of cash flows to high-yield uses is the most fundamental attribute of the M-form enterprise in the comparison of internal with external control processes. It must be appreciated, of course,

* The reasons for avoiding operating involvement have been given elsewhere. A recent comparative study by Allen (1970) of two divisionalized firms broadly supports the general argument. Allen observes that, of the two firms, the high-performing firm had a 'fairly simple but highly selective set of organizational devices to maintain control over its divisions' while the management of the low-performing firm become 'over-involved', in relation to its capacity, in the affairs of its operating divisions (p. 28).

† This internal management consulting unit would ordinarily be made available at the request of the operating divisions as well as at the behest of the general management. Such a unit would presumably possess scarce expertise of a high order. It would be uneconomical for each operating division to attempt to replicate such a capability.

‡ On the reasons for this, see the discussion in O. E. Williamson (1970), pp. 114, 119–21; also March and Simon (1958), p. 35.

that the divisionalized firm is able to assign cash flows to only a fairly narrow range of alternatives at any one point in time. Even if the firm is actively acquiring new activities and divesting itself of old, its range of choice is circumscribed in relation to that which general investors, who are interested in owning and trading securities rather than managing real assets, have access to. What the M-form firm does is trade off breadth for depth in this respect. As Alchian and Demsetz (1972) put it, in a similar context, 'Efficient production with heterogeneous resources is a result not of having *better* resources but in *knowing more accurately* the relative productive performances of those resources' (p. 29).

2.4 Externality adaptation

As noted in section I, spillovers in production or marketing may occur between some of the operating components of an organization. These spillovers may be mitigated by combining the affected parts within a single division. If, however, the resulting division becomes oversized—in that it is administratively unmanageable and effectively defeats the divisionalization concept, with a consequent loss of control in the incentive, auditing and cash flow senses described above—externalities may simply be tolerated or adapted to in other respects. Thus, rather than resort to combination, rules may be devised to attempt to augment positive and attenuate negative spillover effects.

As indicated earlier, interdivisional transfer-pricing rules between successive production stages may sometimes be necessary—especially if the item in question cannot be procured externally at competitive prices. Similarly, the selling and pricing practices of divisions that market products having high cross-elasticity of demand will presumably require mediation by higher-level authority. Divisions that are severely constrained in these or related respects cannot fully be regarded as profit centres—at least in the autonomous degree that this term ordinarily implies.

Divisionalization may nevertheless be meaningful in that *efficiency* performance can still be assessed.* Also, although the spillover aspect of investment proposals will require special attention, the allocation of resources to favour high-yield projects can be conducted in the ways described above.

Of course, in circumstances where the affected parts are very richly connected, divisionlization may not be feasible. An 'oversized' unit operating along traditional functional lines may then emerge. Often, however, a more extensive decomposition of the enterprise is possible than the operating parts of a functionally organized firm would concede. Proposals to divisionalize an integrated system rarely originate with those who are deeply involved with managing a 'complex' system in which everything is (or appears to be) connected with everything else. One of the critical functions of the general management is to discover the decomposability properties of the enterprise and, where circumstances permit (that is the malcoordination losses do not offset the prospective organizational gains), divisionalize accordingly.

3. Transitional Adjustments

The above discussion is conducted mainly in equilibrium terms. For many

* These are the cost centres referred to in section I.

purposes, this is altogether appropriate. Inasmuch, however, as it may take some time for an organization to recognize the need for reorganization, to effect a major structural change, and then become adapted to its operational consequences (which is to say that organizational learning is involved), the period just prior to, during, and immediately following a reorganization along M-form lines is apt to be a disequilibrium interval. Some allowance for the difficulties of adjustment may be needed if the performance consequences of such a change are to be accurately evaluated.

Similarly, the process of effectively integrating new acquisitions within an established M-form enterprise may take time. The incumbent managers of the newly-acquired firm may have been able to negotiate, as a condition of support for the acquisition, that their division be accorded special autonomy. Only as this management is redeployed within the parent organization, reaches retirement, or is otherwise induced to accept a more normal divisionalized relationship can the M-form control apparatus be brought fully to bear. Indeed, as a transitional matter to hasten the divisionalization, the general management may, at its first 'legitimate' opportunity, involve itself more actively in the operating affairs of the newly acquired parts than would, assessed in equilibrium terms, ordinarily be appropriate. The purpose of this effort, presumably, is to effect a more rapid conditioning of attitudes and transformation of procedures than would otherwise obtain — bringing both more nearly into congruence with those existing elsewhere in the firm. Such apparent over-involvement ought not to be regarded as a contradiction to M-form procedures unless the interference is long-continued and widely practised throughout the enterprise. Otherwise it is merely a transitional condition and a violation of M-form operations is not implied.

4. Operational Decision-making

The M-form structure is thoroughly corrupted when the general management involves itself in the operating affairs of the divisions in an extensive and continuing way. The separation between strategic and operating issues is sacrificed in the process; the indicated internalization of capital-market functions with net beneficial effects can scarcely be claimed. Accountability is seriously compromised; a substitution of enterprise expansion for profitability goals predictably obtains (O. E. Williamson 1970, pp. 48–9).

Effective divisionalization thus requires the general management to maintain an appropriate 'distance'. Moreover this holds for the support staff on which the general management relies for internal auditing and management consulting services. Over-involvement upsets the rational allocation responsibilities between short-run operating matters and longer-run planning and resource allocation activities. What March and Simon (1958) refer to as Gresham's Law of Planning—'Daily routine drives out planning' (p. 185)—takes effect when operating and strategic functions are mixed. While the arguments here are familiar and their implications for organizational design reasonably clear, maintaining a separation between these two activities apparently poses severe strain on some managements. A desire to be comprehensively involved is evidently difficult to resist.

F

5. 'Optimum' Divisionalization

Optimum divisionalization thus involves (1) the identification of separable economic activities within the firm, (2) according quasi-autonomous standing (usually of a profit centre nature) to each, (3) monitoring the efficiency performance of each division, (4) awarding incentives, (5) allocating cash flows to high-yield uses, and (6) performing strategic planning (diversification, acquisition, etc.) activities in other respects. The M-form structure is one that *combines* the divisionalization concept with an internal control and strategic decision-making capability. The general management of the M-form usually requires the support of a specialized staff to discharge these functions effectively. It bears repeating however, that care must be exercised lest the general management and its staff become over-involved in operating matters and fail to perform the high-level planning and control functions on which the M-form enterprise relies for its continuing success.

As indicated at the outset of this paper, whether and how to divisionalize depends on firm size, functional separability, and the state of information technology. Also it should be pointed out that our reference here to 'optimum' is used in comparative-institutional terms. As between otherwise comparable unitary or holding company forms of organization, the M-form structure would appear to possess significant advantages. It cannot, however, be established on the basis of the argument advanced here (and elaborated by Williamson 1970) that the M-form structure is the best of all conceivable structures. Organizational innovations may even now be in the making that will make it obsolete in part, but which academics will identify as noteworthy only after several years. A keener sensitivity to organizational innovations and their economic importance than has existed in the past should nevertheless help to avoid the long recognition lags before the significance of the M-form structure and its conglomerate variant became apparent.

III. A CLASSIFICATION SCHEME

The above analysis leads to a (tentative) six-way classification of large corporate structures. We expect that experience with the scheme may reveal certain ambiguities and suggest better definitions; the need to devise still additional categories may also become evident. We think it useful nevertheless to get on with the assignment task and make the refinements as we go. Surely enough is known about internal organization at this time to begin such an effort. The following classification scheme is accordingly proposed.

1. Unitary (U-form)

This is the traditional functionally organized enterprise. (It is still the appropriate structure in most small to lower-middle-sized firms. Some medium-sized firms in which interconnections are especially rich may continue to find this the appropriate structure.) A variant on this structure occasionally appears in which the enterprise is mainly of U-form character but where the firm has become diversified in slight degree and the incidental parts are given semi-autonomous standing. Unless such diversification accounts for at least a third of the firm's value added, such a functionally organized firm will be assigned to the U-form category.

2. Holding Company (H-form)

This is the divisionalized enterprise for which the requisite internal control apparatus has not been provided. The divisions are often affiliated with the parent company through a subsidiary relationship.

3. Multidivisional (M-form)

This is the divisionalized enterprise in which a separation of operating from strategic decision-making is provided and for which the requisite internal control apparatus has been assembled and is systematically employed.

Two sub-categories should be distinguished: type D_1, which denotes a highly integrated M-form enterprise, possibly with differentiated but otherwise common final products; and type D_2, which denotes the M-form enterprise with diversified final products or services. As between these two, a more extensive internal control apparatus to manage spillover effects is needed in the former.

4. Transitional multidivisional (M'-form)

This is the M-form enterprise that is in the process of adjustment. Organizational learning may be involved or newly-acquired parts may not yet have been brought into a regular divisionalized relationship to the parent enterprise.

5. Corrupted multidivisional ($\overline{M}$-form)

The $\overline{M}$-form enterprise is a multidivisonal structure for which the requisite control apparatus has been provided but in which the general management has become extensively involved in operating affairs. The appropriate distance relation thus is missing, with the result that M-form performance, over the long run, cannot reliably be expected.

6. Mixed (X-form)

Conceivably a divisionalized enterprise will have a mixed form in which some divisions will be essentially of the holding-company variety, others will be M-form, and still others will be under the close supervision of the general management. Whether a mixed form is likely to be viable over the long run is perhaps to be doubted. Some 'exceptions' might, however, survive simply as a matter of chance. The X-form classification thus might be included for completeness purposes and as a reminder that organizational survival is jointly a function of rational and chance processes (Alchian 1958). Over the long pull the rational structures should thrive, but aberrant cases will appear and occasionally persist.

That the X-form lacks for rationality properties, however, is probably too strong. For example, a large U-form firm that enjoys monopoly power in its main market may wish to restrict the reinvestment of cash flows back into this market. At the same time it may discover attractive opportunities to invest some part of these funds in unrelated business activities. Diversification could follow, but not in sufficient degree to warrant disestablishment of the main market from central-office control. The diversified parts of the business thus might each be given divisional standing, but the main business retained, for the most part, under its earlier control relationship. Only if the main business itself could be efficiently divided (through product differentiation, geographic territorialization, or other lines), which eventually it may, might divisionalization of this part of the firm's activities be warranted.

IV. RESEARCH OPPORTUNITIES*

Once the classification of the largest 500 industrials according to the scheme proposed in section III and illustrated in the Appendix is completed, it would be of interest to investigate the influence of organization form on firm behaviour and performance. Comparative growth and profit rates among rival firms might be studied. Investment behaviour, including marginal rates of return to alternative sources of funds (Baurmol *et al.* 1970, Friend and Husic 1971), as well as other forms of internal expenditure (hierarchical expense, advertising, R & D, etc.) ought also to be investigated for organization form effects. Executive compensation practices as a function of orgnization form, following along the lines developed by Masson (1971), should also be examined. Evidence relating to slack (internal inefficiency), as this is influenced by organization form and changes in the condition of the environment, should be studied. Internal operating practices, such as cross-subsidization, and 'offensive' marketing practices, such as reciprocity, could also be investigated to determine whether these are affected by organization form. It is probably important, for the purpose of making each of the types of studies suggested, to make allowance for firm-size effects.

Of related interest is the historical evolution of the M-form structure. Chandler (1966) traces much of this in descriptive terms, but a more formal assessment of this organizational innovation would seem useful. Of special interest are the factors that influence the rate of diffusion: What firms with what characteristics were induced to adopt it at what time? It is our impression that the period 1945–50 is the critical period during which the M-form innovation took on quantitative significance, that from 1950–60 it was adopted by many large firms as a defensive measure, and that 1960–70 is the period during which the conglomerate variant of this structure flourished. Historical studies of aggregate business behaviour may, at the least, want to distinguish between prewar and postwar periods, in the expectation that the latter will conform more nearly with the M-form hypothesis.

Considerations of organization form might also usefully be introduced

* For a more extensive development of the matters discussed in this section, including a development of the policy issues, see O. E. Williamson (1972), pp. 28–31.

into the study of bureaucracies more generally, to include non-profit institutions (hospitals, universities, etc.) and the public sector.

APPENDIX*

Our purpose in the Appendix is to give an illustration of each of the organization form types described in section III and indicate some of the sources that can be used for assigning large corporations quite generally to organization form categories. The firms appearing below were all among the largest 200 industrial corporations in the US (as ranked by 1965 sales in the *Fortune* 500 series).

U-form

The U-form structure is a vanishing breed among large US corporations. Reynolds Metals Company is one of the last such firms to make the transformation from a unitary to a divisionalized structure. Inspection of their annual reports together with correspondence from Mr Robert L. Teeter (Assistant Director for Corporate Planning) reveals that the company had maintained a U-form structure from its inception in 1929 until 1969. The company indicates in its *1969 Annual Report* that 'In the past year, our corporate structure was reorganized on a divisional, profit centre basis'. However, it is not clear to what extent operating responsibilities have been delegated to the divisions and whether appropriate rules have been made for harmonizing interdivisional interaction effects. Thus, while Reynolds Metals appears definitely to have been a U-form firm up until 1969, its current classification is uncertain. We provisionally assign it to M'-form status.

Quaker Oats Company is another example of a firm that only recently adopted a divisionalized structure. Although it had begun to diversify into chemicals and toys a number of years ago, this was merely incidental to the main business of the firm as a food processor and distributor. In an announcement dated 23 September 1970, President Robert D. Stuart, Jr stated that the company was being changed 'from a centralized functional [U-form] organization to a substantially decentralized one with profit responsibility delegated to a number of Groups and Divisions'. He went on to note that while some of the organizational changes 'will take place very soon, ... others, such as accounting and management information services, are highly complex and will take longer'. Among the advantages that he imputed to the new structure were that it 'heightens the incentive to succeed by making success at each level more visible ... [and is] readily adaptable to adding new businesses, either internally or through acquisition'. Thus Quaker Oats, which had a U-form structure until 1970, is provisionally assigned to M'-form status at the moment.

* The Appendix is based mainly on efforts of Bhargava to classify the largest 200 industrial corporations in the US as a part of his PhD dissertation. The assignments made here are provisional. Certain cross-checks on the assignments made have yet to be completed.

H-form

The Signal Companies Inc. is an example of an H-form firm. In the *1968 Annual Report*, Forrest N. Shumway, President, reported that the firm's name had been changed from Signal Oil and Gas to the Signal Companies, indicated that in 1968 the firm had acquired one company, created two others, and purchased nearly half of another, and characterized the organizational structure of the corporation in the following terms:

> Each of the Signal Companies functions within a corporate framework but is essentially on its own in day-to-day operations; each has its own slate of officers and Board of Directors. We weave them together and into the parent company by an interlock of directors, and we draw from directors of Signal and the major affiliates for our Executive Committee....
>
> We have been acquiring superior managements among our affiliates.... This permits us to maintain a relatively small corporate staff, which can concentrate on corporate legal and financing matters and serve as a conduit and catalyst for all the companies.
>
> The parent staff also conducts a broadscale corporate advertising and public relations programme to help earn favourable attitudes among the financial community and the general public.

The three major components of the Signal Companies operations arc Signal Oil and Gas Company (petroleum, with 1970 sales of $495 million), Mack Trucks, Inc. (heavy-duty trucks and off-highway equipment, 1970 sales of $534 million), and The Garrett Corporation (aerospace, 1970 sales of $379 million). Other smaller Signal Companies are involved in screw compressors, housing, chemicals, computer components, etc., with aggregate 1970 sales of $78 million. Although the corporate staff performed more than a simple financial aggregation function for these various companies, it had neither the intention nor the capacity to perform the management control functions that we associate with the M-form structure. Rather, through its aggressive acquisition period during the 1960s at least, Signal was organized under an H-form structure. We have been unable to ascertain whether the financial difficulties that Signal has experienced more recently have given rise to any later changes in its corporate structure.*

M-form

As noted, the M-form structure can be split into two types. Type D_1 is one in which manufacturing and/or marketing spillovers exist since common processes or products are involved. General Motors Corp. is illustrative. It was transformed from what was essentially an H-form structure under

---

* That crises reveal the need for more comprehensive controls, which may involve transforming an H-form to an M-form structure, is suggested by Richard A. Smith's treatment of Olin Mathieson in his *Corporations in Crisis* (New York, 1963).

W. C. Durant's leadership (during the period 1908 to 1920)* to an M-form structure under the duPonts and Alfred P. Sloan, Jr in the early 1920s.

Although General Motors was in 1920 and has since remained a diversified company (producing household appliances, diesel locomotives, military vehicles, etc.), its main business throughout the period from 1920 to the present has been automobiles. Some coordination of manufacturing, but especially of marketing, was needed lest the various automobile divisions compete in counterproductive ways (assessed in terms of the effect on corporate profits). The general office in General Motors thus became involved not merely in monitoring and strategic resource allocation (which is characteristics of the general office in any M-form structure), but, being a type-D_1 variant, was also engaged in rule-making and related processes designed to mitigate negative and enhance positive spillovers among the divisions (Chandler 1966, pp. 182–91).

The recent recentralization of certain manufacturing activities at General Motors may be in response to changing technology, perceived control difficulties with the earlier organization, strategic antitrust considerations, or some combination thereof. We lack the necessary information to determine how this is to be interpreted. At present, however, General Motors is still to be regarded as an M-form structure.

The type-D_2 variant is illustrated by Textron.† The firm, formerly Atlantic Rayon Company, had been a textile firm. The company engaged in extensive diversification under Royal Little during the 1950s. It appears mainly to have employed an H-form (or incipient M'-form) structure during this period. By 1960 the decentralized management pattern had been established; growth during the 1960s was mainly internal. Concurrently, the general office began to exercise M-form controls. Thus although it maintains a lean central staff (there being only 115 people at the Textron headquarters in 1970), it closely manages resource allocations and in 1969 group controllers were added to the headquarters staff.

Sales among the four industry groups in 1969 were distributed as follows: aerospace, 37 per cent; consumer products, 26 per cent; industrial products, 21 per cent; and metal products, 16 per cent. While these are a diverse mixture of activities, Textron has remained strictly a manufacturing organization and thus enjoys commonality among its divisions in this respect. Group vice-presidents are easily rotated among the operating companies for this reason.

M'-form

Deere & Company illustrates a firm that has recently been through and appears not fully to have completed a transformation from a functional to an M-form enterprise. Deere was originally a farm-equipment manufacturer

* Chandler (1966) characterizes the early organization of General Motors as 'a loosely knit federation of many operating enterprises' (p. 151). Harlow Curtice observes that prior to 1921, 'Operations were neither integrated nor coordinated' and that in many respects 'the individual units [were] largely out of control'. Sloan and the duPonts devised and implemented what we refer to in the text as the M-form structure.

† In addition to the annual report of Textron, a *Business Week* article ('Textron: built to diversify', 17 October 1970) has been useful for our treatment of Textron.

organized along U-form lines. By 1966, however, it had become diversified and organizationally too complex to be managed along functional lines. The manufacturing and marketing departments were accordingly subdivided into farm equipment, industrial equipment, and consumer products components. This evidently was not wholly successful, however, and the company divisionalized along product lines in 1970.

The Deere & Company management, in an internal memorandum dated 17 February 1970, summarized the changing organization structure of the firm in the following terms:

> Some years ago when the business of Deere & Company and its sub-sidiaries was concentrated almost exlusively in the farm equipment markets of the United States and Canada, an organization based on function, structured primarily on manufacturing, marketing and financial lines, was both appropriate and highly effective. As our business grew, new markets and products became increasingly important to us with our overseas expansion and our addition of industrial equipment and consumer products lines. Each of these additions not only opened new opportunities, but also imposed requirements for new and different ways of operating. In 1966 we began to adjust to those requirements by modifying the original management structure based on functions, adding the Overseas Division and regrouping within the Manufacturing and Marketing Divisions their organizations into farm equipment, industrial equipment and consumer products components.
>
> Another change is now needed: the establishment of operating divisions based on product lines and regional market areas, and the creation of a corporate staff division to provide increasingly effective counsel, services and functional guidance for the operating divisions.
>
> The hoped for benefits of the reorganization include:
>
> 1   Greater recognition and scope for corporate staff activities plus improved coordination of these activities. The complexities of modern technology and professional specialization have made staff functions equal in importance with those of operations as a factor in business success.
> 2   Clear focusing of operating management talents on the development of business opportunities in each of our principal product lines and regional market areas.
> 3   Closer coordination of the manufacturing and marketing functions within each product line and market area.
> 4   More opportunities for developing corporate executives with experience in broad general management responsibilities.
> 5   Divisional accounting to give better knowledge of the return-on-investment performance of the major parts of our business, and to facilitate return-on-investment comparisons among John Deere operating divisions and with other companies in the same industries.
>
> This new management organization clearly is consistent with and gives new emphasis and meaning to the traditional John Deere policy of decentralization of authority and responsibility within a framework

of corporate objectives, policies and communications practices. The senior vice-president in charge of each division has full authority and responsibility within such limits and within the limits of the resources allotted to his division.

Whether Deere will fully attain an M-form structure cannot yet be determined. From 1966 to the present, it is assigned to the M'-form category.

$\overline{M}$-form

Allis-Chalmers Company illustrates a divisionalized firm that, possibly, might have been intended to be an M-form enterprise but in which the general office became excessively involved in operating affairs. Mr Lee P. Appleton, Assistant Secretary and Treasurer, indicated in a letter dated 18 February 1971, that the company had been divisionalized for 'at least twenty years', but went on to observe that the divisionalization concept had recently undergone great change within Allis-Chalmers—as indeed it has.

The 1952 annual report refers only to General Machinery and Tractor divisions. Partly through acquisition and partly by splitting existing divisions, this had grown to six divisions by 1955: Power Equipment, Industrial Equipment, General Products, Construction Machinery, Farm Equipment, and Buda. Nuclear Power and Defense Products divisions were added subsequently. The 1964 Annual Report reported a general reorganization out of which 'twelve integrated operating divisions with full management responsibility' were created. The purported autonomy objective, however, was apparently unrealized.

The company subsequently experienced heavy reverses and was subject to repeated takeover threats. Only after the President and Chairman of the Board resigned and David C. Scott was brought in (from Colt Industries) did the company face up to its actual organizational practices. The 1968 annual report catalogues the problem:

> Before year-end 1969, a total of 5000 non-production personnel will have been released throughout the company. Corporate staff employees —that is people not reporting to profit centres—now total 132, a reduction of more than 1300 from this classification in five months. Most of those formerly classified 'corporate staff' have been transferred to profit centres.
>
> Although decentralization moves were made some four years ago, operating divisions were not held to true profit responsibility. In addition to their own operating expenses, each producing division was charged with a proportionate amount of heavy corporate overhead expense. It is our intention to decentralize Allis-Chalmers fully into true profit centres, where each division and department general manager can be accurately measured in his performance of generating profit.
>
> At present, our operations are structured into seven operating groups, each . . . headed by a senior vice-president or vice-president, who reports to the President.

The reorganization, however, has not by itself been fully effective. The 13 March 1971 issue of *Business Week* observed that the company apparently had need of fresh talent at top and middle-management levels.

While Allis-Chalmers appears clearly to illustrate the $\overline{\text{M}}$-form structure during the 1950s and early 1960s, there is a serious problem of recognizing this corrupted form of an M-form enterprise at the time. Annual reports, press releases, even 'depth' reports in the business magazines rarely expose over-involvement by a general office in the affairs of the operating divisions. A strong indication that this condition prevails can be deduced from question-naire responses in which the size of the general office staff is reported. Not all companies are prepared to respond to such a query, however. Moreover, the size of this staff is merely a first indication. Its composition and the characteristics of the firm need also to be considered. (Thus M-form, type-D_1 firms will usually require larger staffs than will type-D_2; also firms that centralize the R & D function may have what appear to be large staffs, but these may be little involved, in an operating sense, with the operating divisions.)

X-form

Firestone Tire & Rubber Company is one of the most highly integrated firms in the rubber industry. While it had become diversified to the extent that 40 per cent of its sales were in non-rubber products in 1969, its main business has continued to be in tyres. The tyre business is operated along U-form lines, while the other businesses (mainly rubber products, plastics, steel products, and textiles) are set up as product divisions which enjoy quasi-autonomous standing. The X-form classification appears to be appropriate.*

---

* A letter from Glenn D. Cross, Manager of Organizational Planning, observes that 'Our organization structure falls mainly within the functional category although one phase of it, concerning our non-tire activities, is of the division type'. The 1969 Annual Report reports that 'From the very beginning Firestone has been one of the most integrated of businesses. From the ownership of rubber plantations this integration terminates at franchised retail stores dealing exclusively in Firestone manufacturers'.

EXECUTIVE COMPENSATION AND THE OBJECTIVES OF THE FIRM

by

GEORGE K. YARROW

University of Newcastle upon Tyne

INTRODUCTION

One of the few areas of empirical work which have been widely discussed in recent controversies concerning the adequacy of the profit-maximization assumption in the theory of the firm is that dealing with the determinants of executive compensation. Indeed, the more recent studies of executive compensation have been explicitly motivated by the desire to discriminate between alternative theories of the firm. A feature of the studies is the rather loose way in which the various hypotheses are set up and predictions derived from them for the purpose of cross testing. Only Marris (1964) and Roberts (1959) develop the theory of executive compensation in any detail. However, the former deals only with two special cases of the firm's production function, while the arguments of the latter concerning the implications of the profit-maximization hypothesis are not completely correct. The first task of this paper is, therefore, to consider different theories of executive compensation, and in particular to formulate a more rigorous version of the neoclassical (profit maximization) hypothesis, so that their predictions can be compared and distinguished. This is accomplished in section I. A second feature of the empirical studies, arising in part from the theoretical deficiencies mentioned above, is the lack of discussion concerning the appropriate mathematical forms of the equations to be fitted to the data. The problems raised by the omission are considered in sections II and IV. Section II is both a summary and discussion of the more important of the earlier articles. In section III the theories outlined in section I are used to generate some new empirical results which are compared and contrasted with those of previous writers. Finally, section IV contains a more detailed analysis of the problem of the specification of the equations and an explanation of the quite substantial differences between the findings of the present paper and those of the most recent of the articles summarized in section II.

I. THEORIES OF EXECUTIVE COMPENSATION

(a) Neoclassical

By the neoclassical theory is meant that which bases itself on the assumption that the compensation of executives is set at levels which maximize the welfare of shareholders of the firm. Empirical work has largely focused on the compensation of the highest paid executive, so it is on the determination of this variable that the analysis will be concentrated. By definition the quantity of the input is fixed at one unit and, therefore, only the quality of the input can be varied.* The problem is to determine the optimum quality.

Consider a fully idealized neoclassical world in which the quality of the top manager can be represented by a continuous variable Q. For each quality of manager there is a freely competitive market in which the wage is determined by supply and demand. Each individual firm will then be faced with a fixed price s for an executive of quality Q, and it can be assumed that the higher the quality of the manager the higher the wage, that is $s'(Q) > 0$.

---

* Situations in which two or more executives are paid the highest salary will be ignored.

The quality of management will have effects on both the revenue and cost functions of the firm so that total profits will be given by P, where:

$$P(x, Q, z) = \Pi(x, Q, z) - s(Q) \tag{1}$$

and $\Pi(x, Q, z)$ is the profit of the firm before deduction of the wage of the highest paid executive, x is the n-vector of factors of production and z is a vector of other, non-variable, influences. The first-order conditions for profit maximization are:

$$\frac{\partial \Pi}{\partial x_i} = 0 \qquad (i = 1, 2, \ldots, n) \tag{2}$$

$$\frac{\partial \Pi}{\partial Q} = s'(Q) \tag{3}$$

$\partial \Pi / \partial Q$ will be called the net marginal revenue product of the quality of management (NMRPQM) and $s'(Q)$ the marginal cost of the quality of management (MCQM). Condition 3 is shown diagrammatically for firm j in figure 1, on the assumption that all other inputs are used at their optimum levels.

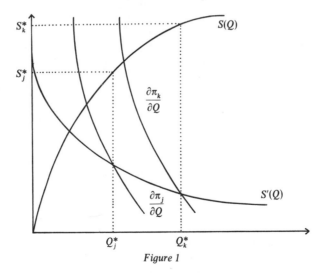

Figure 1

Now all firms face the same curve $s(Q)$. Hence the quality and compensation of the top manager of a given firm will depend upon the factors determining the shape and position of the NMRPQM curve. NMRPQM is a function of Q, x and z. In the empirical section III the only elements of the vector x that will be considered are capital, labour and the size of the administrative staff of the firm. These are all factors that can be expected to be complementary to management, and it will be assumed that $\partial / \partial x_{ij}(\partial \Pi_j / \partial Q_j) > 0$, where x_{ij} is the quantity of the ith factor used by the jth firm. In the absence of disturbing influences there will be a similar firm-to-firm effect. That is, comparing two firms, the one with the higher inputs of the three factors mentioned can be expected to have a higher NMRPQM at all levels of Q, and hence a higher optimum quality of the top manager. It follows, then, that there would be a relationship between the observed (optimum) values of compensation and the inputs of the form:

$$s_j^* = g(x_j^*, z_j)$$

$$\frac{\Delta s_j^*}{\Delta x_{ij}^*} > 0 \quad (i = 1, 2, 3. \ j = 1, 2, \ldots, m) \tag{4}$$

where m is the number of firms and stars indicate profit-maximizing values of the variables.

Consider next two firms with identical factor inputs x^* but different levels of compensation. That is, suppose that $x_j^* = x_k^*$ but $s_k^* > s_j^*$. It must follow that:

$$\frac{\partial \Pi_j(x_j^*, Q, z_j)}{\partial Q} < \frac{\partial \Pi_k(x_k^*, Q, z_k)}{\partial Q} \tag{5}$$

in some interval covering $[Q_j^*, Q_k^*]$ (see figure 1). If inequality 5 holds for all $Q \in (0, Q_k^*)$ then the total profit of firm k, given by

$$P_k^*(x_k^*, Q_k^*, z_k) = \int_0^{Q_k^*} \frac{\partial \Pi_k}{\partial Q} \cdot dQ - s_k^* \tag{6}$$

is greater than the total profits of firm j. While there is no logical argument that can take us, in this way, from the inequality of the NMRPQMs over the interval $[Q_j^*, Q_k^*]$ to a similar inequality relating total profits, unless it is specified that the revenue and cost functions take certain definite mathematical forms, it is an *inference* that is commonly made. In cases in which there is no obvious reason to expect that the NMRPQM and the net average revenue product of the quality of management (NARPQM), defined as the ratio of total profits to the quality of management Q, will not be positively related to one another it seems reasonable to suppose that:

$$P_j^* < P_k^* \tag{7a}$$

Since, by assumption, $x_j^* = x_k^*$, both sides of inequality 7a can be divided by the capital input* to give a similar inequality concerning profitability (denoted by p^*):

$$p_j^* < p_k^* \tag{7b}$$

It is extremely important to keep in mind, however, that inequality 7b is an inference and not a deduction from equation 5. It can only be expected to hold true on the average and in the circumstances outlined above.

Drawing together the various arguments, the predictions of the neoclassi-

---

* The reason for making this step is that it helps to remove the collinearity between profits and the factor inputs and, therefore, makes statistical testing easier.

cal theory can be summarized in the equations:

$$s_j^* = f(x_j^*, p_j^*, y_j)$$

$$\frac{\Delta s_j^*}{\Delta x_{ij}^*} > 0$$

$$(i = 1, 2, 3 \qquad j = 1, 2, \ldots, m) \qquad (8)$$

$$\frac{\Delta s_j^*}{\Delta p_j^*} > 0$$

where y_j is a vector of variables containing elements likely to lead to the relationship between the NMRPQM and the NARPQM being *not* monotonically increasing.

(b) Organization Theory

An alternative theory of executive compensation has been developed by Simon (1957), based on some commonly observed features of large organizations. Only a brief summary of the salient features is given here and the interested reader is referred to the original article. The first step in the analysis is the assumption that the starting salary for trainee managers is constant from firm to firm. It is next assumed that the management team can be split into a number of distinct hierarchical levels numbered $1, 2, \ldots, m$, and that there is a consistent relationship between the compensation of managers at each successive level of the company hierarchy. Specifically, it is supposed that the salary of an executive at level i is equal to h times the compensation of executives at the level below $(i - 1)$ where h is independent of i but depends on the span of control, defined as the ratio of the number of managers in the level below to the number of managers at the given level. Letting h_i be the ratio of salaries at level i to salaries at level $i - 1$ and x_i be the span of control at level i, then if $h_i = x_j^\beta$ it can be shown that

$$s = Y_0 \cdot E_0^\beta \qquad (9)$$

where Y_0 is the salary and E_0 is the number of (trainee) managers at the lowest hierarchical level. Now Y_0 is assumed to be constant and E_0 will be closely correlated with some appropriate measure of the size of the firm, say W. Simon's theory, therefore, predicts a relationship between top executive compensation and firm size of the form:

$$s = \alpha W^\beta \qquad (10)$$

(c) Managerial Theories

Managerial theories of the firm are based on the recognition that managers have objectives other than the maximization of profits or shareholder welfare, and that capital-market imperfections give them discretion to pursue these alternative objectives. They generally take the form of assuming that managers maximize a utility function consisting of several variables, one of which is their level of job security. Job security is taken to depend either on the firm's profits (short-period models) or the market value of the firm's equity (long-period models).*

If these theories are a correct description of some aspects of the decision-making process of the firm, then the degree to which compensation and profits or profitability are related will be important for two reasons, assuming that salary is one component of the managerial utility function. First, to the extent that compensation is influenced by people other than the executives themselves, a high responsiveness of compensation to changes in profits will affect the marginal rate of substitution between the former and the other variables entering the utility function in such a way as to tend to bring the utility-maximizing level of profits closer than it would otherwise have been to the profit-maximizing level. Put more simply, the more responsive is compensation to the level of profits the greater is the incentive for the executive to seek high profits. Second, to the extent to which top management set their own salaries, the responsiveness of profits to compensation may be taken as an indicator of the weight attached to profit directly as an argument of the utility function in its own right, rather than indirectly as a variable that affects the security of managers. The weighting will, to a large extent, be determined by the general normative orientation of management.† For example, they may follow policies close to profit maximization and reward themselves approximately in the way outlined by the neoclassical theory because they feel that this is the way in which they *ought* to behave, and not because they are forced to do so by market forces. For both these reasons, then, the responsiveness of compensation to profits could be an important indicator of the extent to which firms are deviating from profit-maximizing behaviour.

Similar arguments to the above can be advanced concerning the implications of the extent of the relationship between compensation and any other variable that could enter the objective function of management. The most commonly cited of these is sales revenue. In a much-quoted statement, Baumol (1959) claimed that the evidence that 'executive salaries appear to be far more closely correlated with the scale of operations of the firm than its profitability' tended to support his hypothesis that managers maximize the sales revenue of their firm subject to a minimum profits constraint. The reasoning can of course be applied to other measures of the scale of operations of the firm, such as capital stock, instead of to sales, but the general direction and implications of the argument are clear.

II. SURVEY OF PREVIOUS STUDIES

(a) Roberts (1959)

Roberts's book is concerned with more problems than simply the determinants of executive compensation but I shall summarize his findings only on the points relevant to this aspect of his work. The study was based on a

* See G. K. Yarrow, 'Managerial Utility Maximisation under Uncertainty', Warwick Economic Research Paper, Number 20.
† For a full discussion of this point see Nichols (1969).

sample of 410 US corporations for the years 1945, 1948 and 1949, and 989 corporations for the year 1950. It is much more comprehensive in its coverage than all subsequent work and although the data on compensation, drawn from records lodged with the Securities and Exchange Commission, consists only of basic salary plus bonus, this would seem to be a relatively minor problem unlikely to affect the results for the period in question.* Roberts's main conclusions are as follows:

1 The most important determinant of executive compensation is the sales revenue of the firm,
2 Profitability has no significant effect on compensation, and
3 There are no significant industry differences in the relationship between compensation, sales and profits in the major manufacturing industries.†

Doubt will be cast on all three of these conclusions in section III of the paper where new results are presented. However, it is interesting to note that 1 and 2 can be disputed even on the basis of some of Roberts's own data.‡ Using the figures he presents for the 1948–50 averages of compensation, profits, sales and tangible net worth for 77 selected corporations, two log-linear equations were fitted to the data by the method of least squares with the following results:

$$\log Y = 1.547 + 0.354 \log X_1 + 0.198 \log X_3 \qquad (11)$$
$$(3.55)^* \quad (9.43)^* \qquad\qquad (1.56)$$

$R^2 = 0.588$

$$\log Y = 1.669 + 0.353 \log X_2 + 0.236 \log X_3 \qquad (12)$$
$$(3.96)^* \quad (9.83)^* \qquad\qquad (1.91)^*$$

$R^2 = 0.607$

where $Y =$ average annual compensation of highest paid officials in $000s,
$\quad X_1 =$ average gross sales in $00000s,
$\quad X_2 =$ average tangible net worth in $00000s and
$\quad X_3 =$ average annual profits as a percentage of average tangible net worth.

The figures in brackets show the t values associated with the coefficient above them and a star indicates that the coefficient is significantly positive at the 5 per cent level or better. This is the level of significance that will be used throughout the rest of this paper. The two points to note about the equations are that 12 fits the data better than 11, goodness of fit being measured by R^2, and that the coefficient of profitability is significantly

---

* In the period examined there is evidence to show that basic salary plus bonus made up the great bulk of total executive compensation. See, for example, Lewellen (1968).

† Although such differences do become significant for some of the non-manufacturing industries.

‡ Even 3 can only be accepted with caution. Five dummy shift variables were added to equations 11 and 12 to capture industry effects, data being given for six industries. F tests were used to see if this set of variables contributed significantly to the explanatory power of the equation. They did at a 10 per cent, but did not at a 5 per cent level of significance.

positive in 12 at the 5 per cent level, but only significantly positive at the 10 per cent level in 11. The first point indicates that it is some measure of the scale of operations of the firm, to use Baumol's phrase, and not specifically sales revenue, that is the major determinant of compensation. The second suggests that profitability does have a significant effect on compensation. Despite these reservations about Roberts's conclusions, however, it is clear from the *t* values that a measure of the scale of operations of the firm, and not the level of profitability, is the most important explanatory variable.* It should be noted that this in no way invalidates the neoclassical theory.

(b) McGuire, Chiu and Elbing (1962)

McGuire *et al.* took a sample of 45 of the largest 100 industrial corporations, ranked by sales, in the US for the period 1953–9 inclusive. The corporations chosen were those for which data on the compensation of the highest paid executive was available from the magazine *Business Week* for each of the seven years in question. In each year significantly high simple correlations between compensation and sales, and between compensation and total profits, were found. However, because of collinearity between sales and profits, McGuire *et al.* were led to an examination of partial correlation coefficients between compensation and the other two variables. This was done using various lags in the relationship and for first differences of the three variables. Their conclusions were that in most cases sales and executive compensation are significantly correlated at the 5 per cent level, while profits and compensation are not significantly correlated at all. They claimed that their results supported the Baumol sales-revenue-maximization hypothesis.

There are however two problems with this piece of work. First, and more important, taking partial correlation coefficients does not entirely remove the problem of collinearity between sales and profits, because collinearity will tend to lead to large standard errors in the estimates of the coefficients. Hence, possibly significant associations between the variables may not be picked up. Second, the partial correlation analysis only measures the degree to which variables are linearly associated. However, scatter diagrams of compensation against various measures of the size of the firm, and against profits, indicate that the appropriate relationships are curvilinear. To be more precise, compensation appears to be a concave function of sales or profits.

(c) O. E. Williamson (1963)

In his paper, Williamson deals, among other things, with the effect of managerial discretion on compensation. According to his theory of the firm, managers maximize a utility function, which includes as one argument their own remuneration, subject to a minimum profits constraint. He argues

---

* However, the *average* effects of increased profitability on compensation are relatively large. On average a doubling of profitability is associated with a 24 per cent increase in compensation, while a doubling of the size of the firm, measured either by sales or tangible net worth is associated with a 35 per cent increase in compensation.

that increased discretion will lead to higher compensation, and takes as proxy variables for discretion the four-firm sales concentration ratio of the firm's industry C, the height of the barriers to entry for the industry H, as developed by Bain (1956),* and the degree of stockholder diffusion. The equation

$$\log s = b_0 + b_1 \log A + b_2 \log C + b_3 \log H + b_4 \log B + \epsilon \qquad (13)$$

was fitted to the data where:

A = general, selling and administrative expense†
B = a measure of the extent of management representation on the board of directors, which is taken as a proxy for both management 'tastes' and the degree of stockholder diffusion,
ϵ = the error term.

The sampling procedure was to take the two largest firms, in terms of sales, in each of 26 major US manufacturing industries. However, because of data deficiencies, especially on account of the unavailability of figures for the barriers-to-entry variable, only 25–30 observations were available for the three years concerned, which were 1953, 1957 and 1961. The executive compensation figures, as in the McGuire *et al.* paper, were taken from *Business Week*. Williamson found that the coefficients b_1 and b_2 were significantly positive at the 2.5 per cent level or better in all three years, b_3 was significantly positive at this level in 1953 and 1957 but b_4 was not significantly different from zero in any year, even at the 5 per cent level. When the profit rate was added to equation 13 as an extra variable it was found that its coefficient was significantly positive only in 1957,‡ and had a negative sign in 1961, while the concentration ratio and entry barrier variables remained significantly positive at the 10 per cent level or better in every year.

The main point of interest in Williamson's results for this paper is his finding that industry variables have significant effects on compensation, thus casting doubt on the generality of Roberts's conclusions discussed earlier. The problem will be taken up in section III below. On the other hand the most important deficiency of the work lies in the small size of the sample, while the formulation of the profit-maximizing theory is less than adequate.

(d) Lewellen and Huntsman (1970)

The conclusions of this, the most recent study of executive compensation, are in marked contrast to the results discussed in parts (a)–(c). Lewellen and Huntsman fitted the two equations

$$\frac{s}{K} = \frac{b_0}{K} + b_1 \frac{P}{K} + b_2 \frac{R}{K} + \epsilon \qquad (14)$$

$$\frac{s}{K} = \frac{b_0}{K} + b_1 \frac{V}{K} + b_2 \frac{R}{K} + \epsilon \qquad (15)$$

* H takes the value 1 for low barriers to entry and the value e for high or substantial barriers to entry.
† Williamson makes the assumption that the profit-maximizing compensation level will be a function only of A and an index of special ability Z. Compare this with section I(a) above.
‡ Williamson does not specify at what level but 2.5 per cent seems to be implied.

to a sample of 50 of the largest 100 industrial corporations in the US
where R = the sales revenue of the firm
  K = the book value of the firm's total assets
  P = reported after-tax profits of the firm
  V = market value of the firm's outstanding common stock
all measured in millions of dollars, and s is measured in dollars. Each
equation was fitted to the data twice in each year; once with s defined as basic
salary plus bonus, and once using a much more sophisticated measure of
executive compensation which takes into account the present values of
items such as pension awards, deferred compensation, stock options, etc.
Both variables were taken from Lewellen's earlier extensive work (1968) on
the measurement of compensation. The 50 corporations in the sample were
the largest, in terms of sales, for which all the data was available in each of
the years the equations were fitted (1942, 1945, 1948, 1951, 1954, 1957, 1960
and 1963).* The capital stock variable appears in the denominator of each
term to remove as much as possible of the collinearity between the independent variables, sales and profits.

Lewellen and Huntsman found that the profit and market value variables
were significantly positive at the 5 per cent level or better for all the runs in
which the dependent variable was basic salary plus bonus, and for six of the
eight years when the more sophisticated compensation measure was used.
On the other hand b_2 was not significantly different from zero at this level
in any equation or year, and was negative in approximately half the runs.
A second important feature of the results was that, except in the first two
years, the cruder measure of executive compensation gave the better fit
to the data, again using the coefficient of determination as the criterion. The
increase in R^2 obtained by taking s as basic salary plus bonus was quite marked
in some years.† Lewellen and Huntsman concluded by claiming that their
results supported the view that managers aim to maximize the profits of their
firm, rather than its sales revenue.

However, as Lewellen and Huntsman argue at two points in their paper,
there are both theoretical and empirical grounds for believing that compensation is a concave function of profits and/or sales. Their justification for
adopting linear forms of their basic equations seems to be the assumption that
they are dealing with firms which do not vary widely in size and that, therefore, it is reasonable to use a linear approximation to the true curve over the
relevant intervals of the independent variables. Although the sample only
includes corporations in the *Fortune* top 100 this assumption is not valid
since there are still large differentials in both the absolute and relative levels
of sales and profits of the firms. For example, in 1963, the latest year of the
study, the profits of the first corporation in the *Fortune* list were nearly 60
times those of the 100th corporation, and this is almost certainly less than
the relative differential between the most profitable and least profitable
firms in the sample in any year. Over a range of the independent variable as
large as this the concavity of the relationship would be expected to manifest

---

* The smallest of the 50 corporations in 1968 was ranked 94th in *Fortune* magazine's list for
that year.
  † The largest increase was in 1957 when R^2 was more than doubled from 0.439 to 0.929 for
equation 14 and from 0.440 to 0.922 for equation 15.

itself, unless it was virtually non-existent. The results of section III indicate that the basic equation has a fairly substantial degree of concavity, and thus a linear approximation as used by Lewellen and Huntsman may lead to serious specification errors.

Further, since sales and total assets tend to be closely correlated with one another, the insignificance of b_2 would seem to show that compensation does not depend upon any measure of the size of the firm other than total profits. This contradicts not only the results of other studies but also the predictions of the neoclassical theory developed above. Possible explanations of the insignificance of the coefficient are specification error and the fact that variations in the ratio of sales to assets tend to depend on factors such as the type of technology in use, the degree of vertical integration of the firm, etc., none of which are necessarily connected with compensation in any way.

III. SOME NEW RESULTS

The following analysis is based on a sample of 85 large US industrial corporations for the years 1963, 1965 and 1968. The sample was not random but depended on the availability of compensation data for the years in question. The great majority of the firms appear in the top 150 of the *Fortune* list, and the smallest was ranked 317th in 1963.* The source of the compensation data was *Business Week*, as in the McGuire *et al.* and Williamson studies. The figures published are for basic salary plus bonus together with some other elements of compensation such as deferred payments. Stock options are not included although very recently *Business Week* has started publishing information about these. No attempt has been made to adjust deferred payments to present values as was done by Lewellen (1968). The data on compensation are, therefore, very crude and the errors involved are probably greater than those of previous studies using the same source since basic salary plus bonus as a percentage of total compensation has been declining over time (Lewellen 1968). On the positive side, the findings of Lewellen and Huntsman give support to the view that empirical results may be rather insensitive to the actual measure of compensation used, and this tends to be confirmed by some of the findings of the present paper (see section IV). Data on sales, profits, capital and number of employees were taken from the *Fortune* list of the largest 500 industrial corporations. The sources of figures for general, selling and administrative expense were Moody's Industrials and Extel cards, and as they were not always available for all the firms in the sample, it was impossible to use 85 observations in each of the regression equations. In fact the maximum number of observations available was 72 in 1963, 79 in 1965 and 78 in 1968.

The starting point of the regression analysis is equation 8. In addition to the variables in that equation it is desirable to include the level of sales revenue to test the claims, made by Roberts and McGuire *et al.*, that sales is the major determinant of compensation. Unfortunately to include all these variables in one equation would lead to very substantial collinearity

* A list of the corporations in the sample is available on request.

and correspondingly large standard errors of the estimates. To partially ease the problem, only two of the variables that tend to be correlated closely with the scale of operations of the firm have been included in any one equation. The first set of equations to be fitted to the data for each of the three years is as follows:

$$\log s = b_0 + b_1 \log R + b_2 \log A + b_3 \log p + \epsilon \qquad (16)$$

$$\log s = b_0 + b_1 \log L + b_2 \log A + b_3 \log p + \epsilon \qquad (17)$$

$$\log s = b_0 + b_1 \log K + b_2 \log A + b_3 \log p + \epsilon \qquad (18)$$

$$\log s = b_0 + b_1 \log (IK) + b_2 \log A + b_3 \log p + \epsilon \qquad (19)$$

where R = sales in year t in \$00 000s
L = number of employees in year t
K = book value of total assets at end of year t in \$00 000s
IK = invested capital at end of year t in \$00 000s
A = general, selling and administrative expense in year t in \$00 000s
s = compensation of the highest paid executive in year t in \$000s and
p = percentage after-tax rate of return on invested capital in year $t - 1$.

Several points should be noted concerning the above equations. First, a loglinear specification has been adopted to allow for the curvilinear relationship expected from both theoretical reasoning (see Lewellen and Huntsman 1970) and scatter diagrams of compensation against any of the 'scale of operations' variables. It is also the appropriate specification if the organization theory of section I(b) is correct (see equation 10). The equations are of the same form as those used by Williamson.

General, selling and administrative expense has been included in all the equations for two reasons, both based on its usefulness as a proxy for the size of the 'staff' of the firm. First, 'staff' is the factor of production probably most complementary to top management and hence, if the neoclassical theory is correct, it would be expected to have an important effect on compensation. Second, from the point of view of the organization equation (10), this is the size variable that would be expected to best represent the number of managers at the lowest level of the hierarchy. Indeed, we may say that the prediction of the Simon theory is that b_2 will be significantly positive and all the other coefficients will not be significantly different from zero.

As general, selling and administrative expense is positively correlated with sales, capital and labour force,* not all the collinearity has been removed from the independent variables. This is the cost of including the former in every equation for the reasons outlined above. The extent of the problem can be assessed by examining the simple correlation coefficients shown in table 1. Although they are far from negligible, they do not rule out meaningful measurements of the separate effects of the two size variables included in every equation.

If profitability affects compensation it is likely to do so after a certain interval, since the firm's performance will be difficult to predict in advance

---

* Among other things, general, selling and administrative expense will depend upon the size of one part of the labour force, so the two variables overlap.

Table 1. Simple correlation coefficients between log A and log R, log L, log K and log IK

		log R	log L	log K	log (IK)
1963	log A	0.747	0.540	0.628	0.591
1965	log A	0.739	0.600	0.655	0.610
1968	log A	0.729	0.662	0.599	0.565

or record immediately. For example, the *Business Week* information shows that bonuses awarded for year t, say, are often not paid until year $t + 1$.* All other variables have therefore been lagged one year behind profitability. The equations were tried with no lag with very little difference in the results, thus confirming the finding of McGuire *et al.* that introducing short lags has very little effect. It is clear that lagging compensation one period behind the size variables would have virtually no effect on the conclusion because the latter are so highly correlated with their own previous values.

The equations were also run using the valuation ratio, defined as the ratio of the market value of the firm's outstanding common stock to its invested capital,† in place of profitability, since it can be argued that the former is a better performance measure which takes into account expectations of future returns. Again it was found that this alteration to the equations made little difference to the results, confirming a similar conclusion of Lewellen and Huntsman. Only the results concerning profitability will, therefore, be presented.

The vector y in equation 8 has been absorbed into the error term on the assumption that these variables are independent of the variables included in the equations. The point will be taken up again at a later stage where the assumption will be relaxed.

The coefficients of the four equations with their associated t values are set out in table 2. Once again using the coefficient of determination as the criterion, the best fit to the data is obtained when either total assets or invested capital is used in the equation. In all three years R^2 falls when either of them is replaced with sales or number of employees. In 1963 and 1968 the use of invested capital gives a better fit than the use of total assets, and vice versa in 1965, although the differences are relatively small. Hence, it can be concluded that a measure of the capital input is more closely correlated with compensation than the sales of the firm, which is exactly what would be predicted by the neoclassical theory.‡ The claims that sales revenue is the major determinant of compensation would, on the other hand, seem to be false, and the explanation of the significant correlations found between the two variables in this and earlier studies may be that the former is closely correlated with one of the real determinants of the latter, the capital input. The conclusion tends to contradict the implied predictions of Baumol's hypothesis about the objectives of firms, but there is a possible counter-

* Observed relationships between performance and bonus do not necessarily imply a corresponding relationship between performance and total compensation, since an increase in bonus may coincide with a reduction in basic salary or other elements of compensation.

† The market value of the firm's common stock was calculated using the median price of common stock in calendar year $t - 1$.

‡ See equation 8 above.

Table 2. Estimates of the coefficients of equations 16 to 19. The associated t values are shown in brackets underneath and a star indicates significance at the 5 per cent level using a one-tailed test. Sample sizes are 72 in 1963, 79 in 1965 and 78 in 1968

Year	Constant	log R	log L	log K	Coefficient of log IK	log A	log p	R^2
1963	3.036	0.149				0.103	0.084	0.365
	(7.63)*	(2.61)*				(1.62)	(0.96)	
	2.968		0.089			0.178	0.073	0.331
	(5.90)*		(1.74)*			(3.46)*	(0.81)	
	2.815			0.160		0.114	0.113	0.397
	(6.97)*			(3.28)*		(2.14)*	(1.30)	
	2.823				0.169	0.113	0.112	0.420
	(7.21)*				(3.73)*	(2.26)*	(1.33)	
1965	3.263	0.100				0.126	0.118	0.303
	(7.83)*	(1.71)*				(2.12)*	(1.20)	
	3.312		0.058			0.167	0.107	0.288
	(7.08)*		(1.14)			(3.31)*	(1.08)	
	3.001			0.138		0.106	0.149	0.341
	(7.28)*			(2.74)*		(2.02)*	(1.55)	
	3.081				0.128	0.118	0.142	0.339
	(7.75)*				(2.69)*	(2.37)*	(1.48)	
1968	3.150	0·139				0.138	0.019	0.398
	(7.35)*	(2.43)*				(2.46)*	(0.22)	
	3.432		0.065			0.195	−0.014	0.363
	(7.36)*		(1.26)			(3.75)*	(−0.16)	
	2.855			0.164		0.139	0.045	0.441
	(6.83)*			(3.48)*		(3.03)*	(0.55)	
	2.861				0.175	0.140	0.036	0.461
	(7.31)*				(3.92)*	(3.24)*	(0.46)	

argument based on the fact that sales levels are heavily dependent on the extent to which the firm is vertically integrated and, therefore, are not always the best measure of the scale of operations. The implication of the argument is that the scale of operations, and not sales revenue, is what managers are intent on maximizing. Perhaps a better formulation of Baumol's thesis that avoids the problem of the degree of vertical integration would be to assume that the size variable in the management objective function was value added rather than sales. However, it would be impossible for us to look at the effect of value added on compensation because of the unavailability of data.

The significantly positive coefficient of general, selling and administrative expense in eleven out of the twelve runs is again in accordance with the neoclassical theory and is not predicted by the sales-maximization hypothesis. It is also consistent with organization theory and Williamson's model (1963) of the firm, but it should be noted that the 'pure' organization theory approach predicts that only the coefficient of this variable should be significant.* The 'pure' organization theory is, therefore, not consistent with the significantly positive coefficients of capital and sales. It can be concluded then that, at best, organization theory is only a partial explanation of the level of executive compensation.

* See equation 10 and the comment earlier in this section.

Finally, and perhaps most important, it should be noted from table 2 that profitability is not significant in any of the equations for any of the years, although its coefficient does tend to be larger, and the corresponding value of the t statistic closer to the critical value, in equations 18 and 19. Part of the reason for the latter phenomenon may be errors in the measurement of the capital input.* The analysis, therefore, confirms the results of those studies that found profits, or profitability, had no significant effect on compensation. One of the predictions of the neoclassical theory is therefore not confirmed by the regression results, and the evidence in table 2 would seem to fit in best with some managerial theory of the firm that emphasized the scale of operations and the size of the staff hierarchy among the objectives of management,† or alternatively with some mixed managerial-cum-organizational theory.

However, such a conclusion would be overhasty, as we shall now try to demonstrate. The rejection of the neoclassical theory on the basis of the insignificance of b_3 in equations 16 to 19 is only valid if the assumptions made in simplifying equations 4 and 8 are justified. The most important of them was that y is independent of the other variables on the right-hand side of equation 8, and can therefore be incorporated into the error term for the regression analysis. This assumption is implicitly made in the McGuire *et al.* and Lewellen and Huntsman articles when they pool all their data from different industries without testing to see if the procedure may lead to errors. As mentioned above, the work of Williamson suggests that some industry variables have marked effects on compensation, although Roberts could find no significant industry effects in his sample. Further, there are strong reasons for believing that industry affects the relationship between compensation and profitability. Firms in a given industry will tend to be faced with common factors in, for example, their demand and cost conditions. In these circumstances there is more reason to assume that the NMRPQM and the ANRPQM will be monotonically related than for firms drawn from heterogeneous industries. Empirical work shows that there are regular and systematic differences between the mean profitabilities of firms in different industries, and yet there may be no reason to suppose that at a given quality the NMRPQM should be lower in the less profitable industry.

Ideally, the desirable course is to group together firms with similar product lines and to fit separate regression lines to each group. The procedure eliminates some of the effects of elements of y on the compensation-profitability relationship. Unfortunately it was not feasible on the basis of the present sample because of the wide range of industries involved and the small number of firms in each. Nor was it feasible, for the same reason, to allow slope or intercept dummy variables into the equations to catch product group effects. To test whether pooling of firms was justified, therefore, only a partial disaggregation of the sample was made. Firms were classified as either producers of consumer goods or of capital goods. A firm was assigned to the former category if over 50 per cent of its sales were accounted for by

---

* If there are errors in the measurement of capital it can be shown that the estimator of b_3 in equations 18 and 19 tends to be asymptotically biased upwards when $b_1 > b_3$. A proof is available on request.

† The latter is included in the objective function in Williamson's theory.

consumer goods, and to the latter category otherwise. The breakdown of sales into these two items was made on the basis of product line descriptions obtained mainly from Moodies Manual of Investments. The following equation was then fitted to the data:

$$\log s = b_0 + b_1 D + b_2 \log W + b_3 \log A + b_4 \log p + b_5 D \log W$$
$$+ b_6 D \log A + b_7 D \log p + \epsilon \qquad (20)$$

where W is a measure of the scale of operations of the firm* and D is a dummy variable taking the value 1 for firms in consumer goods industries and the value 0 for the others. In fact four variants of equation 20 were tried, W being defined as sales revenue, labour force, total assets and invested capital in turn. The comparative performance of the four scale variables, measured by R^2, was much the same as for equations 16 to 19 except that the relative superiority of the capital variables over the others was enhanced. The results are, therefore, quoted only for the cases in which sales and invested capital were used as the scale variable. They are shown in table 3. Although only one of the extra variables in one of the years (b_5 in 1965) is significantly different from zero, their introduction changes the results in quite a marked way. Using an F test, the hypothesis that $b_1 = b_5 = b_6 = b_7 = 0$ is rejected, even at the 1 per cent level of significance, in every case. Therefore, as a set, the dummy variables add significantly to the explanatory power of the equations, a fact also reflected in the large increase of the coefficient of determination. The reason the individual coefficients do not turn out to be significant would appear to lie in the high collinearity of the terms containing D in equation 20. The collinearity is demonstrated in table 4 which shows the correlation matrices between these variables for the case where invested capital is the scale variable. As confirmation of the conjecture the equations have been run again omitting $D \log W$, $D \log A$ and $D \log p$. The results are shown in table 5. The coefficient of D is then significantly positive in every equation and comparison of the coefficients of determination with those of tables 2 and 3 shows that most of the increase in them can be accounted for by the introduction of the one variable.

Returning now to table 3 we may note several points. First, the superiority of capital over sales as the scale variable, in terms of the explanatory power of the equation, has been considerably enhanced, providing further evidence against the sales-maximization hypothesis. Second, the coefficient of the scale variable has been increased whereas the coefficient of general, selling and administrative expense has been reduced, and, with one exception, has become insignificant. Indeed, in three of the equations, increases in the latter have a negative effect on compensation for consumer goods firms. This is contradictory to both the neoclassical and organization theories.

However, the results below suggest that the finding may be due to an incorrect specification of the equation through insufficient disaggregation. Third, the coefficient and associated t value of $\log p$ have tended to be increased by the disaggregation, but the sign of the coefficient of $D \log p$ is always negative and in three cases the absolute value of the latter is greater than that of the

* It should be remembered in what follows that the validity of the significance tests on the coefficients depends on the assumption of homogeneity of the variance of the error term between the two classes of firm.

Table 3. Estimates of the coefficients of equation 20. Interpretation and sample sizes are the same as in table 2

Year	Scale variable	b_0	b_1	b_2	b_3	Estimate of b_4	b_5	b_6	b_7	R^2
1963	R	3.060 (5.68)*	−0.156 (−0.18)	0.197 (2.14)*	0.038 (0.47)	0.050 (0.42)	0.045 (0.35)	0.002 (0.01)	−0.011 (−0.06)	0.441
	IK	2.936 (5.22)*	0.190 (0.25)	0.235 (3.76)*	0.036 (0.62)	0.146 (1.34)	0.048 (0.49)	0.015 (0.14)	−0.175 (−1.10)	0.540
1965	R	2.811 (4.39)*	1.006 (1.11)	0.144 (1.52)	0.096 (1.25)	0.202 (1.21)	0.060 (0.49)	−0.134 (−0.79)	−0.173 (−0.89)	0.364
	IK	2.788 (5.37)*	0.647 (0.81)	0.141 (2.22)*	0.106 (1.89)*	0.225 (1.81)*	0.189 (1.76)	−0.219 (−1.63)	−0.156 (−0.85)	0.452
1968	R	2.145 (4.19)*	1.172 (1.29)	0.275 (3.11)*	0.025 (0.37)	0.104 (0.78)	−0.140 (−1.11)	0.110 (0.73)	−0.181 (−1.07)	0.489
	IK	2.483 (5.52)*	0.650 (0.84)	0.236 (4.16)*	0.077 (1.66)	0.129 (1.10)	0.095 (1.00)	−0.100 (−0.90)	−0.159 (−1.08)	0.607

Table 4. Correlation matrices

1963	D	Dlog(IK)	Dlog A	1965	D	Dlog(IK)	Dlog A
Dlog IK	0.988			Dlog IK	0.989		
Dlog A	0.992	0.994		Dlog A	0.992	0.995	
Dlog p	0.973	0.963	0.967	Dlog p	0.975	0.969	0.967

1968	D	Dlog(IK)	Dlog A
Dlog IK	0.990		
Dlog A	0.994	0.995	
Dlog p	0.963	0.942	0.952

Table 5. Estimates of the coefficients of equation 20 with $Dlog\,W$, $Dlog\,A$ and $Dlog\,p$ omitted

Year	Scale variable	b_0	b_1	Estimate of b_2	b_3	b_4	R^2
1963	R	2.871 (7.53)*	0.250 (2.94)*	0.229 (3.78)*	0.025 (0.37)	0.042 (0.05)	0.438
	IK	2.604 (7.22)*	0.305 (3.98)*	0.253 (5.43)*	0.042 (0.86)	0.068 (0.88)	0.527
1965	R	3.091 (7.18)*	0.189 (2.24)*	0.154 (2.49)*	0.078 (1.25)	0.104 (1.10)	0.347
	IK	2.830 (7.32)*	0.251 (3.04)*	0.196 (3.90)*	0.063 (1.23)	0.135 (1.49)	0.413
1968	R	2.940 (7.20)*	0.240 (3.24)*	0.208 (3.59)*	0.725 (1.29)	0.007 (0.09)	0.473
	IK	2.519 (7.19)*	0.326 (4.83)*	0.268 (6.14)*	0.067 (1.63)	0.020 (0.30)	0.592

former. Thus, the effect of profitability on compensation is quite different in the two groups of industries.* In consumer goods there appears to be no relation between the two, whereas in capital goods there is a positive association although it is only significant in one run.

The above conclusions indicate that separate regressions should be run on the two groups of industries and that the estimates of table 2 are unreliable. However, fitting two separate equations would be open to the same objections as the pooling of data from all industries, for each of the two broad categories of firms includes a diverse range of industries each with its own demand and cost conditions, market structure, etc. Such a procedure would only be justified if it were first shown that the coefficients of the equations (and also, to be completely correct, the variance of the error term) were not significantly different, by using, for example, the analysis of covariance.†

* Since the coefficient of $D\log p$ was always insignificant, these differences cannot be said to be significant. However, this was probably due to the collinearity problem outlined earlier. To avoid it separate equations could be run for the two industry groups but this has not been done for the reason given in the text.

† The results below indicate that pooling would not be justified in one case.

The purpose of the partial disaggregation gone through above is simply to cast doubt on the conclusions of studies based upon the pooling of data from all industries. It is desirable, then, to fit separate equations to each industry group but, as mentioned before, the sample is seriously deficient for this purpose. There are, however, some industry groups which contain larger numbers of firms, so it was decided to take a subsample of firms which belonged to product groups containing five or more members and use it to test for industry differences in the compensation equation. The criterion produced a sample of 31 firms which belonged to one of the following broad industry groupings: non-ferrous metals, tyres and rubber, oil, steel and chemicals.* Data were available for 27 of the 31 in 1963, 28 in 1965 and 28 in 1968. There are obvious dangers in generalizing from such a small sample in such a restricted range of industries and the results obtained should, therefore, be considered indicative, rather than conclusive, where they concern the validity of the various alternative hypotheses.

The following two equations were fitted to the data for each of the three years:

$$\log s = b_0 + b_1 \log W + b_2 \log A + b_3 \log p + \epsilon \qquad (21)$$

$$\log s = b_0 + b_1 D_1 + b_2 D_2 + b_3 D_3 + b_4 D_4 + b_5 \log W + b_6 \log A$$
$$+ b_7 \log p + \epsilon \qquad (22)$$

As before, W is first defined as sales and then as invested capital. It was necessary to use only shift dummy variables because of the small size of the sample. With more observations in each industry it would have been possible to follow the better course of performing an analysis of covariance. The dummy variables are defined as:

D_1 = 1 for all firms in the oil industry and = 0 for all other firms,
D_2 = 1 for all firms in the steel industry and = 0 for all other firms,
D_3 = 1 for all firms in the tyre industry and = 0 for all other firms,
D_4 = 1 for all firms in the chemical industry and = 0 for all other firms.

The results for equation 21 are shown in table 6. They can be compared with those for the same equations (equations 16 and 19) fitted to the full sample as shown in table 2. The major differences are that, in the subsample, general, selling and administrative expense is never significant, profitability becomes significant in 1965 and the coefficient of determination is much higher in every year.

The results for equation 22 are shown in table 7. The introduction of the industry dummy variables changes the coefficients quite radically. With one exception, at least two of the dummies are significantly different from zero and general, selling and administrative expense is significantly positive in every year. The coefficient of determination rises quite sharply but the most interesting change is that profitability becomes highly significant in 1963 and 1965. Indeed in 1963 it is the variable with the largest coefficient and t value and a doubling of profitability is associated with an increase of over 70 per cent in compensation. Only in 1968, which is also the year the equation gives the poorest fit to the data, is profitably insignificant, although it is

---

* Note that all the firms included in the subsample are from the capital goods sector.

Table 6. Estimates of the coefficients of equation 21 using only firms in the subsample.

Year	Scale variable	b_0	Estimate of b_1	b_2	b_3	R^2
1963	R	1.999	0.333 (2.51)*	−0.023 (−0.23)	0.166 (0.92)	0.438
	IK	2.547	0.244 (2.75)*	0.026 (0.32)	0.177 (0.99)	0.461
1965	R	2.618	0.195 (1.94)*	0.040 (0.58)	0.268 (1.95)*	0.485
	IK	2.875	0.156 (2.42)*	0.060 (1.12)	0.284 (2.14)*	0.521
1968	R	2.185	0.320 (2.95)*	0.000 (0.00)	0.116 (0.70)	0.536
	IK	2.963	0.210 (3.03)*	0.078 (1.49)	0.030 (0.18)	0.544

interesting to note that even here the magnitude of the coefficient is not much smaller than that of the coefficients of the scale variables. Thus a doubling of profitability has, on the average, about the same effect as a doubling of the invested capital of the firm. Again the use of invested capital in the equation gives a better fit in each year than the use of sales, but the differences are not great.

At this stage it is necessary to repeat the warning that not too much reliance should be placed upon the results from such a restricted sample. Their importance lies in the implication that the neoclassical theory might give quite good predictions when industry variables are taken into account. Further work based on larger samples is obviously needed to enable separate equations to be fitted to the data for each industry.

IV. THE SPECIFICATION OF THE COMPENSATION EQUATION

It has been mentioned above that there are theoretical and empirical reasons for believing that the correct specification of the equation relating compensation to the independent variables is one which allows for a curvilinear relationship. When a loglinear equation was fitted to the pooled data, profitability turned out to be insignificant, thus reinforcing the findings of the work prior to that of Lewellen and Huntsman. Lewellen and Huntsman, however, found profitability had a highly significant effect on compensation, and it is of interest to examine why their results differ so much from our own and from those of earlier studies. There are three possible reasons for the difference:

Table 7. Estimates of the coefficients of equation 22 using only firms in the subsample

Year	Scale variable	b_0	b_1	b_2	b_3	Estimate of b_4	b_5	b_6	b_7	R^2
1963	R	2.124	−0.185 (−0.87)	0.748 (3.71)*	−0.262 (−1.76)	−0.400 (−2.56)*	−0.019 (−0.14)	0.260 (2.88)*	0.736 (4.24)	0.776
	IK	1.469	−0.284 (−1.41)	0.651 (3.88)*	−0.190 (−1.20)	−0.392 (−2.58)*	0.107 (1.07)	0.196 (2.41)*	0.726 (4.46)*	0.789
1965	R	1.066	−0.632 (−3.34)*	−0.354 (−2.42)*	−0.452 (−3.21)*	−0.365 (−2.28)*	0.299 (2.50)*	0.144 (1.73)*	0.321 (2.21)*	0.695
	IK	0.950	−0.749 (−4.12)*	−0.358 (−2.79)*	−0.327 (−2.39)*	−0.420 (−2.90)*	0.284 (3.38)*	0.173 (2.70)*	0.399 (3.08)*	0.745
1968	R	1.111	−0.428 (−1.92)	−0.083 (−0.45)	−0.277 (−1.70)	−0.387 (−2.44)*	0.323 (2.19)*	0.133 (1.35)	0.240 (1.09)	0.649
	IK	1.257	−0.483 (−2.20)*	−0.023 (−0.14)	−0.126 (−0.77)	−0.363 (−2.40)*	0.271 (2.61)*	0.185 (2.43)*	0.259 (1.24)	0.674

1 It might be due to the different specification of the equation. It has already been argued that the linear specification used by Lewellen and Huntsman is incorrect.

2 It may be due to differences in the sample.

3 It may be due to differences in the compensation data. On this score more reliance can be placed on Lewellen's data than on that derived from *Business Week*.

The three possibilities will be considered in turn.

First note that the implication of the Lewellen and Huntsman results is that the underlying compensation equation is:

$$s = b_0 + b_1 P \qquad (23)$$

However, because of the multicollinearity problem in their original equation, which also contained sales as an independent variable, the actual equation fitted was 14. Now if equation 23 is the correct specification, division of both sides by total assets yields:

$$\frac{s}{K} = \frac{b_0}{K} + b_1 \frac{P}{K} \qquad (24)$$

Fitting both equations 23 and 24 to the full sample gave the results shown in table 8. Two points should be noted. First, if equation 23 is the correct

Table 8. Estimates of the coefficients of equations 23 and 24

Year	Constant	P	Coefficient of $1/K$	P/K	R^2
1963			193.1 (20.34)*	-4.73×10^{-5} (-0.17)	
	182.6 (21.90)*	3.76×10^{-4} (10.12)*			0.565
1965			228.1 (16.43)*	-2.60×10^{-4} (-0.85)	
	198.5 (20.62)*	2.93×10^{-4} (8.05)*			0.441
1968			205.8 (14.62)*	5.58×10^{-4} (2.35)*	
	232.8 (19.42)*	3.08×10^{-4} (7.11)*			0.379

specification then dividing through by total assets and fitting this second equation should have little effect on the estimates of the coefficients. The results, however, show the estimates of b_1 to be wildly different, probably due to the fact that division by K effectively removes any 'size of the firm' influences from the equation. Second, b_1 is only significantly positive in equation 24 for 1968 and is negative for the other two years. While the first point indicates specification error, the second can only be the result of data or sample differences since this coefficient in the Lewellen and Huntsman study was always significantly positive. To explore the problem further, 36 firms were taken from the Lewellen and Huntsman sample for which compensation data was available from *Business Week*. Equation 14 was then fitted to the data for this subsample and the results are shown in table 9. The coefficient of the profitability variable is highly significant in all three years, and if we compare the coefficients and their *t* values in table 9 with the results Lewellen and Huntsman obtained, using their full sample and their own data, for 1963 we find them to be very similar.* This suggests that it is the sample differences,and not the data differences, which are the cause of the variations of the results.† It can, therefore, be concluded that the sample, as well as the specification, has a very important effect on the estimates–another warning against relying too heavily on estimates derived from small samples.

CONCLUSIONS

The present paper is preliminary to a more extensive analysis of the problem in question using British data and a sample with larger numbers of observations in each industry group. Because of the sample deficiencies the conclusions to be drawn from it can only be considered tentative. They are still useful, however, in that they are directly comparable to those of the studies outlined in parts (b) to (d) of section II. The tentativeness of the conclusions may be salutary as previous writers have tended to claim too much for their results. For example, Lewellen and Huntsman claim that 'The evidence presented ... can be interpreted as support for the notion that a highly industrialized economy characterized by a diverse set of suppliers of capital, sizeable aggregations of productive resources and a professional managerial class can in large measure be analysed by models which are based on the assumption of profit-seeking behaviour.' McGuire *et al.* on the other hand claim that on the basis of their evidence 'Baumol's thesis is supported'.

What then can be said of the results of this paper? The firmest conclusion seems to be that Simon's organization theory is by itself not a complete explanation of the determination of executive compensation. If it were, only the coefficient of general, selling and administrative expense should have been significantly positive in the equations and it would be difficult to explain why capital, industry and perhaps profitability have significant effects on compensation. This is not to imply that organization theory has no role to play in the explanation of compensation but only that, at best, its role is a partial one.

The neoclassical theory comes out rather better. Although profitability

* The Lewellen and Huntsman equation for 1963, with compensation defined as basic salary plus bonus, was:

$$s/K = 155.3(1/K) + 6.78 \times 10^{-4}(P/K) - 15.6 \times 10^{-4}(R/K)$$
$$\quad\quad (9.24)* \quad\quad\quad (3.91)* \quad\quad\quad\quad (-1.08)$$

† Lewellen and Huntsman found that when they replaced their crude measure of compensation with a more sophisticated one there was no improvement in the fit of the equation to the data, which tends to reinforce the point.

is insignificant when all the data is pooled, and both profitability and general, selling and administrative expense are insignificant when the sample is split into consumer goods firms and capital goods firms, it has been argued that this is probably the result of insufficient disaggregation. When the regression line is allowed to shift its intercept from industry to industry, as in equation 22, the predictions of the theory as embodied in equation 8 were all verified in two of the three years, and only one of them failed to be correct in the third year. The sample was small, non-random and based on only five industries so it must be left to further research to see if the results hold more generally.

Table 9. Estimates of the coefficients of equation 14 for the subsample of 36 firms

Year	$1/K$	Coefficient of P/K	R/K
1963	146.4 (8.04)*	6.47×10^{-4} (3.67)*	-4.94×10^{-4} (-0.36)
1965	152.2 (7.75)*	6.14×10^{-4} (3.57)*	-7.50×10^{-4} (-0.54)
1968	170.0 (7.75)*	6.61×10^{-4} (3.88)*	7.85×10^{-5} (0.06)

The comments on the neoclassical theory are also relevant to the question of the validity of managerial theories of the firm. The results indicate that the lack of a significant relationship between compensation and profitability that has often been found may be the outcome of a specification error arising from a rather casual identification of differences in profits and profitability between firms with differences in the marginal productivity of their managers. If the findings from the five-industry subsample generalize, it would be necessary to conclude, if one believed the managerial theories to be correct, that either managers place a relatively high weight on profits in their preferences or that there is a relatively high incentive for them to seek higher profits. Both conclusions imply that the firm will be operating closer to the profit-maximization point than if there were only a slight or non-existent relationship between compensation and profitability. However, it does not necessarily mean that profit is being maximized, as Lewellen and Huntsman seem to suggest, since there can still be other arguments in the utility function as well as profits or compensation.

Finally, it can be concluded that sales revenue does not appear to be the major determinant of executive compensation, as has often been claimed. Capital input, when used in place of sales, gives a better fit to the data. However, Baumol's observation that the scale of operations of the firm is a major determinant of compensation is not thereby contradicted.

AN ECONOMETRIC STUDY OF PRICE-FIXING, MARKET STRUCTURE AND PERFORMANCE IN BRITISH INDUSTRY IN THE EARLY 1950s

by

*ALMARIN PHILLIPS**

I. INTRODUCTION

Empirical studies of the relations between industry profitability and various measures of industry structure have appeared in numbers in recent years. Following Bain's (1951) seminal work are more or less similar studies of United States manufacturing industries by Schwartzman (1959), Stigler (1963), Fuchs (1961), Weiss (1963), Hall and Weiss (1967), Collins and Preston (1968, 1969), Mann (1966, 1970, 1971), Miller (1967, 1969), Comanor and Wilson (1967), George (1968), Kilpatrick (1968), MacAvoy, McKie and Preston (1971) and Shepherd (1972). While criticisms of the conclusion that concentration ratios and the degree to which entry is barred are positively related to profit rates have been expressed by Brozen (1970, 1971) and Coase (1972), it is probably correct that most industrial economists feel that statistically significant—albeit small—relationships have been demonstrated.

Unpublished works by Long (1970) and Greenberg (1972) support this conclusion. Long finds that trade association activities, measured by the number of trade association employees per firm, are also positively related to profit rates. Greenberg concludes that the strongest relationship between price-cost margins and concentration occurs in industries in which the dispersion of firm size is relatively high and the number of firms is relatively small. Studies of commercial banking markets by Edwards (1964), Kaufman (1966), Phillips (1967) and Bell and Murphy (1969), among others, suggest that concentration is positively associated with the pricing of bank services, though Flechsig (1965) has argued that a regional rather than a concentration effect is being revealed.

Without disputing that concentration and entry barriers are related to the level of profits or prices, I have argued elsewhere (Phillips 1971) that the underlying model used by industrial economists represents a 'naive Cournot-like' approach to the subject. Industry performance is viewed as a simple and static function of industry structure and conduct, with both of the latter taken as essentially exogenous variables. Further, it is common to conceive of conduct as being uniquely related to structure, leaving only differences in structure as an explanation of differences in performance.

O. E. Williamson (1965) has developed a theoretical model in which the frequency of interfirm communications aimed at establishing collusive agreements among firms is related to profit levels and the rate of change in profits with respect to time. Thus, conduct is taken as a function of the state of demand and is partially endogenous to the system describing interrelations among performance, structure and conduct. Long's conclusions concerning trade association activities are based on an implicit hypothesis rejecting a unique relation between structure and conduct, but there is no suggestion that the latter is in any way endogenous to the system.

II. THE MODEL

This study is based on the view that, at any point in time, performance is

* I am indebted to Mrs Lesley Hancox for her help with the computational tasks and Mr Oliver Coles for his research assistance.

functionally related to structure and conduct, but that the latter tend to change over time in response to performance. While a partially endogenous system of interrelations over time is, in fact, envisioned, the model itself relates to but a single year due to data limitations.

Two dimensions of conduct are involved. One is a 'propensity to attempt price-fixing agreements'; the other, the 'effectiveness of price-fixing agreements' when such attempts are made. More specifically, the first aspect of the model assumes that:

$$\Pi = \Pi (CR, B, PD, D, EPF) \tag{1}$$

and

$$EPF = EPF (N, H, \Pi) \tag{2}$$

where Π is a measure of profitability, CR is a concentration measure, N is the number of firms, B measures the substantiality of entry barriers, PD is the degree of product differentiation, D is market demand, EPF is the effectiveness of price-fixing agreements and H is a measure of the 'homogeneity of values' among the firms in the industry.*

For industries comprised of profit-maximizing firms, it is anticipated that:

$$\partial\Pi/\partial CR > 0 \tag{1a}$$

$$\partial\Pi/\partial B > 0 \tag{1b}$$

$$\partial\Pi/\partial PD > 0 \tag{1c}$$

$$\partial\Pi/\partial D > 0 \tag{1d}$$

$$\partial\Pi/\partial EPF > 0 \tag{1e}$$

and

$$\partial EPF/\partial N < 0 \tag{2a}$$

$$\partial EPF/\partial H > 0 \tag{2b}$$

$$\partial EPF/\partial \Pi > 0 \tag{2c}$$

The anticipated relations of (1a), (1b), and (1d) require no explanation. That of (1c) asserts that product differentiation should tend to increase profits and is based on the elemental notion that the greater the product differentiation the lower the (positive) cross-demand elasticities among firms and the lower the (negative) subjective own-demand elasticities within each of the firms. Given the magnitude of market demand and production costs, product differentiation should lead to higher profit potentials.

The partial relationship of (1e) is virtually tautological. If firms prefer more profits to less† and if attempts are made to fix prices in order to achieve firm objectives, effective price-fixing should, in and of itself, tend to increase profits.

Relationship (2a) posits that attempts at price-fixing should be more effective when the number of firms is small. Stigler (1964) and Phillips

---

* The meaning of the term 'homogeneity of values' will become clearer as the discussion proceeds. See, however, Phillips (1961, 1962) for earlier treatment.

† Some of the empirical results below raise questions as to the truth of such an assumption.

(1962) provide the theoretical foundations for the expectation. The expectation of (2b) that greater 'homogeneity of values' gives rise to higher profits rests also on Phillips' arguments. If firms have similar cost and demand conditions, similar views on future industry growth, the level of entry-preventative prices, etc., and if there is little disparity in the relative importance of profits, sales growth and other managerial preferences in the objective functions which underlie the decisions of the several firms, agreements are easier to reach and to maintain than where such conditions do not exist.

O. E. Williamson (1965) and Phillips (1962) provide an explanation for (2c). When firms are realizing high profits, there is little temptation to 'break' from interfirm agreements. 'Rules of the game' tend to be adhered to, and 'cheating' on price is less frequent than when profits are low.

The second aspect of the model contains (1), as above. Ideally, its second equation would express the propensity to attempt price-fixing agreements in terms of structural variables, the level of profits, and the change in profits with respect to time. That is, attempts at price-fixing should arise from decreases in profits as much, if not more, than from just low levels of profits. Data limitations prevent the use of such a model, however, and the second equation of the second aspect is:

$$PPFA = PPFA\ (N, H, \Pi) \tag{3}$$

where *PPFA* is the propensity to attempt price-fixing agreements. Here the anticipated directional relationships are:

$$\partial PPFA/\partial N > 0 \tag{3a}$$

$$\partial PPFA/\partial H < 0 \tag{3b}$$

$$\partial PPFA/\partial \Pi > 0 \tag{3c}$$

The expectation of (3a) is that the existence of large numbers of firms tends to lead to attempts to fix prices, even though the same conditions make effective price-fixing more difficult. Similarly, from (3b), more attempts at price-fixing should occur when value systems are disparate than when they are homogeneous. Conflicting values lead to conflicting behaviour, rivalry and overt attempts to stifle the rivalry. Relationship (3c) attempts to capture the dependence of price-fixing attempts on profits. It omits, as noted above, the change in profits with respect to time, relying instead on the possibly incorrect assumption that low levels of profits at a given time are positively associated with current and recently past decreases in profits.

III. THE DATA

Price-Fixing

Data on the effectiveness of price-fixing and on attempts to fix prices came from a survey on industrial trade associations carried out by Political and Economic Planning (1959) in the years 1953–6. In one part of the survey 50 large firms and over 600 small firms were interviewed 'to find out what associations mean to them in their day-to-day conduct of business (p. xii).

Government departments, public corporations, local authorities and hospital groups were similarly interviewed.

Among the questions asked in the interviews were some relating to price-fixing. Particular associations were listed by those buying from its member firms according to whether or not a price-fixing agreement existed and, if so, according to whether it was 'effective' or 'less effective'. There was also a recording of whether the buyers could or could not obtain the same goods at prices set ostensibly independently by non-member producers. Some 1300 associations of manufacturers, classified by Census of Production industry groups, were covered.

The PEP report shows only aggregate data, for rather obvious reasons. Excluding Order V, metal manufacture, many of the products of which were subject to price-setting by the Iron and Steel Board, 58 Minimum List Heading industries were found to have associations with price agreements. Within these industries, 122 products were found to be subject to 'effective' agreements, and 105 other products to 'less effective' agreements. Overall, 243 of the 1300 associations were reported as attempting to fix prices (pp. 161–2). Because of the limited sample of buyers and because some of the sampled buyers might have been unaware of price-fixing, PEP concluded that their finding on the extent of price-fixing 'errs if anything on the conservative side' (p. 163).

The worksheets underlying the PEP aggregates were examined and the data were reassembled by individual industry. Trade associations were further classified into industry-wide associations, on the one hand, and associations representing sub-product classes or particular geographic areas, on the other. The result was a list of trade associations, industry-wide and other, by SIC Minimum List Heading industries, with each association identified as 'effective', 'less effective' and 'unreported'. The latter might in fact be a price-fixing association which was not so reported by buyers.

PPFA was defined simply as the number of trade associations reported as attempting to fix prices in a given industry, regardless of whether it was 'effective'. *EPF* was defined in a more complicated—and a more subjective—way. Industry-wide associations with 'effective' agreements were assigned a weight of 300; with 'less effective' agreements, a weight of 150. Sub-industry associations were given a weight of 100 for 'effective' agreements and of 50 for 'less effective'. The sum of these weights for each industry was then divided by the number of associations in the industry to yield the *EPF* variable. Thus, industry-wide price-fixing is given triple weight relative to sub-industry price-fixing, and 'effective' agreement is given double weight relative to 'less effective'. *PPFA* and *EPF* had non-zero values for 27 of the industries for which structural data were available. The concentration ratio for one of these was based on the largest five firms rather than the largest three firms.

Concentration and Number of Firms

Three-firm concentration ratios (*CR*) for 1951 were taken from Evely and Little (1960). The number of firms (*N*) are those reported by Evely and Little, and are directly from the 1951 Census of Production. There were 71 industries for which these data were available, including 26 of the 27 industries for which *PPFA* and *EPF* could be determined. The remaining industry was the one for which a three-firm concentration ratio was lacking.

Barriers to Entry and Product Differentiation

Two variables were chosen as measures of barriers to entry. The first was average plant size for 1951 (*APS*), computed by Evely and Little as the number of employees (in thousands) divided by the number of plants in the industry. On the assumption of a positive relation between *APS* and the minimum efficient size of plant, *APS* was introduced as a proxy for the minimum efficient size.

The second measure of entry barriers was the ratio of advertising and market research expenditures to sales (*A/S*) for each industry. These are reported in Summary Tables 6 and 7 of the 1951 Census of Production, but the data pertain to 1948. Comanor and Wilson (1967) and Miller (1969) use the advertising–sales ratio in their studies of US manufacturing industries, arguing that because of brand loyalties and the cumulative effects of past advertising, new firms require high initial working capital and incur high advertising costs to enter an industry with intensive advertising programmes. Alternatively, *A/S* could be viewed as a measure of the degree of product differentiation among the firms in an industry.

Demand

The demand variable (*GO*) used was gross output in 1954 less gross output in 1948, divided by gross output in 1948.

Homogeneity of Values

Trade associations, it is assumed, arise in industry not solely to provide 'merriment and diversion', but also as an organisational response to problems found to be common among a number of firms. An industry with but a single association suggests that the firms have found one organization effective in dealing with their common problems. Where several independent associations exist, there is evidence that different groups of firms have found that special organizations are more effective in dealing with their own special problems. In this sense, the number of trade associations in an industry (*TA*) can be used as an indicator of homogeneity. The greater the number of associations, the more separable—that is, the less homogeneous—are the values of the included firms.*

Producer Goods and Consumer Goods Industries

From the product descriptions of the Census of Production industry classes,

* The ratio of the average size of the three largest firms to the average size of all other firms and the ratio of value added/gross output for the three largest firms to value added/gross output for all other firms were also tried as homogeneity measures. The latter was conceived of as a measure of differences in the degree of vertical integration. Neither proved to have explanatory value.

each industry was classified as a producer good or consumer good industry. The variable (*PRO-CON*) was introduced as a dummy, with producer goods assigned a value of one and consumer goods a value of zero.

Profitability

Census of Production data do not include rates of return on assets or stock holder equity. Following Collins and Preston (1968, 1969) the price-cost margin (Π) is used alternatively. Conceptually, Π is the ratio of profits to sales. Viewed on a unit basis, and with the assumptions that it is long-run costs that are reported, that long-run marginal costs are constant and that firms profit maximize, Π can be viewed as the Lerner measure of monopoly power.

Census data, however, do not permit computation of a pure profit to sales ratio. The data for Π are computed as valued added less wages and salaries divided by gross output. Accordingly, the ratio is actually that of the sum of profits, rents, interest, depreciation, non-wage advertising costs and other miscellaneous costs to gross output. Collins and Preston report significant simple correlation between the price-cost margin and rates of return for the industries in their study for which both were available. As used here, Π is an average of the price-cost margins for 1948, 1951 and 1954.

IV. EMPIRICAL RESULTS

Table 1 gives OLS results for the 26 industries for which both structural data are available and price-fixing was reported. There is some indication of positive concentration and advertising effects and of a negative concentration-advertising interaction effect. If anything, effective price-fixing has a positive effect on the price-cost margin. None of the $\bar{R}^2$ values is significant at the 5 per cent level, however. The number of variables is large relative to the number of observations and, as shown in table 6, substantial multicollinearity exists among *CR*, CR^2, *A/S*, and *CR·A/S*.

In table 2, results are given for 71 industries, with the actual *EPF* and *PPFA* values for each industry. That is, *EPF* and *PPFA* have zero values for the 45 industries for which PEP respondents did not report any price-fixing. Here all the $\bar{R}^2$ values, while not high, are significant.

The *CR* and *A/S* effects are consistently positive, as expected. The *APS* effect is negative and significant, indicating that the partial effect of plant size is contrary to that anticipated. Similarly, while none of the coefficients is significant at the 10 per cent level, the concentration–advertising interaction term is again consistently negative. So, too, is the coefficient of the *GO* term. The *EPF* variable—expressed as a natural number rather than in the log form because of the 45 zero values—has a positive sign, though the effect is not significant by the usual criterion. The producer good/consumer good dichotomy produces a hint of higher margins among the producer goods industries.

The *EPS* and *PPFA* variables undoubtedly suffer from reporting error. In particular, it is not clear that associations for which no price-fixing was

Table 1. OLS regressions of the price-cost margin on structural and price-fixing variables—26 industries (figures in parentheses are t statistics)

Regression	Constant	CR	CR^2	APS	A/S	CR·A/S	GO	EPF	ln EPF	PPFA	PRO-CON	$\bar{R}^2$
1	0.098	+0.0011 (1.93)	+0.00000 (0.34)	-0.0174 (0.20)	+15.95 (1.99)	-0.2629 (2.13)	+0.0065 (0.16)	+0.0002 (0.84)	—	—	—	0.002
2	0.048	+0.0010 (0.47)	+0.00000 (0.36)	-0.0388 (0.46)	+16.63 (2.20)	-0.2628 (2.26)	+0.0035 (0.09)	—	+0.0186 (1.57)	—	—	0.009
3	0.096	+0.0011 (0.51)	+0.00000 (0.32)	-0.0380 (0.40)	+17.24 (2.14)	-0.2842 (2.31)	+0.0109 (0.27)	—	—	-0.0004 (0.07)	—	-0.004
4	0.089	+0.0018 (2.23)	—	-0.0246 (0.30)	+15.88 (2.03)	-0.2608 (2.17)	+0.0051 (0.13)	+0.0002 (0.85)	—	—	—	0.048
5	0.040	+0.0016 (2.16)	—	-0.0469 (0.58)	+16.54 (2.24)	-0.2606 (2.20)	+0.0020 (0.05)	—	+0.0185 (1.61)	—	—	0.130
6	0.089	+0.0018 (2.23)	—	-0.0111 (0.14)	+17.14 (2.18)	-0.2822 (2.35)	+0.0094 (0.23)	—	—	-0.0001 (0.02)	—	0.012
7	0.083	+0.0017 (2.10)	—	-0.0177 (0.21)	+17.26 (2.17)	-0.2661 (2.21)	-0.0060 (0.15)	+0.0001 (0.49)	—	—	+0.0253 (1.00)	0.048
8	0.040	+0.0016 (2.04)	—	-0.0406 (0.51)	+17.44 (2.35)	-0.2599 (2.30)	-0.0091 (0.23)	—	+0.0165 (1.41)	—	+0.0238 (1.03)	0.132
9	0.086	+0.0017 (2.11)	—	-0.0116 (0.14)	+18.18 (2.34)	-0.2798 (2.37)	-0.0072 (0.17)	—	—	-0.0016 (0.29)	+0.0311 (1.25)	0.040

Table 2. OLS regressions of the price-cost margin on structural and price-fixing variables—71 industries with actual price-fixing data (figures in parentheses are t statistics)

Regression	Constant	CR	CR^2	APS	A/S	$CR \cdot A/S$	GO	EPF	PPFA	PRO-CON	$\bar{R}^2$
1	0.137	+0.0021 (1.67)†	−0.00001 (0.99)	−0.1015 (2.06)†	+5.180 (2.58)	−0.0683 (1.42)	−0.0094 (1.17)	+0.0002 (1.43)	—	—	0.259
2	0.137	+0.0022 (1.73)†	−0.00001 (1.07)	−0.0925 (1.86)†	+5.188 (2.54)	−0.0697 (1.43)	−0.0092 (1.23)	—	+0.0018 (0.43)	—	0.237
3	0.131	+0.0021 (1.69)†	−0.00001 (0.93)	−0.1126 (2.22)†	+5.481 (2.69)*	−0.0727 (1.50)	−0.0102 (1.26)	+0.0002 (1.17)	—	+0.0146 (0.95)	0.258
4	0.130	+0.0022 (1.76)†	−0.00001 (1.01)	−0.1075 (2.10)†	+5.545 (2.69)*	−0.0750 (1.53)	−0.0109 (1.34)	—	+0.0008 (0.18)	+0.0181 (1.17)	0.242
5	0.147	+0.0010 (2.22)†	—	−0.1127 (2.22)†	+5.609 (2.76)*	−0.0730 (1.51)	−0.0118 (1.50)	+0.0002 (1.27)	—	0.0155 (1.01)	0.260
6	0.147	−0.0010 (2.13)†	—	−0.1063 (2.05)†	+5.669 (2.73)*	−0.0744 (1.50)	−0.0126 (1.57)	—	+0.0013 (0.30)	+0.0191 (1.23)	0.240

* Significant at the 1 per cent level
† Significant at the 5 per cent level
‡ Significant at the 10 per cent level

reported did not, in fact, attempt to fix prices but remained unreported because of either bias in the sample of buyers from whom the reports were obtained or the buyers' lack of awareness of price-fixing.

Table 3 gives OLS estimates of EPF and $PPFA$ based on variables from the underlying model. Price-fixing appears more effective where the number of trade associations is small. In the sense used here, price-fixing is more effective, that is, where little heterogeneity in values exists. The effect of number of firms has the expected sign, but is not significant. In the OLS form, no relationship between price-cost margins and EPF appeared.

Table 3. OLS estimates of price-fixing variables (figures in parentheses are t statistics).

	Price-fixing variable	Constant	N	$\ln N$	TA	$\ln TA$	$\bar{R}^2$
1	$\ln \hat{EPF}$	5.410	—	−0.083 (0.64)	—	−0.782 (3.13)*	0.29
2	$PP\hat{F}A$	−0.323	−0.001 (1.63)	—	+0.374 (5.62)*	—	0.52

* Significant at the 1 per cent level.

The $PPFA$ variable, as anticipated, is larger where the number of trade associations is large. Heterogeneity in values leads to frequent attempts to fix prices, but makes effective price-fixing more difficult. The effect of the number of firms has the opposite sign from that expected, but again is not significant.

The regressions of table 4 utilize the estimated EPF and $PPFA$ values. The CR, APS and A/S effects are much as those of table 2, with plant size still showing a negative association with the margins. The $CR \cdot A/S$. interaction term has the negative coefficient previously found, but its significance is greater when the estimated price-fixing data is employed. Both the GO and $PRO-CON$ variables have greater significance and indicate that lower rates of output growth and the producer goods classification are associated with higher margins. The CR^2 term has a consistently negative coefficient when it is included, but the t statistic is relatively small, probably because of the high correlation between CR and CR^2.

Use of the estimated values for EPF and $PPFA$ alters the role of these variables in the regressions. Effective price-fixing tends to raise the price-cost margins, while price-fixing attempts seem more numerous when margins are low. In both cases, these are the anticipated results.

Because the price-cost margins (Π) and EPF and $PPFA$ are interdependent, the OLS regressions are not properly indentified. In terms of the model, two-stage least squares is the preferred estimating method. But TSLS estimates had to be restricted to the 26 industries for which price-fixing was reported, placing a great burden on that small number of observations, particularly because of the multicollinearity among the variables.

Table 5 gives the TSLS results. The CR^2 term has been omitted to alleviate the multicollinearity problem and because of the small and probably insignificant effects shown in the OLS regressions. Still, the estimated

Table 4. OLS regressions of the price-cost margin on structural and price-fixing variables—71 industries with estimated price-fixing data (figures in parentheses are t statistics)

Regression	Constant	CR	CR^2	APS	A/S	$CR \cdot A/S$	GO	$\ln E\hat{P}F$	$PP\hat{F}A$	$PRO \cdot CON$	$\bar{R}^2$
1	0.080	+0.0021 (1.70)‡	−0.00001 (1.09)	−0.0978 (2.00)‡	+5.328 (2.65)†	−0.0750 (1.55)	−0.0111 (1.39)	+0.0170 (1.45)	—	—	0.260
2	0.152	+0.0026 (2.10)†	−0.00002 (1.41)	−0.1028 (2.12)†	+5.358 (2.70)*	−0.0784 (1.64)	−0.0108 (1.37)	—	−0.0094 (1.98)‡	—	0.280
3	0.096	+0.0009 (1.88)‡	—	−0.0965 (1.97)‡	+5.462 (2.71)*	−0.0753 (1.56)	−0.0131 (1.68)‡	+0.0175 (1.50)	—	—	0.253
4	0.175	+0.0010 (2.14)†	—	−0.0998 (2.05)‡	+5.502 (2.75)*	−0.0777 (1.62)	−0.0132 (1.70)‡	—	−0.0086 (1.81)‡	—	0.269
5	0.060	+0.0021 (1.69)‡	−0.00001 (0.96)	−0.1190 (2.36)†	+5.836 (2.89)*	−0.0826 (1.72)‡	−0.0124 (1.55)	+0.0199 (1.70)‡	—	+0.0228 (1.53)	0.275
6	0.143	+0.0026 (2.16)‡	−0.00002 (1.33)	−0.1267 (2.54)‡	+5.918 (2.98)*	−0.0871 (1.84)‡	−0.0121 (1.55)	—	−0.0109 (2.30)†	+0.0251 (1.70)‡	0.301
7	0.073	+0.0024 (2.16)†	—	−0.1190 (2.36)†	+5.981 (2.97)*	−0.0832 (1.73)‡	−0.0141 (1.82)‡	+0.0205 (1.76)‡	—	0.0241 (1.62)	0.276
8	0.164	+0.0011 (2.49)†	—	−0.1250 (2.50)†	+6.076 (3.05)*	−0.0869 (1.83)‡	−0.0144 (1.87)‡	—	−0.0102 (2.15)†	+0.0263 (1.77)‡	0.293

* Significant at the 1 per cent level
† Significant at the 5 per cent level
‡ Significant at the 10 per cent level

Table 5. TSLS regressions of price-cost margins and structural and price-fixing variables (figures in parentheses are standard errors)

Regression	Dependent variable	Constant	CR	N	TA	APS	A/S	CR·A/S	GO	PRO-CON	ln EPF	PPFA	Π
1a	$\hat{\Pi}$	−0.0228 (0.1052)	+0.0014 (0.0009)	—	—	−0.0900 (0.1071)	+15.79 (8.21)	−0.2329 (0.1310)	−0.0072 (0.0435)	—	+0.0421 (0.0354)	—	—
1b	ln $\hat{EPF}$	+3.458 (1.192)	—	−0.0002 (0.0004)	−0.0684 (0.0471)	—	—	—	—	—	—	—	+3.704 (5.642)
2a	$\hat{\Pi}$	+0.1152 (0.0525)	+0.0019 (0.0009)	—	—	−0.0252 (0.0884)	+16.86 (8.46)	−0.2905 (0.1293)	−0.0044 (0.0431)	—	—	−0.0092 (0.0074)	—
2b	$P\hat{P}FA$	−0.0903 (1.9044)	—	−0.0009 (0.0006)	+0.3699 (0.0753)	—	—	—	—	—	—	—	−0.8784 (9.0155)
3a	$\hat{\Pi}$	−0.0337 (0.1047)	+0.0014 (0.0009)	—	—	−0.0941 (0.1109)	+16.20 (8.66)	−0.2279 (0.1356)	−0.0155 (0.0457)	+0.0144 (0.0289)	+0.0448 (0.0358)	—	—
3b	ln $\hat{EPF}$	+3.198 (1.109)	—	−0.0002 (0.0004)	−0.0644 (0.0464)	—	—	—	—	+0.4725 (0.4211)	—	—	+4.995 (5.121)
3c	ln $\hat{EPF}$	+3.582 (1.147)	—	−0.0000 (0.0004)	−0.0800 (0.0486)	—	—	—	—	—	—	—	—
4a	$\hat{\Pi}$	+0.1064 (0.0507)	+0.0018 (0.0008)	—	—	−0.0233 (0.0857)	+18.26 (8.25)	−0.2859 (0.1255)	−0.0162 (0.0443)	+0.0405 (0.0269)	—	−0.0097 (0.0073)	—
4b	$P\hat{P}FA$	−1.1113 (1.6631)	—	−0.0010 (0.0006)	+0.3859 (0.0707)	—	—	—	—	—	—	—	+4.1929 (7.7991)
4c	$P\hat{P}FA$	−0.4302 (1.7995)	—	−0.0008 (0.0006)	+0.3582 (0.0762)	—	—	—	—	+0.8383 (0.6605)	—	—	−1.3010 (9.1443)

standard errors in table 5 are inflated because of multicollinearity. In summary, the CR and APS effects found in the OLS regressions reappear in the TSLS estimates. The A/S effect shows the same positive sign, but is roughly three times as large. The $CR \cdot A/S$ interaction term, on the other hand, remains negative in its effect and is also roughly three times as large. By themselves, concentration and advertising intensity tend to be positively related to price-cost margins, but when they are combined so that their joint value is large, they are associated with lower margins.

The TSLS regressions show the negative relation between output growth and margins and provide limited evidence that the producer good industries have higher margins than do the consumer goods industries.

Effective price-fixing, which tends to occur where the number of trade associations, and, perhaps, the number of firms are small, has a positive effect on the margins. Effectiveness may also vary positively with the margins. Attempts at price-fixing occur more often when there are a large number of associations, a small number of firms and, if anything, when margins tend to be low. Except for the number-of-firms effect on attempts at price-fixing, these are all the anticipated results. The TSLS regressions also show more effective price-fixing and more attempts at price-fixing among the producer goods industries, but this could well be the results of the PEP sample of buyers, which was limited to firms and excluded consumers.

V. EVALUATION

The predictions of the model with respect to the propensity of firms to enter price-fixing agreements and the effectiveness of price-fixing agreements are generally borne out. Yet the statistical results must be taken with caution. Neither the EPF nor the $PPFA$ variable is defined in an ideal way, and multi-collinearity makes meaningful statistical tests of significance quite difficult. The most that can be said in support of the results is that they are fairly consistent when different variables were entered in the regressions, when EPF and $PPFA$ were extended by estimation to industries for which data were lacking, and when either OLS or TSLS methods of estimation were used. Further efforts to find relations between conduct variables and industry performance are obviously warranted—and obviously difficult for want of data on conduct.

Aside from the price-fixing relationships, the signs of the $APS, CR \cdot A/S$, $GO, PRO\text{-}CON$ and though its significance is questionable, the CR^2 coefficients capture special interest. These are not consistent with the expectations of the model nor with the results of studies of United States industries.

The CR^2 and $CR \cdot A/S$ terms were introduced because previous studies, especially those of Bain (1951), Mann (1966, 1971) and Comanor and Wilson (1967), suggest a compounding effect on profitability when both concentration and entry barriers are high. For the industries covered here, the reverse effect is observed. If, based loosely on the regressions of table 4, the CR coefficient is taken to be $+0.002$, the CR^2 coefficient is -0.000015, the A/S coefficient is $+5.5$, and the $CR \cdot A/S$ coefficient is -0.08, on average the partial effect of increases in concentration on price-cost margins becomes

Table 6. Matrix of simple correlation coefficients

	CR	CR²	N*	TA*	APS	A/S	GO	CR·A S	ln EPF*	PPFA*	Π	ln ÊPF	PP̂FA
CR	+1.00	—	—	—	—	—	—	—	—	—	—	—	—
CR²	+0.97	+1.00	—	—	—	—	—	—	—	—	—	—	—
N*	−0.53	−0.41	+1.00	—	—	—	—	—	—	—	—	—	—
TA*	−0.29	−0.29	+0.38	1.00	—	—	—	—	—	—	—	—	—
APS	+0.45	+0.44	−0.33	−0.34	+1.00	—	—	—	—	—	—	—	—
A/S	+0.09	+0.04	−0.03	−0.10	−0.13	+1.00	—	—	—	—	—	—	—
GO	+0.41	+0.45	−0.19	−0.02	+0.30	−0.03	+1.00	—	—	—	—	—	—
CR·A S	+0.32	+0.26	−0.19	−0.21	+0.06	+0.93	+0.03	+1.00	—	—	—	—	—
ln EPF*	+0.19	+0.15	−0.21	−0.40	+0.36	−0.20	+0.11	−0.13	+1.00	—	—	—	—
PPFA*	−0.01	−0.05	+0.07	+0.72	−0.04	−0.13	−0.05	−0.12	−0.07	+1.00	—	—	—
Π	+0.07	+0.01	+0.06	−0.19	−0.22	+0.48	−0.16	+0.42	+0.10	+0.01	+1.00	—	—
ln EPF	+0.32	+0.30	—	—	+0.21	+0.05	+0.19	+0.14	—	—	+0.14	+1.00	—
PP̂FA	−0.13	−0.15	—	—	−0.14	−0.08	−0.11	−0.12	—	—	+0.07	—	+1.00

* Based on 26 industries used in TSLS regressions

negative after CR reaches about 48* The partial effect of increases in A/S becomes negative when CR reaches about 56.† If the CR^2 coefficient is taken as zero, increases in concentration are associated with decreases in the margin after A/S reaches $+0.025$.

If, based on the table 5 regressions, the CR coefficient is $+0.0015$, the A/S coefficient is $+16.00$ and the $CR \cdot A/S$ coefficient is -0.25, the concentration effect is negative after A/S reaches $+0.006$ and the A/S effect is negative after CR reaches 60. Thus, unlike the results from the studies of United States industry, high concentration and high barriers to entry appear to combine to produce negative effects on profitability for the sampled British industries in the early 1950s.

It is difficult to conclude that monopoly power and the potential for profits in fact decline as market concentration and entry barriers reach high levels. Three alternative explanations come to mind. First, the results may be due to data deficiencies, particularly in the concentration data as measures of market structure. If industries in Great Britain with high concentration and large plants are, in fact, industries which tend to compete more with foreign firms for the British market and for export markets, the domestic concentration ratio would be a misleading structural measure. In such circumstances, high domestic concentration and large plants could be associated with low margins, and with relatively high advertising expenditure being used to maintain within the domestic market some degree of product differentiation based on preferences for British products.

This possibility cannot be wholly dismissed. Yet the information on the industries with high combined concentration and advertising given in table 7 provides little supportive evidence. These industries seem to be at least as effective in their fixing of prices as are the other industries. Foreign competition, it would be supposed, would make price-fixing more difficult. The industries, on average, also show substantially higher rates of output growth than do the others. While this is not necessarily inconsistent with a high degree of foreign competition, it indicates that the industries were not being faced with such severe competition that foreign-made products were displacing them. It also appears that the industries with high combined concentration and advertising had plants no larger than the average for all industries and price-cost margins which are somewhat higher. Finally, the industries in the list are not typically ones in which international competition seems likely to be intense.

A second possible explanation is that postwar controls, both formal and informal, brought about the unusual results. Determining how government policies in this period constrained the exercise of monopoly power would be difficult, if not impossible. Nonetheless, preliminary findings by Holtermann (1972) based on 1963 data are remarkably similar to those formed here. The variance of the profit-to-sales ratios used by Holtermann have no significant relationship with five-firm concentration ratios when neither a squared concentration term nor a concentration-advertising interaction term is

* This is evaluated using the mean A/S ratio of approximately 0.007.

† Because advertising is included in the price-cost margin, the *net* effect of changes in A/S on the margin is $\partial \Pi / \partial (A/S) - 1$. This evaluation is based on the assumed net coefficient of $+4.5$ rather than $+5.5$.

Table 7. Structural and performance data on 16 industries with above $+0.25$ $CR \cdot A/S$ values

Industry	CR	A/S	APS	ln $\hat{E}PF$*	GO	Π	$\hat{\Pi}$†
Fertilizers and disinfectants	59	0.014	0.14	—	1.45	0.18	0.21
Batteries and accumulators	74	0.009	0.41	—	0.51	0.19	0.16
Watches and clocks	60	0.006	0.14	—	0.43	0.21	0.21
Musical instruments	46	0.030	0.06	—	0.44	0.27	0.25
Asbestos	59	0.010	0.37	—	0.58	0.31	0.21
Biscuits	26	0.012	0.32	—	1.30	0.18	0.18
Cocoa, chocolate and sugar confectionery	39	0.010	0.42	—	1.64	0.17	0.18
Margarine	79	0.004	0.18	—	4.81	0.23	0.15
Cattle, dog and poultry foods	53	0.008	0.08	—	2.77	0.11	0.20
Vinegar and other condiments	62	0.020	0.06	—	0.33	0.27	0.24
Starch	82	0.021	0.14	—	1.49	0.19	0.18
Wine, cider and soft drinks	18	0.021	0.04	—	0.41	0.26	0.24
Printing and publishing	25	0.014	0.17	—	1.02	0.28	0.19
Toys and games	40	0.008	0.12	—	0.69	0.21	0.20
Sports requisites	29	0.011	0.06	—	0.21	0.20	0.21
Film studios	41	0.013	0.10	—	−0.35	0.22	0.22
Mean, high $CR \cdot A S$ industries	50	0.013	0.18	3.88	1.11	0.22	0.20
Mean, all industries	36	0.007	0.18	3.77	0.79	0.18	0.18

* Confidentiality prevents disclosure of individual items.

† Based on OLS regression 7, table 4.

included. With either or both of the latter included, the concentration effect becomes significantly positive and the coefficients for the squared concentration and the interaction terms are negative. With the addition of capital-output ratios and investment-sales ratios, Holtermann obtains corrected coefficients of determination approaching 0.60, with 113 industries covered. These results weaken the argument that the 1951 performance was just a postwar anomaly.

The third explanation—and that which seems most plausible in view of Holtermann's findings—is that the performance of the high-concentration/high-entry-barrier industries reflects something other than profit-maximizing behaviour. Following O. E. Williamson (1963), Marris (1963), Baumol (1967) and Liebenstein (1966), it can be conjectured that what is being observed is a group of industries with firms so isolated from market pressures that managerial discretion and 'X-inefficiency' appear. Advertising is relatively high—both to bar potential entrants and to achieve growth. Prices are set high enough to maintain at least average profits, even given possible cost inefficiencies, but neither price nor cost behaviour is such that profits are maximized. The combination of concentration and product differentiation gives rise to little overt rivalry within the industries. Even in their purchasing the firms fail to minimize costs, with the result that producer goods' margins are higher than consumer goods margins. Monopoly is there, but is exercised so as to achieve goals different from maximum profits.

Whatever the correct explanation, it is certain that strong caveats are necessary when questions of appropriate public policy are considered. None of the empirical studies has succeeded in explaining a high proportion of the variance in actual or potential profitability. Even if they had, other performance measures are often relevant for policy purposes. Structural variables are certainly important ingredients to studies aimed at aiding policy decisions, but we are far from the point that more detailed and 'industry specific' inquiries can be abandoned.

REFERENCES

Adelman, M. (1969), 'A note on the H-measure as a numbers equivalent', *Review of Economics and Statistics,* 51 (1), 99–101.

Alberts, W. W. and Segall, J. E. (eds) (1966), *The Corporate Merger* (Chicago: University of Chicago Press).

Albouy, M. and Breton, A. (1968), 'Interprétation économique du principe du maximum', *Revenue française de Recherche Opérationnelle,* 14.

Alchian, Armen (1958), 'Uncertainty, evolution, and economic theory', *Journal of Political Economy,* 58, 211–22.

Alchian, Armen and Demsetz, Harold (1972), 'Production, information costs and economic organization,' *American Economic Review,* forthcoming.

Allen, Stephen A., III (1970) 'Corporate divisional relationships in highly diversified firms,' in *Studies in Organization Design* ed. Jay W. Lorsch and Paul R. Lawrence (Homewood, Ill.; Irwin), pp. 16–35.

Ansoff, II. I. and Brandenburg, R. G., 'A language for organizational design: Part II', *Management Science,* 17, B-717–31.

Ansoff, H. I., Brandenburg, R. G., Portner, F. E. and Radosevich, R. (1971), *Twenty Years of Acquisition Behaviour in America* (London: Cassell).

Arrow, K. J. (1965), *Aspects of the Theory of Risk Bearing* (Helsinki: Yojö Johnssonin Säätiö).

Arrow, K. and Kurz, M. (1970), *Public Investment, The Rate of Return, and Optimal Fiscal Policy* (Baltimore: Johns Hopkins Press).

Bain, J. S. (1951), 'Relation of profit rates to industry concentration', *Quarterly Journal of Economics* (August).

Bain, J. S. (1956), *Barriers to New Competition* (Harvard University Press).

Bain, J. S. (1968), *Industrial Organization* (New York: Wiley).

Barnard, Chester I. (1946), 'Functions and pathology of status systems in formal organizations', *Industry and Society,* ed. W. F. Whyte, pp. 46–83.

Baumol, W. J. (1967), *Business Behavior, Value and Growth* (New York: Harcourt, Brace and Johanovich).

Baumol, W. J., Heim, Peggy, Malkiel, B. G. and Quandt, R. E. (1970), 'Earnings retention, new capital, and the growth of the firm', *Review of Economics and Statistics,* 52, 345–55.

Bell, Frederick W. and Murphy, Neil B. (1969), 'Impact of market structure on the price of a commercial bank service', *Review of Economics and Statistics* (May).

Bishop, R. L. (1952), 'Elasticities, cross elasticities, and market relationships', *American Economic Review,* 42 (5), 779–803.

Borch, K. H. (1968), *The Economics of Uncertainty* (Princeton, New Jersey: Princeton University Press).

Borden, N. H. (1942), *The Economic Effects of Advertising* (Homewood, Ill.: Irwin).

Bower, Joseph L. (1971), 'Management decision-making in large diversified firms', (unpublished manuscript).

Brozen, Yale (1970), 'The antitrust task force deconcentration recommendations', *Journal of Law and Economics* (October).

Brozen, Yale (1971), 'Bain's concentration and rates of return revisited', *Journal of Law and Economics* (October).

Butters, J. K., Lintner, J. and Cary, W. L. (1957), *Effects of Taxation on Corporate Mergers* (Boston: Graduate School of Business Administration, Harvard University).

Caves, R. E. (1967), *American Industry: Structure, Conduct, Performance,* second edition (Englewood Cliffs, NJ: Prentice-Hall).

Caves, R. E. and associates (1968), *Britain's Economic Prospects* (London: Allen & Unwin).

Chandler, Alfred D., Jr. (1966), *Strategy and Structure* (New York).

Churchill, N. C., Cooper, W. W. and Sainsbury, T. (1964), 'Laboratory and field studies of the behavioral effects of audits', in *Management Controls: New Directions in Basic Research,* ed. C. P. Bonini *et al.* (New York: McGraw-Hill), pp. 253–67.

Coase, Ronald H. (1972), 'Industrial organization: a proposal for research', in *Policy Issues and Research Opportunities in Industrial Organization,* ed. Victor R. Fuchs (New York: National Bureau of Economic Research).

Cochran, W. G. (1963), *Sampling Techniques* (New York: Wiley).

Collins, Norman R. and Preston, Lee E. (1968), *Concentration and Cost-Price Margins in Manufacturing Industries* (Berkeley: University of California Press).

Collins, Norman R. and Preston, Lee E. (1969), 'Price-cost margins and industry structures', *Review of Economics and Statistics* (August).

Comanor, W. S. and Wilson, T. (1967), 'Advertising, market structure and performance', *Review of Economics and Statistics* (Nov.), pp. 423–40.

Comanor, W. S. and Wilson, T. (1969), 'Advertising and the advantages of size' *American Economic Review* (Papers and Proceedings) **59** (May), 87–98.

Cowling, Keith and Cubbin, John (1971), 'Price, quality and advertising competition: an econometric analysis of the U.K. car market', *Economica* (November).

Cowling, Keith and Cubbin, John (1972), 'Hedonic price indexes for cars in the U.K.', *Economic Journal* (September).

Cowling, Keith and Rayner, A. J. (1970), 'Price, quality and market share', *Journal of Political Economy* **78** (5) (November/December).

Cyert, R. M. and March, J. G. (1963), *A Behavioral Theory of the Firm* (Englewood Cliffs, NJ: Prentice-Hall).

Dewing, A. S. (1921), 'A statistical test of the success of consolidations', *Quarterly Journal of Economics* (November).

Dixon, W. J. and Massey, F. J., Jr (1957), *Introduction to Statistical Analysis* (New York: McGraw-Hill).

Dorfman, R. (1969), 'An economic interpretation of optimal control theory', *American Economic Review* (December).

Dorfman, R. and Steiner, P. O. (1954), 'Optimal advertising and optimal quality', *American Economic Review,* **44** (5), 826–36.

Doyle, P. (1968), 'Advertising expenditure and consumer demand', *Oxford Economic Papers,* **20** (3), 395–417.

Drucker, Peter (1970), 'The new markets and the new capitalism', *The Public Interest,* 21, 44–79.

Economists' Advisory Group (1967), *The Economics of Advertising* (London: The Advertising Association).

Edwards, Franklin R. (1964), 'Concentration in banking and its effects on business loan rates', *Review of Economics and Statistics* (August).

Eis, C. (1969), 'The 1919–1930 merger movement in American industry', *Journal of Law and Economics* (October).

Else, P. K. (1966), 'The incidence of advertising in manufacturing industries', *Oxford Economic Papers,* **18** (1) 88–110.

Evely, R. and Little, I. M. D. (1960), *Concentration in British Industry* (London: Cambridge University Press).

Fisher, G. R. (1969), 'Review of growth, profitability and valuation', *The Economic Journal* (June).

Fisher, L. (1966), 'Some new stock market indexes', *Journal of Business.*

Flechsig, Theodore G. (1965), 'The effect of concentration on bank loan rates', *Journal of Finance* (May).

Friend, Irwin, and Husic, Frank (1971) '*Efficiency of Corporate Investment* (Working Paper No. 4–71) (Rodney L. White Center for Financial Research, University of Pennsylvania).

Fuchs, Victor R. (1961), 'Integration, concentration, and profits in manufacturing industries', *Quarterly Journal of Economics* (May).

Gaskins, D. W. (1971), 'Dynamic limit pricing: optimal pricing under threat of entry', *Journal of Economic Theory,* 3.

George, K. D. (1968), 'Concentration, barriers to entry and rates of return', *Review of Economics and Statistics* (May).

Gibrat, R. (1931), *Les Inégalités Économiques* (Paris: Sirey).

Gort, M. (1959), *Diversification and Integration in American Industry* (Princeton: Princeton University Press).

Gort, M. (1969), 'An economic disturbance theory of mergers', *Quarterly Journal of Economics* (November).

Gort, M. and Hogarty, T. F. (1970), 'New evidence on mergers' *Journal of Law and Economics* (April).

Gould, J. H., *Diffusion Processes and Optimal Advertising Policy*, in Phelps (1970).

Greenberg, Warren (1972), 'The performance trade-off between number and size distribution of firms within industries' (unpublished PhD dissertation, Bryn Mawr College).

Guth, L. A., (1971) 'Advertising and market structure revisited', *Journal of Industrial Economics,* **19** (2), 201–19.

Hadley, G. and Kemp, M. C. (1971), *Variational Methods in Economics* (North-Holland).

Hall, Marshall and Weiss, Leonard W. (1967), 'Firm size and profitability', *Review of Economics and Statistics* (August).

Hart, P. (1962), 'The size and growth of firms', *Economica* (February).

Hart, P. and Prais, S. J. (1956), 'The analysis of business concentration: a statistical approach', *Journal of the Royal Statistical Society*.

Heflebower, Richard B. (1960), 'Observations on decentralization in large enterprises', *Journal of Industrial Economics*, **9**, 7–22.

Hindley, B. V. (1969), 'Capitalism and the corporation', *Economica* (November).

Hindley, B. V. (1970), 'Separation of ownership and control in the modern corporation' *Journal of Law and Economics* (April).

Hogarty, T. F. (1970), 'The profitability of corporate mergers', *Journal of Business* (July).

Holtermann, S. E. (1972), 'Market structure and economic performance', (unpublished manuscript, London Graduate School of Business Studies).

Horowitz, I. (1970), 'A note on advertising and uncertainty', *Journal of Industrial Economics*, **18** (April).

Hotelling, H. (1929), 'Stability in competition', *Economic Journal*, **39**, 41–57.

Houthakker, H. and Taylor, L. D. (1970), *Consumer Demand in the U.S., 1929–70*, second edition (Cambridge, Mass.).

Ijiri, Y. and Simon, H. A. (1971), 'Effects of mergers and acquisitions on business firm concentration', *Journal of Political Economy* (March).

Ireland, N. J. (1972), *Concentration and the Growth of Market Demand: A Comment on Gaskin's Limit Pricing Model* (mimeographed) University of Warwick.

Ironmonger, D. S. (1960), 'New commodities, quality changes and consumer behaviour', (PhD Dissertation, University of Cambridge).

Jacquemin, A. (1971), *Product Differentiation and Optimal Advertising Policy: A Dynamic Analysis* (Working Paper No. 7107) (Louvain: Institut des sciences économiques).

Jacquemin, A. (1972), 'Market structure and the firm's market power', *The Journal of Industrial Economics*, No. 2.

Johnson, H. G. (1967), 'The economics of advertising', *Advertising Quarterly*, no. 13 (Autumn), pp. 9–15.

Johnson, H. W. and Simon, J. L. (1969), 'The success of mergers: the case of advertising agencies', *Bulletin of the Oxford Institute of Economics and Statistics* (May).

Kaldor, N. (1950), 'The economic aspects of advertising', *Review of Economic Studies*, **18**, 1–27.

Kaldor, N. and Silverman, R. (1948), *A Statistical Analysis of Advertising Expenditure and the Revenue of the Press* (London: Cambridge University Press).

Kamien, M. I. and Schwartz, N. L. (1971a) 'Limit pricing and uncertain entry', *Econometrica* (May).

Kamien, M. I. and Schwartz, N. L. (1971b), 'Theory of the firm with induced technical change', *Metroeconomica* (September–December).

Kamien, M. I. and Schwartz, N. L. (1972a), 'Market structure, rivals' response, and the firm's rate of product improvement', *The Journal of Industrial Economics* (April).

Kamien, M. I. and Schwartz, N. L. (1972b), 'Uncertain entry and excess capacity', *American Economic Review* (December, forthcoming).

Kamien, M. I. and Schwartz, N. L. (1972c), 'Timing of innovations under rivalry', *Econometrica* (January, forthcoming).

Kaufman, George (1966), 'Bank market structure and performance', *Southern Economic Journal* (April).

Keenan, M. (1970), 'Models of equity valuation: the great serm bubble', *Journal of Finance* (May).

Kelly, E. M. (1967), *Profitability of Growth Through Mergers* (University Park Pa: Pennsylvania State University).

Kilpatrick, Robert W. (1968), 'Stigler on the relationship between industry profit rates and market concentration', *Journal of Political Economy* (May-June).

Kuehn, A. A. (1961), 'A model for budgeting advertising', *Journal of Business* (January). Reprinted in *Mathematical Models and Methods in Marketing*, ed. F. Bass *et al.* (New York: Irwin).

Kuehn, D. A. (1969), 'Stock market valuation and acquisitions: an empirical test of one component of managerial utility', *Journal of Industrial Economics*, **17** (2), 132–44.

Lambin, J. J. (1970a), 'Advertising and competitive behaviour: a case study', *Applied Economics*, **2** (4).

Lambin, J. J. (1970b), 'Optimal allocation of competitive marketing efforts: an empirical study', *Journal of Business* (October).

Lancaster, K. (1966), 'A new approach to consumer theory', *Journal of Political Economy,* **74** (April).

Lewellen, W. G. (1968), *Executive Compensation in Large Industrial Corporations* (New York: National Bureau of Economic Research).

Lewellen, W. G. and Huntsman (1970), 'Managerial pay and corporate performance', *American Economic Review* (September).

Liebenstein, Harvey (1966), 'Allocative efficiency vs "X-efficiency"', *American Economic Review* (June).

Lintner, J. (1971), 'Optimum or maximum corporate growth under uncertainty', in Marris and Wood (1971).

Livermore, S. (1935), 'The success of industrial mergers', *Quarterly Journal of Economics* (November).

Long, William F. (1970), 'An eoonometric study of performance in American manufacturing industry' (unpublished PhD dissertation, University of California at Berkeley).

Luce, R. D. and Raiffa, Howard (1958), *Games and Decisions* (New York: Wiley).

MacAvoy, Paul W., McKie, James W. and Preston, Lee E. (1971), 'High and stable concentration levels, profitability and public policy: a response', *Journal of Law and Economics* (October).

Ma, R. (1960), 'Births and deaths in the quoted public company sector in the UK 1949–53', *Yorkshire Bulletin of Economic and Social Research.*

Mann, H. Michael (1966), 'Seller concentration, barriers to entry and rates of return in thirty industries, 1950–1960', *Review of Economics and Statistics* (August).

Mann, H. Michael (1970), 'Asymmetry, barriers to entry and rates of return in twenty-six concentrated industries, 1948–1957', *Western Economic Journal* (March).

Mann, H. Michael (1971), 'The interaction of barriers to entry and concentration: a reply', *Journal of Industrial Economics* (July).

Mann, H. M., Henning, J. A. and Meehan, J. W. (1967), 'Advertising and concentration: an empirical investigation', *Journal of Industrial Economics,* **16**, 34–9.

March, J. G. and Simon, H. A. (1958), *Organizations* (New York: Wiley).

Markham, J. W. (1955), 'Survey of the evidence and finding on mergers' in National Bureau of Economic Research (1955).

Marris, Robin L. (1963), 'A model of "managerial" enterprise', *Quarterly Journal of Economics,* **77**, 185–209.

Marris, R. (1964), *The Economic Theory of Managerial Capitalism* (London: Macmillan).

Marris, R. and Wood, A. (eds) (1971), *The Corporate Economy, Growth, Competition and Innovative Power* (London: Macmillan).

Masson, R. T. (1971), 'Executive motivations, earnings, and consequent equity performance', *Journal of Political Economy,* **79**, 1278–92.

McGuire, Chiu and Elbing (1962), 'Executive incomes, sales and profits', *American Economic Review* (September).

Miller, R. A. (1967), 'Marginal concentration ratios and industrial profit rates: some empirical results of oligopoly behaviour', *Southern Economic Journal* (October).

Miller, R. A. (1969), 'Market structure and industrial performance: relation of profit rates to concentration, advertising intensity, and diversity', *Journal of Industrial Economics* (April).

Monsen, R. J. and Downs, A. (1963), 'A theory of large managerial firms', *Journal of Political Economy,* **73**, 221–36.

Mueller, D. C. (1969), 'A theory of conglomerate mergers', *Quarterly Journal of Economics,* **83**, 643–59.

National Bureau of Economic Research (1955), *Business Concentration and Price Policy* (Princeton: Princeton University Press).

Nelson, R. L. (1959), *Merger Movements in American Industry, 1895–1956* (Princeton: Princeton University Press).

Nerlove, M. and Arrow, K. J. (1962), 'Optimal advertising policy under dynamic conditions', *Economica* **29**, pp. 129–42.

Newbould, G. D. (1970), *Management and Merger Activity* (Liverpool: Guthstead).

Neyman, J. (1938), 'Contribution to the theory of sampling human population', *Journal of the American Statistical Association.*

Nichols, T. (1969), *Ownership, Control and Ideology* (London: Allen and Unwin).

Pashigian, P. (1968), 'Limit price and the market share of the leading firm', *The Journal of Industrial Economics* (July).

Peel, D. (1972), 'The non-uniqueness of the Dorfman–Steiner condition: a note', (Mimeo, University of Leeds).

Peles, Y. (1971), 'Rates of amortization of advertising expenditures', *Journal of Political Economy* (September/October).

Penrose, E. T. (1959), *The Theory of the Growth of the Firm* (Oxford: Blackwell).

Phelps, E. S. (ed.) (1970), *Microeconomic Foundations of Employment and Inflation Theory* (New York: W. W. Norton).

Phelps, E. S. and Winter S. G. (1970), 'Optimal price policy under atomistic competition', in Phelps (1970).

Phillips, Almarin (1961), 'A theory of interfirm organization', *Quarterly Journal of Economics* (November).

Phillips, Almarin (1962), *Market Structure, Organization and Performance*, (Cambridge, Mass.: Harvard University Press).

Phillips, Almarin (1967), 'Evidence on concentration in banking markets and interest rates', *Federal Reserve Bulletin* (June).

Phillips, Almarin (1971), 'Structure, conduct and performance—and performance, conduct and structure', in *Industrial Organization and Economic Development: Essays in Honor of Edward S. Mason*, ed. J. W. Markham and G. Papanek (Boston: Houghton Mifflin).

Political and Economic Planning (1957), *Industrial Trade Associations* (London).

Pontryagin, L. S. (1962), *Ordinary Differential Equations*, (London–Pergamon Press).

Pontryagin, L. S., Boltyanskii, V. G., Gamkrelidze, R. S. and Mischenko, E. F. (1962), *The Mathematical Theory of Optimal Processes* (New York: Wiley).

Prais, S. J. (1972), 'The share of the largest 100 manufacturing firms in Britain, 1909–70' (unpublished paper, NIESR).

Rand Corporation (1955), *A Million Random Digits* (New York: Free Press).

Reekie, D. (1970), 'Some problems associated with the marketing of ethical pharmaceutical products', *Journal of Industrial Economics*, 49 (1), 33–49.

Reid, S. R. (1968), *Mergers, Managers, and the Economy* (New York: McGraw-Hill).

Roberts, D. R. (1959), *Executive Compensation* (Glencoe, Ill.: Free Press).

Rosenberg, R. (1971), 'Profit constrained revenue maximisation: note', *American Economic Review*, 61, 208–9.

Ruff, L. E. (1969), 'Research and technological progress in a Cournot economy', *Journal of Economic Theory*, 1.

Samuels, J. M. (1965), 'The size and growth of firms', *Review of Economic Studies*, 32.

Samuels, J. M. and Smyth, D. J. (1969), 'Profits, variability of profits and firm size', *Economica* (May).

Samuels, J. M. and Tzoannos, J. (1969), 'Takeovers and share price evaluation', *Business Ratios*, 2.

Scherer, F. (1971), *Industrial Market Structure and Economic Performance* (Chicago: Rand McNally).

Schnabel, Morton (1970), 'A note on advertising and industrial concentration', *Journal of Political Economy*, 78 (5).

Schumpeter, J. (1942), *Capitalism, Socialism and Democracy* (New York: Harper and Row).

Schwartzman, David (1959), 'The effect of monopoly on price', *Journal of Political Economy* (August).

Shepherd, William G. (1972), 'The elements of market structure', *Review of Economics and Statistics* (February).

Simon, H. A. (1957), 'The compensation of executives', *Sociometry* (March).

Simon, H. A. and Bonini, C. P. (1958), 'The size distribution of business firms', *American Economic Review* (September).

Singh, A. (1971), *Takeovers: Their Relevance to the Stock Market and the Theory of the Firm* (London: Cambridge University Press).

Singh, A. and Whittington, G. (1968), *Growth, Profitability and Valuation* (London: Cambridge University Press).

Smith, D. (1971), 'The performance of merging banks', *Journal of Business* (April).

Smith, K. V. and Schreiner, J. C. (1969) 'A portfolio analysis of conglomerate diversification', *Journal of Finance*, 24, 413–29.

Solow, R. M. (1971), 'Some implications of alternative criteria for the firm', in Marris and Wood (1971).

Stigler, G. J. (1961), 'The economics of information', *Journal of Political Economy,* **49** (3), 213–25.

Stigler, George J. (1963), *Capital and Rates of Return in Manufacturing Industries* (Princeton: Princeton University Press).

Stigler, G. J. (1964), 'A theory of oligopoly', *Journal of Political Economy,* **72** (1).

Stigler, G. J. (1968), *The Organization of Industry* (Homewood, Ill.: Irwin).

Taplin, W. (1959), 'Advertising appropriation policy', *Economica,* N.S. **26**.

Telser, L. (1962), 'The demand for branded goods as estimated from consumer panel data', *Review of Economics and Statistics,* **44**.

Telser, L. G. (1964), 'Advertising and competition', *Journal of Political Economy,* **72** (6), 537–62.

Thisse, J. (1972), 'Un modéle dynamique de la firme avec différenciation du produit', *Recherches Économiques de Louvain,* no. 1.

Tzoannos, J. and Samuels, J. M. (1972), 'Mergers and takeovers: the financial characteristics of companies involved' (Paper presented at Manchester Business School, November 1969, at AUTA Conference, Bristol, September 1970. To be published in *Journal of Business Finance,* Autumn 1972).

Utton, M. A. (1970), *Industrial Concentration* (Harmondsworth: Penguin).

Utton, M. A. (1971), 'The effect of mergers on concentration: UK manufacturing industry 1954–65', *Journal of Industrial Economics* (November).

Vernon, J. M. (1971), 'Concentration, promotion and market share stability in the pharmaceutical industry', *Journal of Industrial Economics* (July), pp. 246–66.

Weiss, Leonard W. (1963), 'Average concentration ratios and industrial performance', *Journal of Industrial Economics* (July).

Westerfield, Randolph (1970), 'A note on the measurement of conglomerate diversification', *Journal of Finance,* **25**, 909–14.

Weston, J. F. (1953), *The Role of Mergers in the Growth of Large Firms* (Berkeley: University of California Press).

Weston, J. Fred (1970), 'Diversification and merger trends', *Business Economics,* **5** (January), 50–7.

Whittington, G. (1971), *The Prediction of Profitability* (London: Cambridge University Press).

Williamson, J. (1966), 'Profit, growth and sales maximisation' *Economica,* **33**, 1–16.

Williamson, J. H. (1967), *Endogenous Technical Progress and the Theory of the Firm* (mimeographed).

Williamson, O. E. (1963), 'Managerial discretion and business behavior', *American Economic Review,* **53**, 1032–57.

Williamson, O. E. (1964), *The Economics of Discretionary Behavior: Managerial Objectives in a Theory of the Firm* (Englewood Cliffs NJ: Prentice-Hall).

Williamson, O. E. (1965), 'A dynamic theory of inter-firm behavior', *Quarterly Journal of Economics* (November).

Williamson, O. E. (1970), *Corporate Control and Business Behavior* (Englewood Cliffs, New Jersey: Prentice-Hall).

Williamson, O. E. (1971a), 'The vertical integration of production: market failure considerations', *American Economic Review,* **61**, 112–25.

Williamson, O. E. (1971b), 'On the limits of internal organization, with special reference to the vertical integration of production' (unpublished manuscript).

Williamson, O. E. (1972), 'Antitrust enforcement and the modern corporation', in *Policy Issues and Research Opportunities in Industrial Organization,* ed. V. Fuchs (New York), pp. 16–33.

Yarrow, G. K., 'The effects of profits tax changes on revenue-maximizing firms' (mimeo).

DATE DUE